CHURCH SWEET HOME

Also by Monica Lee

The Percussionist's Wife:
A Memoir of Sex, Crime & Betrayal

How to Look Hot & Feel Amazing in Your 40s:
The 21-Day Age-Defying Diet, Exercise
& Everything Makeover Plan

Truth, Dare, Double Dare, Promise or Repeat:
On Finding the Meaning of "Like" in 1982

Church Sweet Home

A Renovation
to Warm the Soul

Monica Lee

BOOKS

CHURCH SWEET HOME

Copyright © 2020 by Monica Lee

All rights reserved. No part of this book may be used or reproduced in any manner whatsoever without written permission except in the case of brief quotations embodied in critical articles and reviews.

ISBN 978-0-9861-9433-7 (paperback)

Cover art by Monica Lee
Print book interior design by Monica Lee
Mindfulmonica.wordpress.com

For believers

*If you have faith the size of a mustard seed,
you will say to this mountain,
"Move from here to there," and it will move;
and nothing will be impossible for you.*

~ Matthew 17:20 (NRSV)

Contents

Preface xi
1 In the beginning 1
2 Like a grain of mustard seed 9
3 Bells of pure gold 12
4 Do not let your hearts be troubled 16
5 Rise and measure the temple 20
6 Awaiting a better home 22
7 The wise lay up knowledge 26
8 The pearl of great price 31
9 Revelations 39
10 The repairer of the breach 49
11 He cuts off every branch that bears no fruit 53
12 The calling of the first disciples 66
13 Faith is the assurance of things hoped for 73
14 Remembered in all generations 79
15 Therefore, do not be foolish 91
16 For the lack of wood, the fire goes out 100
17 The one who is unwilling to work shall not eat ... 112
18 Gather up the leftover fragments so nothing will be lost 115
19 The lost is found 126

20 The good Samaritan	130
21 A whole heavenly army	139
22 A light unto my path	149
23 The garden of Eden	158
24 The house on the rock	171
25 Formed out of dirt	183
26 Your silver and gold multiply	187
27 Trampling down the waves of the sea	193
28 A stairway resting on the earth	204
29 Plagues of Pharaoh	208
30 Tower of Babel	213
31 Down onto the floor	220
32 Workers in the vineyard	230
33 One who is faithful in very little is also faithful in much	234
34 The golden calf	244
35 The road to Damascus	250
36 That which is left shall escape	257
37 So shall your storage places be filled with plenty	260
38 They prepare the table, they spread the rugs	268
39 The trials of Job	281
40 Rebuilding the temple	287
41 Sixty cubits long, twenty wide and thirty high	295
42 Because you have kept my word about patient endurance	303
Epilogue	323
Acknowledgements	327

About the Author..329
Reading Guide...331

Preface

When you start looking for them, you see them everywhere—abandoned churches.

Church attendance in the United States is down—way down. Only about one out of four Americans shows up to church at least three out of every eight Sundays, and that includes Catholics who still consider attending weekly Mass to be a sacred obligation. Commitment to showing up at church is worse among Protestant denominations. In the 1950s, nearly three-quarters of Americans identified themselves as Protestants. In 2016, the number is less than one in three.

Church attendance is even worse in other English-speaking countries:

—According to a national survey in Australia, church attendance of at least once a month declined from 44 percent to 17 percent between 1950 and 2007.

—Weekly attendance at religious services in Canada was just 13 percent, according to a 2013 national poll. That 13 percent includes all faiths, not just Christians. Just after World War II, two-thirds of Canadians polled said they had attended a religious service in the previous seven days. Even in the mid-1980s, about one-third of Canadians could still be found in a worship service on any given week.

—In the United Kingdom, a 2007 survey found that only 7 percent of the population considered themselves practicing Christians. That same survey found two-thirds of U.K. adults had no connection with *any* religion. About 30 Church of England parish churches are declared "closed for regular public worship" each year.

As more people join the ranks of the secular world, faithful congregations shrink to the point of being unable to support a pastor. Instead of the gift of a gathering place, their worship space becomes a burden saddled by heating and cooling bills, maintenance and repairs. The congregation merges with another one nearby, and the building goes on the market.

But church buildings are unique. Large sanctuaries have towering windows, a bunch of little Sunday School rooms (probably decorated with bad paneling and ugly suspended ceilings) and maybe a commercial kitchen. Who needs such a strange space? Who wants an altar and a baptismal font? Who has the kind of cash required to do an aggressive renovation? Another denomination in town might find the space useful, but growing churches with money to spend often want high-tech modern spaces with gargantuan entryways in suburban locales, not poorly maintained traditional ones in city centers or small towns.

In many cases, these cast-off buildings become warehouses. Pews are sold. The beautiful windows are boarded up. Yards are ignored and overgrown. Or, even more catastrophically, they're demolished.

This was the likely destiny of the 126-year-old Methodist church in a small village in southern Wisconsin that my husband Tyler and I acquired in November 2017.

Like many other Protestant denominations in the United States, the United Methodist Church membership plummeted in recent decades. Based on the teachings of Englishman John Wesley, the Methodists began forming churches in America in the 18th century and became the largest protestant denomination in the country by the mid-19th century; nearly every hamlet in the country had a Methodist presence. U.S. membership peaked in the 1970s and has dropped 30 percent since then. One source estimated modern U.S. Methodist churches are losing a thousand members a week. Among all Christian denominations, Wisconsin ranks near the bottom in state statistics measuring church attendance. That leaves a lot of empty churches, especially ones formerly occupied by Methodists.

But more and more, creative developers like Tyler and I are crawling through the proverbial open windows left by these closed church doors. All around the world, churches, temples and synagogues are being converted into houses, condos, co-ops, and apartment buildings. Good statistics are hard to find, but according to one nationwide real estate tracking firm, church sales in the United States nearly doubled between 2010 and 2015 while the number of church redevelopment projects more than tripled. More than 6,800 religious buildings have been sold in the past five years and more than 1,400 are currently for sale in the United States, according to another commercial real estate database. Anecdotally, the nation's capital received thirty-one applications to change buildings from a place of worship to something else in 2014 and 2015, according to the local newspaper of record. In New York City, no fewer than sixteen such conversions were reported recently.

But few churches are easily turned into homes, and the hurdles are many. A quick look through the Pinterest website reveals some spectacular transformations, the sort of metamorphosis that inspired me. But you'll also find some horrors of awkwardly chopped-up spaces, dark rooms, strange window configurations and thoughtless appropriation of church symbols—like an altar reused as a bar. Ugh.

Every good renovation of an historical building requires some reverence for the original construction, but this presents a unique obstacle in a church conversion. A church is more than brick and mortar; a worship space is the repository for deep emotions and memories of life's most important moments for generations of members. Respect for the building's former life is crucial.

Anyone who buys an old church also must be aware of maintenance issues. Shrinking congregations with limited income are not able to prioritize repairs. It is almost a given that a buyer will encounter surprises, whether crumbling exterior brickwork, a disintegrating foundation or shoddily constructed additions done over decades or even centuries.

For us, our church conversion called us to stewardship—of a former congregation's worship space *and* our own resources. From disrepair and construction dust, we claimed an architectural gem to enjoy and kept the building safe for another generation—another generation of our family. This is our story.

1
IN THE BEGINNING

TINY SNOWFLAKES FELL ON the northern Illinois landscape when we woke on October 28, 2017.

"What are we *doing* here?" I asked out loud, not expecting any answer.

We were squatting in my husband's second cousin's yard—a green square acre surrounded by harvested cornfields. Our home since January was a forty-foot fifth-wheel camper. The first six months on the road, we traveled America's west coast visiting some of the country's most picturesque national parks, stopping at iconic roadside sites and imbibing the most delicious offerings of coastal vineyards.

That's when the proverbial good news and bad news was delivered.

The good news: we were going to be grandparents! My stepdaughter, who not long ago had told us she would *never* marry and *never* would have children, announced this joyous but highly unexpected news. We were thrilled, but we also suspected our unmoored status would hinder forging important bonds with our new granddaughter.

The bad news: Tyler's long-time and highly valued assistant in his insurance agency quit to pursue a full-time career. I was tapped to handle the agency's paperwork and customer service. As a little girl, I played office at a desk with a notebook, a pencil, a stapler and a telephone. But juggling dozens of accounts and reams of files proved troublesome—at best—in a 358-square-foot camper.

This drove our decision to give up the nomadic life and once again become homeowners. Weeks of scouring online real estate listings and several showings revealed only this: We couldn't afford what we really wanted. And what we *could* afford would require tens of thousands of dollars in renovations to remove the previous owners' bad taste.

We came close to making an offer on a tiny-but-could-be-renovated house with a miles-off view of a lake. But a second showing fell through when someone else beat us to an offer.

Ugh.

That very afternoon, my discouraged-but-ever-persistent husband found an interesting listing in the commercial category of a nearby real estate firm: an old Methodist church was for sale only fifteen miles from where my stepdaughter lives.

I had wanted to buy and renovate an old church for ages—not as long as I had been playing office as a little girl, but for at least a couple of decades. The cathedral ceilings, wide-open loft-like layout and character details like stained glass appealed to me.

In fact, Tyler and I had looked seriously at a church only a year before. The 125-year-old structure on a tree-lined street in Pecatonica, Illinois, piqued our curiosity. An electrician, plumber, plasterer and window installer provided renovation cost guesstimates. We were what they call in the trade, "serious buyers." I wanted that church so bad then. I thought it would be the perfect answer to a wish I'd made ten years before.

It was a tumultuous year. My life was so ridiculous and unbelievable, I wrote a book about it. When I recorded these wishes, I was no longer coupled and before I met Tyler. Theoretically, this list reflected my true wishes, unaffected by anyone else.

Near the top of the list, I wrote that I wanted to live in a loft in the city.

Well, that didn't happen.

When we were considering the church in Pecatonica, I lived in a big box of a house in the suburbs. It had nine-foot ceilings and what some might consider an open floor plan, but no one would consider it loft-like.

The church in Pecatonica was a smokin' deal. By hot, I mean it would have cost less than most cars. Let's just say it needed *a lot* of work, otherwise known as a blank canvas to take on every Pinterest dream associated with "loft," "barn," "converted church" and "open floor plan." The church sat in the center of the village, within walking distance of the post office, hardware store and local watering hole. And I thought it was my alliterative destiny to become Monica from Pecatonica.

I kept everything about that church in an accordion file with folders labeled "flooring," "taxes," "real estate" and "budgets." As we made our offer, contingent on an inspection, we salvaged a chunk of the flooring to get it tested for asbestos. Asbestos was a common building material in the mid-20th century. And it causes cancer.

The church flooring was full of the stuff.

We rescinded our offer.

I was disappointed, no denying it. But for about three weeks, it felt like buying a lottery ticket and daydreaming about your most extravagant fantasies. In the end, I was like, "better to have loved and lost than never to have loved at all." You know the drill.

We opted to sell our home and travel the country in our RV, foregoing the idea of buying a church. I threw my disappointed energy into cleaning out the house in anticipation of selling it. I dumped a ton of paperwork and went to the local Goodwill at least seventeen times to donate our accumulated junk. What we valued but couldn't bring with us in the camper, we packed into a cargo trailer.

The folder of information about the church we decided not to buy made its way into the trailer. Sure, it was meaningless, and it should have joined my other paperwork in the dumpster. But I still had a secret desire for a church. I believed words had real power in the universe. I think there's a big difference between praying "God, just get me through tomorrow" and "God, please bless me." One is a desperate plea, and one is a hopeful prayer. Words matter. Intentions have power.

In the moments between looking online at the Methodist church and seeing it in person, I remembered that folder of information about the Pecatonica church. And I thought I remembered precisely where I'd stored it. I dug up the key to the cargo trailer, and I put my hands on that folder within five seconds of looking. Between the shade-less lamps and plastic storage tubs labeled "winter clothes," I'd filed the paperwork of dreams right inside the door.

It was Saturday, which is like a workaday-Wednesday for a real estate agent, and Tyler found one willing to show us the Methodist church within an hour.

On our way to having dinner with Tyler's brother, we stopped by the church to have a look.

It was exactly what we were looking for. The layout featured a 26-by-38-foot sanctuary with an overflow area we envisioned as a kitchen and a main-floor master bedroom. Standing inside the serene sanctuary, more of our vision became clear. Bereft of typical church furnishings such as pews, pulpits and altars, I could imagine a beautiful great room with a raftered ceiling. The only visual noise was the gaudy gold trim and a fifteen-foot-tall red velvet curtain. Upstairs from the overflow, we could have another bedroom and an office. The wide-open full basement of nine-foot ceilings and three egresses seemed suitable for more bedrooms and anything else we needed.

The church in its "for sale" condition.

The building, we found out later, had been built 126 years before, and it looked every bit as solid as anything lovingly constructed in the 19th century. The much newer roof was in great condition (except for the bell tower roof which the seller disclosed was "rooted," which we took to mean was "rotted"). And the extra-large wooded lot left room for Tyler's dream garage. Even better than the high ceilings, this church was cheap. Cheap enough that we could buy it for cash and have enough money left over to fill the blank slate with features we loved.

We left the church that afternoon with a mission. Instead of counting souls, our mission was to count our pennies. I brought a piece of paper and a pencil along with the budget from the folder of dreams we'd created a year before for the Pecatonica church. We bellied up to the bar, and Tyler ordered tequila shots for two.

Tequila is my hard liquor of choice, and Tyler must have believed he needed some liquid courage.

We wrote down what would soon become known as the "Tequila Budget." We estimated we'd need $5,000 to re-do the ceiling, $30,000 for an awesome kitchen, $20,000 to improve the landscaping and on and on. We talked about everything from the bell tower to the basement flooring. When in doubt, we guessed high.

When we added it all up, the total sum—including 126-year-old church and brand-new attached three-car garage—came to $248,600. This was more than $100,000 *less* than we'd spent on our first home together a decade earlier. If we did it right, our church would have 100,000 times more character than the cardboard box in the suburbs we bought the first time.

That cardboard box served its purpose. We lived in a good school district and a village of low crime—perfect for raising Tyler's teenage son. But when my adored stepson grew up, we no longer needed such a characterless structure. We craved something unique.

A quick look at comparable properties in the neighborhood revealed we had enough margin to make money if things didn't work out and we had to sell a church converted into a residence. But by now, I had fallen in love with the bell tower and the planned quartz countertops and the warehouse-inspired bathroom makeover. I already didn't want to sell it.

"We need to take another look at it," my practical husband said.

And then he ordered another shot of tequila.

THE AFTERNOON OF THE Tequila Budget had been six weeks before the snowflakes. In the meantime, there was a second visit to the church, and an offer with no contingencies was made (asbestos be damned!), requesting a response in twenty-four hours. The church, being a church, took three days to respond, but the answer was yes. We were thrilled. They had accepted an offer $30,000 below asking price. We had already saved money! We had requested a closing date of no later than October 31, 2017, but we emphasized we could close immediately; we had *cash*.

We spent days dreaming of lighting fixtures and polished hardwood floors and furniture layouts. Truth be told, my husband also spent many hours studying the pictures we'd taken of the interior of the church and thinking up ways to run the plumbing and electrical work. He was the real brains of this operation; I was just the grunt labor and, on good days, the window dressing. He even met with the building inspector and talked about rezoning regulations and building permits and water meters.

Tyler is good at construction projects, but he is no good at waiting. Living in a camper amid northern Illinois' falling autumn temperature meant we had to quickly make the church habitable. Otherwise, we would have nowhere to live while we worked. As the days turned to weeks, he began calling every day our real estate agent (who was earning only a tiny commission on our miniscule offer). Then he began calling the title company. Finally, he called the pastor directly.

Tracking down proper paperwork to sell a 126-year-old building that has been owned by a church that's changed affiliations at least once and then merged with another congregation is tricky, it turns out. How tricky? About two months and half months of tricky.

When our offer was about to expire on Halloween, the seller ominously requested two more weeks. All Hallows' Eve, or the evening before All Saints' Day known popularly as Halloween, is the time in the liturgical year dedicated to remembering the dead, including saints ("hallows"), martyrs and all the faithful departed. Though frustrated, we didn't want our deal to die. We were faithful. But "two more weeks" sounded like a warning.

Home remodeling fans surely recall the infamous line from Tom Hanks in the movie *The Money Pit*. Everything was going to take two weeks. Construction. Reconstruction. Repairs. Finishing. Everything was "two weeks." In the beginning, the unfortunate homeowner asks a contractor, "When I do get the permits, how long will the job take?"

"Two weeks," the contractor says.

"Two weeks? Two weeks?"

"You sound like a parakeet there. 'Two weeks! Two weeks!'" the contractor mocks.

"Well, two weeks. It—it's amazing," says Tom Hanks' character, shaking his head.

"'It's amazing' nothing," the contractor says under his breath as he drives away in a pickup truck. "It'll be a regular miracle."

At this point in the game, we were depending on that miracle. Without it, our water lines in the camper would freeze, and we'd be two shivering homeless grandparents-to-be.

2
LIKE A GRAIN OF MUSTARD SEED

WHEN WE TOLD PEOPLE we were buying a church, some reacted with envy. "Oh, that sounds like an absolute dream!"

Others reacted with horror. "Why would you want to live in a church?"

Whether they said it or not, *everyone* thought we were crazy. "Sounds interesting. Good luck."

As a native of Minnesota, I'd learned "interesting" was the Minnesota Nice way of saying "scarier than three feet of wet snow on October 30 when the snowblower's broken." Even if they didn't say "interesting," their eyes betrayed their opinion about our sanity.

We were a couple in our 50s who were enjoying a second marriage. Which is to say we had already thrown a couple of partners to the curb for various infractions. If a remodeling project could break up other marriages, ours was not immune. And maybe we weren't up to the task physically. Tyler had tackled a similar whole-house remodeling project decades earlier, and he triumphed with a palatial result. But he wasn't twenty-something anymore, and not all his body parts are natural. And I had *never* been able to lift more than thirty pounds. Our joints now crackled like crisped-rice cereal, and our butts had spread like peanut butter.

Besides the collateral damage to our relationship and bodies, we pondered the financial risks. What if there were termites? What if the foundation was cracked? What if the wiring was so ancient it would have to be completely updated? These sorts of dilemmas cost money. A *lot* of money.

Maybe we *were* crazy.

But I didn't think so.

I spent a little time talking Tyler into rehabbing a church.

"This is the only way to get what we really want. Otherwise, we're just buying someone else's foolhardy decorating decisions."

"Imagine how awesome our great room will be. We can buy an eighteen-foot tall Christmas tree. Our children will love it!"

"It'll be great exercise. Why buy a membership to a gym when we can work out in our own house?"

"We'll never find a property so cheap. Heck, even the land itself is worth what we're paying."

"We can get this done without a mortgage. It'll be all ours in two years!"

Honestly, that's all it took to convince Tyler. He liked challenges. In the insurance world, I called him the dragon slayer because the bigger the account, the more hair on it, the more he liked it. Big risks reaped big rewards.

Plus, he wanted to please me. He's a great husband like that.

I especially scoffed at the notion that a church might be haunted. One naysayer asked if I was going to burn sage.

Harrumph. Sage. No.

Why would ghosts want to haunt a church? Only someone who didn't *attend* church would suggest such a thing.

Church buildings are places of joy. Babies get baptized. Couples get married. Children sing songs, and people celebrate holidays and

Note those chandeliers. You'll see them again.

anniversaries. Yes, people have funerals in churches, too. Funerals are sad. But people who have church funerals believe they're going to Heaven; they're not going to hang around a church pissed off about the afterlife. And we had established, as definitively as you can without breaking ground, that no cemetery had ever been part of the property, so we were confident we wouldn't have Poltergeist-like incidents.

(Then I looked up what a sage-smudging ritual involved. Sage smoke absorbs conflict, anger, illness or evil, according to Google results. Couldn't hurt to take a metaphysical shower, right?)

I have been accused of being naïve Pollyanna, so maybe when I said I was convinced we could successfully tackle this job, save money in the process and love our new digs, well, maybe I was wrong.

But I was also a fatalist who believed it did no good to resist the inevitable. Any house we purchased, or any lifestyle we adopted, could get us killed or cost us money or make us miserable. Not to mix metaphors, but if we were going to go down in flames, we were going down in a church.

3
Bells of pure gold

The belfry had the potential to be our first money pit.

A belfry is the part of a bell tower or steeple in which bells are housed.

Ask not for whom the bell tolls. It tolls for thee.

Bells toll. Pay the toll. Bad things take a toll.

Originally, the seller wanted the bell excluded from the sale of the church building. But with a little bit of research on eBay, my husband convinced the congregation that removing the bell would probably cost more than it was worth. When they accepted our offer, which included the bell, we were thrilled to become its new owners. But the bell was going to exact a toll.

Without any inspection, we knew the belfry had problems. Remember, the seller had mistakenly described it as "rooted." We hoped it was "rooted," actually. My husband, ever the insurance agent, had visions the tower would fall, and we'd be liable for killing someone. Being solidly rooted is what we wanted in a good belfry.

Wear and tear were evident.

But the roof of the belfry indeed proved problematic, which was obvious standing even twenty-five feet away. Shingles curled all around the edges, and a piece of flashing was tearing away.

Our third showing of the church involved my enterprising husband wearing a hazardous materials suit, goggles, a face mask and wielding a big flashlight. Oh, and a hammer.

Looking like the Stay Puft Marshmallow Man, Tyler climbed a stepladder in the second-floor closet that led to the belfry. A couple of whacks at the trapdoor, and he was inside.

Unfortunately, he could see the sky. Coffee-can sized holes dotted the roof's perimeter around the bell. On days with worse weather, rain was likely pouring into those holes. And who knows what else!

Well, we found out what else.

Stan the squirrel.

The mummified and dust-covered rodent's wide-open mouth betrayed the terror he must have felt in his last moments.

The real estate agent and I were standing along the far wall while Tyler poked around. We had no interest in coming face to face with a bat.

Tyler found Stan. But he didn't find any bats.

Oh, joy! We didn't have bats in our belfry after all! (I told that joke ad nauseam for days afterward. And I'm not promising I won't use it again.)

In the privacy of our bed in the early-morning hours as we dreamed of our church, Tyler initially cooked up the idea that he could use the emergency stairs that were attached to a different side of the house to repair the belfry. He described in alarming detail how he could move the stairway around the building, climb up twenty-five feet, deconstruct the belfry piece by piece around the bell and rebuild the roof.

In the chilly days of November in Wisconsin.

I forced him to recount his brilliant plan in excruciating detail to our children in the hopes that they would dissuade him of such lunacy.

In the light of day, and after the encounter with Stan, he knew professionals needed to be involved.

First, he called three area roofers. Roofers sneer at heights. Or, at least, they have the equipment to mount such a repair. Keep in mind, we didn't even officially own the property yet. Tyler, with his salesman-like charm, persuaded the roofers to have a look. One of them followed through, emailing a quote for reroofing the entire church.

Um, that's not what we wanted. We wanted you to reroof the belfry.

Tyler was undeterred, which is what we would need if we ever hoped to finish this project. He discovered an entire profession created for just such a project: steeplejacks.

A steeplejack is a craftsman who scales tall buildings to repair chimneys, church spires, cupolas, clock towers and—fortunately for us—bell towers.

The first steeplejack looked at pictures of the belfry and provided a highly detailed quote within a week: $50,000.

We wanted to cry. That figure was more than we were paying for the entire church building!

Tyler didn't give up, though, and the second steeplejack—a pro with a mission who signed his quote with "in His Service"—confessed he couldn't promise he could do it for less than $50,000 until he could inspect the belfry. Just erecting the scaffolding would take a day to accomplish. Besides paying for him and two assistants (at $2,400 a day), we'd have to shell out for the materials, of course.

Of course.

But we loved the bell tower that would soon be ours. And I loved my husband. Avoiding having his broken body at the bottom of a set of rickety steps was worth $2,400 a day to me.

And, as if guided by a divine scheduler, the pro with a mission would be available in November.

This coincidental schedule opening only made us more impatient to close on the church. But perhaps the divine scheduler could see a bigger picture than we could.

4
DO NOT LET YOUR HEARTS BE TROUBLED

BACK AT OUR CAMPER, the prospect of freezing temperatures became ever more real. We debated how long it would take for us to acquire a habitation permit from the village.

The building inspector told Tyler he required an operational bathroom, kitchen and bedroom before he would allow us to occupy the church.

Well, we had a toilet in the basement.

We didn't even have running water. The congregation had turned it off sixteen months before when they vacated the church building to merge with another congregation in a nearby city. They took all the pews, the pulpit, the altar and both the bathroom and kitchen sinks. The basement kitchen countertops were unmoored from the walls.

On the third showing at the church when we found Stan the squirrel, Tyler and I discovered puddles in the basement. The caretaker, who noticed us at the church as he drove by, came inside to tell us the basement always got water when it rained. *Shouldn't a caretaker do something about that?* I wondered silently.

A basement prone to flooding was probably not a great place for a bed.

Tyler spent a month scheming how to construct a bathroom shower and install new (or newish) sinks. He consulted with an electrician. He called an HVAC guy to schedule a furnace check. And he pondered how to protect our sleeping area from construction dust. We could take our time once we moved in, but speed was of the essence to make it livable.

Every day the church failed to conjure up the necessary documents for closing the deal put us more on edge. Tyler would lay awake at two o'clock in the morning thinking about hundred-year-old lead pipes and drain vents. For me, the sleeplessness came at the beginning of the night. I would watch HGTV for hours before retiring for the evening, and then I'd lay awake re-arranging the location of the main floor laundry and dining room table. Or I'd scroll through pages on Pinterest looking at rustic accent walls, vaulted bedroom ceilings and DIY entryways only to dream about them later.

In retrospect, I believe God was giving us a break. An opportunity to catch our breaths and think. A few weeks of rest. But at the time, the delay was maddening. Here we'd finally gotten our heads around the idea that we weren't going to live in the camper and travel the country indefinitely, and we'd decided to jump back into the real estate market. We'd found a property we were confident we couldn't lose money on no matter what Wall Street did to Main Street. We'd created a renovation plan. We'd determined we could agree on the style of our kitchen backsplash, the fireplace mantel and the color of the paired sectionals with which we planned to furnish the great room. But we couldn't do anything other than shop.

This was problematic since we no longer owned a garage in which to store the amazing deals Tyler scored on Amazon Prime and Craigslist. On a brief business trip, we visited an expansive architectural salvage store with historic doors and unique bathroom fixtures, but we couldn't buy any of it with nowhere to put our treasures. Tyler found an amazing store of used construction materials in greater Chicago selling twenty-three pieces of solid wood kitchen cabinets in the perfect shade of cream. But upon inspection, they were a perfect shade of yellow, so we didn't buy them. But we were awed by bathroom vanities in every shade of the rainbow and the doors in widths from twenty-seven inches to thirty-two inches. Too bad we didn't know exactly how wide we'd need our doors. Or how many for that matter.

The visits to second-hand shops cemented our decision renovate with as many pieces of recycled materials as we could find. We'd sold most of our furniture when we vacated our home a year before, and we were horrified by how little other people valued our belongings. We'd vowed never to buy new un-upholstered furniture again (but we would still say yes to upholstered furniture of unknown origin, not so much).

Our lack of storage space didn't prevent Tyler from finding an ornate Mirror, Mirror on the Wall for the front entryway. At the same estate sale, he scored a bathroom faucet, sink and vanity from Craigslist. He purchased two-by-fours and built eight sawhorses. He stashed these finds, in the garages of his cousin and his mother (sometimes over their objections).

AFTER SIX WEEKS OF scheming and waiting, on November first, the day after we agreed to an extension of our closing date, Tyler began shopping for an apartment. He'd toyed with, then rejected the idea a couple of times based on the trouble of the moving and demands for long-term leases and long commuting distances to the work site of the church. But now, after purchasing propane in three-figure volumes, he was serious.

He had lowered his standards enough to entertain all options however unsavory. Finally, he found something we thought could work: a one-bedroom house that allowed pets (to accommodate our aging miniature schnauzer) located just two blocks from our church. Not a moment too soon, we completed the application and set up a time to look at the place. The morning of our walk-through, the garden hose that supplied water to our camper) froze. Campers don't plan trips to northern Illinois in November for a very good reason.

The rental house was tiny but functional. There was room enough for our king-sized bed, lots of natural light and, unbelievably, a wine refrigerator and jetted tub. In this case, "cozy" was a mansion compared to the meager 358 square feet in our RV. Judging by the dirt in the corners, it was clearly a rental property, but who needed pretty? We were going to build pretty into the church. As with all things related to real estate, it had the three attributes we most wanted: location, location, location. We agreed to the terms on the spot and scheduled a day to move in: November eleventh, four days before we planned—hoped? —to close on the church.

While we were town, we accomplished our first maintenance task, an act the church granted us permission to do even though we weren't officially owners: Tyler extended the downspouts on the church to coax water away from the foundation and the basement.

5
RISE AND MEASURE THE TEMPLE

As we waited impatiently for the church to gather closing documents, we reviewed the freshly minted survey for our lot.

To our surprise, we were about to become owners of *three* lots. Together, our triangle-shaped property comprised about a third of an acre. The church building sat on the corner where two streets intersected (there had never been a parking lot; apparently parishioners used street parking or the elementary school's lot kitty corner to the church). This positioning would allow us to build a garage in the backyard with a curb cut on the west side of the lot, avoiding the ugly maw of a double garage door overwhelming our front door as so many suburban homes without alleys have. Before we purchased our former residence, I'd vowed never to buy such a monstrosity. But alas, that's how modern houses are plated and constructed nowadays.

There would be no welcoming porch though. Our front door was 3.78 feet over the property line. Technically, our light sconces on either side of the front door were streetlights. Instead, we planned a screened porch off the to-be-built garage overlooking our side yard.

Some math revealed 5,033 square feet of livable space, including the basement. This was roughly fourteen times the size of the camper in which we'd resided for nearly ten months.

Part of me felt guilty for giving up the minimalist lifestyle. When people asked why we'd moved, we often told them our house had gotten too big; we rarely walked into entire rooms.

But the truth was, we just hated that house. We'd paid more for it than it was worth, and then the 2008 Recession hit and stole even more equity from us. Spending any money to make the home more our own and with less mass market appeal felt wasteful and pointless. The longer we stayed there, the less it felt like home. Getting out was a relief.

The part of me that didn't feel guilty about taking on so much house felt positively giddy about it. The camper's tight quarters weren't great for entertaining. There was too little room to prepare meals, much less serve them. Overnight guests sleeping in our living room awakened at the first grind of coffee beans. I was excited to create inviting guest spaces in our new home, and with a grandchild on the way, I wanted plenty of space to spread out the crib, toys and other paraphernalia accumulated by modern parents.

I longed for our king-sized bed. The camper only had room for a queen, and Tyler and I more than filled it. *Cozy* had started to become *cramped.*

Tyler began to resent the landmines I'd created everywhere by stuffing belongings into every conceivable space; I wished for cupboards to organize dishware, toiletries and shoes without having to pull every last thing apart to get to the bottom of a pile.

Amid the many coordinates and numbers, the survey didn't capture how that square footage would create a sanctuary for a family.

6
AWAITING A BETTER HOME

WE SPREAD OUT THE move into our little rental house over three days. We spent the first day cleaning.

Oh, the house just two blocks from our church looked clean enough. No garbage. The floors appeared swept. The cupboards probably had been wiped out. Probably.

But my Virgo husband wasn't one to trust others' cleaning. One of a Virgo's principle traits is perfectionism. If a Virgo sets out to do something, he typically doesn't rest until it's done very (very!) well. That's a good trait when it comes to cleanliness (and church reconstruction).

He brought five gallons of concentrated Simply Green. Five *gallons*.

We scrubbed literally every surface, and what we didn't scrub, we swept or vacuumed. The whispery spider webs disappeared from ceiling corners. Scrounge on the bathroom floor lifted. Greasy dust no longer stuck to ceiling fans that had clearly never been touched, let alone dusted, by the previous resident.

This was a good warm-up for the church, which had sat empty for sixteen months and had 126 years to accumulate gunk. Ceiling fan dust would be the least of it.

ON THE SECOND AND third day of our move, we transferred our meager belongings from the camper and urgent items from the cargo trailer into our tiny rental house. Our most critical need: a bed. We would need restful slumber if we hoped to survive renovating a church.

We'd packed our big, beautiful king-sized Sleep Number bed into the cargo trailer the day before we moved from our suburban cardboard box. The camper had room for only a queen-sized bed, so we bid farewell to the best bed we ever owned when we moved out.

We had carefully packed our Sleep Number bed's unique combination of foam, air pillows, zippered compartments and inflation device into the cargo trailer. The last thing to go in was the first thing to come out.

Amid sleeting flurries in southern Wisconsin, we coaxed the pieces of the bed from storage and into the little house. We slammed shut the cargo trailer doors and parked our camper on the now-muddy gravel driveway inside the garage foundation. A garage had once stood on this lot, but now, only the cement-block foundation remained. After much cold-handed grunting and groaning, we affixed a boot on the tire and paddle locks on the trailer doors.

Tyler had built a platform for the bed in our new bedroom out of two-by-fours and plywood (the original platform remained in the trailer). We set to work assembling our bed.

After sorting out all the pieces, we realized we were missing one: the inflation device.

An air bed isn't much of a bed without air.

Ugh.

Back to the cargo trailer to pinpoint the apparatus.

"What does it look like," I implored, while climbing over boxes and craning to see the labels on bins.

Clearly, I wasn't paying attention eleven months before when we disassembled the bed.

"It's the size of a bread box," Tyler instructed.

Believe me, a bread box is a needle when the 30-foot cargo trailer is the haystack. Especially when the air is filled with ice-cold wet sleet.

Eventually, we found the contraption, repacked and re-secured the trailer, and retreated to the warmth of our little rental house. Once we had all the pieces, the parts went together easily. As we lay on our beloved king-sized bed looking at the spiderweb-free ceiling, we felt content. I was amazed at how quickly I felt comfortable in our little rental. It felt like a mansion compared to the RV, and I swiftly reacclimated to house living.

In three days, we would close on the church, and we could start our project at long last.

Or so we thought.

TWO WEEKS AFTER WE originally planned to close on the church (just two weeks!), no closing had been scheduled. The church still didn't have the paperwork it required to designate authorized signatures.

Tyler had had it. He was anything but understanding.

Sure, we were protected from the elements now, but really! We wanted to close on the church two months ago! Should we walk away from the deal?

Though we entertained conspiracy theories that the congregation really didn't want to sell the church, we knew in our hearts they just weren't as motivated to wrap things up as we were. We decided to give them incentive. We offered to extend our offer for two more weeks (admitting to ourselves it would be a regular miracle if we closed that quickly), but we also lowered our offering price. Now our good deal was even better.

We sweated it out for twenty-four hours while we awaited a response, but the church accepted. So now we had a few thousand more in our budget and two more weeks to plan how to spend it.

As we relaxed in front of the TV one evening in our little rental house, I asked Tyler how he was feeling about things.

"Excited," he said right away. "And scared."

7
THE WISE LAY UP KNOWLEDGE

My beloved husband knew well what it meant to renovate a house and why anyone about to tackle such an undertaking should proceed with caution.

In the 1980s, Tyler's first whole-house renovation project began with Boone County's oldest operational tobacco farm.

He and his wife at the time purchased the property in northern Illinois for just the price of a new car from two bachelor brothers who had grown tobacco there for decades. Now in their 80s, one brother lived in a nursing home; the other planned to join him.

The farm's distinctive tobacco barn had hinged foot-wide openings that locked from the inside with a wooden peg. The brothers would open the slats to dry the tobacco hanging inside. They smoked their product. Every outbuilding had Zig Zag-brand cigarette rolling paper packages stuffed in every crevice.

The farmhouse had no heat except a warm-morning stove connected to a fuel oil tank. In each room, one light switch connected to a single bulb hanging from the ceiling. Old horsehair plaster covered walls and ceilings. The Douglas fir flooring and trim could be refinished; the baseboards were distinctive. The main floor's three rooms were connected to the second half-story by a steep stairway. The basement was a five-foot-deep hole with a dirt floor.

With no plumbing, the "running water" was a well pump. The brothers hauled pumped water inside for drinking and bathing. When Tyler had the well tested, it was like death syrup—the levels of live bacteria and chloroform so high as to be practically toxic (chloroform was used an anesthetic in the Civil War). The "bathroom" was a two-hole outhouse on skids so the brothers could move it when the pit beneath it filled.

When Tyler acquired the property, he first emptied the place of decades of cigarette rolling papers and other junk accumulated by two old bachelors. The unfinished half-story had two old iron beds with four-inch thick mattresses. Tables on each side of the bed were piled high with identical clothing for the brothers: bib overalls, stained V-neck T-shirts and union suits in varying degrees of wear. Behind the tobacco barn, near a plow and disc (put into use in their time by mules) stood a stack of aluminum pie tins as tall and as wide Tyler.

"There must have been more than a thousand," Tyler mused when he told me about his project. Here his story deviated a bit from renovation concerns to memories of this property.

"Back there was a stump, too, the brothers used for butchering chickens," he recalled. "I did, too. There was a broad-head ax hanging in the tobacco barn that I still have, and I used it to cut the heads off the chickens I grew in the yard. My grandma Blair helped me. I chopped the heads off, dipped them in a cauldron of boiling water, and Grandma did the feathers. I can still see her there in a lawn chair plucking feathers."

"Did they taste good, those chickens?" I asked, thinking of a book I'd read recently about how free-range chickens in decades past have so much more flavor than today's mass-market chicken breasts.

"They were the best chickens I've ever eaten," he remembered.

Tyler returned to remembering his renovation experience and the difficult physical labor required to pull off such an undertaking. After cleaning up the property, he knocked all the horsehair plaster and lath off the walls of the farmhouse, installed 100-amp electrical service and wired the whole house. Tyler had taken vocational classes on electrical work and picked up real-world experience by wiring rental housing and cabins with his grandfather. He installed a high-tech (at the time) Swedish wood stove outside and ran HVAC channels to heat the entire house.

He then ran PVC pipe throughout the structure to bring running water from a new well inside to the kitchen, two bathrooms and a second-floor laundry. As the days turned into weeks, he installed his own septic system. The neighbor dug the trenches with a backhoe, Tyler laid the pipe and rock, and a guy came out to set the tank.

The septic system passed inspection. The plumbing passed inspection. The electrical passed inspection. Now it was habitable.

The basement was another phase. Years before, his parents figured out a masterful method to keep teenaged Tyler busy: he dug out their entire basement by hand. He put that experience to good use when he dug out the tobacco farmhouse basement the same way, removing the dirt with a little elevator into the back of a pickup truck. Once it was deep enough to stand up in, he poured a cement floor.

My enterprising husband is one to go big or go home. He likes big steaks, big trucks and, fortunately for me, big women (or at least tall ones; I'm 5-foot-10). Our RV is among the biggest on the road and, of course, he's fond of big houses, too.

This first renovation project was no different. Once he had the farmhouse livable, he decided he needed more space. He built a 24-by-36-foot two-story addition, the main floor for a family room and the second floor for a master bedroom. (He deconstructed the Swedish wood stove and moved it to heat the addition.) He then built a three-car garage on the other side of the farmhouse.

When I say, "he built it," I'm being literal. He would frame one wall and invite a buddy or a relative to help him stand it up. People who know Tyler won't be surprised he paid his buddies in beer. A lot of beer.

Tyler at work on the tobacco farm, circa 1985.

The entire project took just less than two years. Five years after he and his wife bought it, they moved to Minnesota. They sold the old tobacco farm for ten times what they'd paid for it.

Ironically, Tyler's old tobacco farmhouse transformation was big enough to house a whole congregation—let's call it *cathedral big*. We drove by it not long after we'd purchased our 126-year-old church, and there was a cross, a flag and a rustic sign out front that read "Eternal Light Fellowship/Faith Hope Family/Sunday Worship 10:30 a.m."

The current owner had turned it into a church.

The Eternal Light Fellowship found a home
in Tyler's first renovation.

8
THE PEARL OF GREAT PRICE

EVERY THANKSGIVING, I MAKE Tyler talk about what he has been thankful for in the past year. I hate to think of the holiday as only an opportunity to stuff oneself, watch football and read Black Friday ads. Usually, on our way to a feast of turkey and pecan pie, we counted down the Top 10 people and experiences for which we're grateful.

This year, Thanksgiving fell smack in the middle of our two-week hiatus from getting our hands on the keys to our new old church. We had to be thankful for finding the church, if not grateful for getting started on the project. We had no choice but to travel to enjoy a feast. Our little rental house was so small, it didn't have room for a table, and I don't think anyone would have enjoyed standing around the kitchen island to dine. Instead, we drove to Tyler's mother's house and counted our blessings along the way: Very happy to have sold our house in the suburbs. Grateful for becoming grandparents. Thankful we had the opportunity to travel a bit before resettling. Excited to begin work on our little 126-year-old church.

On Black Friday, Tyler rose before the sun to wait in line at the nearby Home Depot. He returned home with orders before I'd sipped my first coffee:

"Help me get this thing unloaded."

The *thing* was a tool chest. Or, more precisely, *another* tool chest. If I had a thing for books (and I did), Tyler had a thing for tools. Every time he used a tool to fix something or save us the cost of hiring someone to do the work, he reminded me: "I couldn't have done that without the thingy-whatsit, you know. Aren't you glad I have so many thingy-whatsits?" Only he didn't say *thingy-whatsit*. All his tools had specific names and uses that somehow eluded me. I understood hammers and screwdrivers; I could even differentiate between a flat-head screwdriver and a Phillips screwdriver. But I could never remember the difference between a wrench and a pliers. And God help me if he started lauding the values of various kinds of saws.

All these various implements required storage (of course—what's jewelry without a jewelry box?). We might need a screwdriver or a wrench or a pliers (or a measuring tape or a sledgehammer) to transform our church into a house so thank goodness he had found a toolbox at Home Depot, right?

"It was too good a deal to pass up."

Sort of like the church, I suppose.

For all the buildup to closing day, the closing confab itself was uneventful. We arrived at the designated location for the handoff of the keys, and within forty-five minutes, we'd paid our cash, signed the papers, and shook hands with our long-suffering real estate agent and the poor pastor who just wanted to write sermons, not track down 100-year-old paperwork. The church was ours.

We drove straight back to our rental house, where Tyler dropped me off so I could change into something more ... suitable for demolition.

"Grab a couple of cups," he instructed as he put the truck into gear. "I'll meet you at the church."

I changed into my new pink work boots (yes, because if I'm going to get dirty, I might as well do it in style) and grabbed two red Dixie cups. I leashed poopy puppy, our 10-year-old miniature schnauzer, and we walked the two blocks to the church.

Meanwhile, Tyler stopped at the liquor store (conveniently, only two blocks from the church in the *other* direction) and invested in the finest bottle of champagne, er, sparkling wine, the village had to offer.

Tyler was fingering the key to the front door when I arrived.

"Oh, you waited for me." I smiled.

We entered and sat in an abandoned office chair and a 25-year-old padded banquet chair in the middle of our sanctuary, sipping "champagne" from our plastic cups.

"Here's to the church," Tyler toasted.

"The church," I said, looking around the quickly dimming room. We'd turned on the electricity (and, glory be, it worked) but we couldn't find switches to the sanctuary lights. As the winter sun began to set, the room took on a romantic atmosphere.

"Are you ready for this?" he asked.

Methodists don't have confessionals, so I had to own up in the dimming light of the sanctuary.

"*Now* I'm scared."

THE LIST OF "FIRST things to do" at our old church had grown long.

First, there was demolition.

First, we had to pick up and clean.

First, we had to do yard work.

First, we needed to address the deteriorating belfry.

But what happened first—*really* first—was moving in all of Tyler's tools.

For the regular handyman, this might take three or four hours. With Tyler, it took three or four days.

We fished all his toolboxes from our cargo trailer where they had been stored since January. Then we transported all the tools that had arrived at our rental house via the productive guys at UPS and the Postal Service in the time we'd been there; thanks to Amazon Prime, Tyler was on a first-name basis with the UPS guy by the second day. We retrieved sawhorses Tyler had built and stored at his cousin's house and his mother's. He then twice visited Home Depot for sheets of plywood, doodads and locking mechanisms to secure everything.

When he was done (or as done as any man with a penchant for tools who still had money in his pocket could be), the sanctuary of the church (a 26-by-36-foot space) was filled with toolboxes, plywood work tables, sawhorses, saws and duplicates of just about every tool known to man. Or at least known to this woman.

Just the array of screwdrivers boggled my mind.

At one point in the demolition, Tyler needed a very heavyweight hook. A little bit of digging revealed exactly the hook he needed, a medieval-looking device suitable for hanging a dead knight from the rafters.

"What is that?!"

"It's a come-along." (I didn't ask what a come-along was. I later learned it's a hand-operated winch.)

"Why do you have *that?*"

"We needed it for the racecar."

Of course. For the racecar.

Yes, my Renaissance Man husband had grease monkey blood in his veins. A few years before, he and his brother raced stock cars on the dirt racetrack in northern Illinois near our home at the time. Every weekend all summer long, they'd spend their evenings driving a $500 piece of junk around a quarter-mile racetrack wearing out tires. Invariably, by the end of the night, the vehicle would be inoperable for one reason or another (an encounter with another beat-up race car operated by a competitive wild man will do that), and the hunk of metal would have to be loaded onto a trailer so it could be returned home for repairs. And that's the story on how my husband came to have an enormous, scary-looking come-along.

Please do not ask why he *still* had an enormous, scary-looking come-along, four years after he quit racing. But the answer explains why it took us three or four days to unpack his tools.

CHURCHES HAVE SAINTS, AND our saint was St. John.

Even Jesus couldn't do everything by himself. He gathered twelve apostles, among the first was John, one of the sons of Zebedee. Our St. John was a follower, too, an excellent follower of Tyler's orders.

The third time we visited the church, after making an offer but two months before we closed the deal, Tyler and I visited the local grocery store. It was just a glorified convenience store known for selling bacon-wrapped beef tenderloins, but hey, we could get sugar or a can of soup or, heck, a beer in a pinch. Tyler quizzed the cashier as we departed.

"Do you know anyone looking for work?"

She gave him a bewildered look. Maybe she thought he was asking something nefarious.

"I'm renovating a building, and I need some help."

"Help? Like what kind of help?"

"You know ... carrying things, moving things around, demolition. That kind of work."

"Hmm, I don't know." She made a show of looking like she was thinking about fellows who would be willing to carry things.

"Well, if you think of anyone, would you give them my number?"

"Sure," she said, writing Tyler's name and number on a slip of paper. "Maybe I know someone."

I chided Tyler as we left the store. "Why do you think the cashier is the only person in town who knows people who do manual labor?" I asked.

"She's the only person in town I have talked to!"

"No one is ever going to call you. She threw that piece of paper away as soon as we left the store."

"Well, maybe so, but it can't hurt to ask."

Lo and behold, a guy called Tyler a few days later. He introduced himself as Johnny and said he heard Tyler needed some help on a building project.

"See!" Tyler told me later.

At the time, we had hoped to close on the church in a matter of days. We didn't know it would take weeks. He told Johnny to give him a call in three or four days. Every single time, Johnny followed through. He called three or four days later, and Tyler filled him in on the latest delay.

We couldn't be so lucky, I thought, to find a guy in the very town we were buying a property who would be willing to be Tyler's hired man.

But sure enough, Johnny showed up in his work clothes on the second day, and boy, could he work. Best of all, he was the most cheerful order-taker I'd ever seen.

"Move that." "Take that over there." "Help me pick this up." "Take that apart."

Whatever Tyler asked, Johnny carried out.

While carrying loads of garbage, I lowered my voice and told Johnny I hoped it was OK, taking Tyler's orders (I'm not implying *I* was irked to be taking orders, please don't misunderstand).

"No, we get along great," Johnny chirped. "We're on the same wavelength."

If Johnny wasn't a saint, he was at least an angel.

AS IF TO ILLUSTRATE His countenance upon us, the sun shined brightly those first few days we owned the church. The late November Wisconsin weather was unseasonably warm, so we made hay while the sun shined. Well, brush. We made brush.

View looking toward back of the church.

We drove by the church a hundred times or so while we waited for our deal to go through. Without the keys to get inside, we focused on the exterior, and we came to detest the arborvitaes (over)growing near the entryway. They needed more than a trim; an extraction was called for. A chainsaw (one of Tyler's many saws) was put into service, and down came the overgrown bushes. Johnny and I scurried like ants, hauling the pieces of trunk and greenery to the backyard burn pile.

Tyler then turned his attention to the row of bushes lining the sidewalk (and growing through our exterior staircase to the second floor). Even Tyler (yes, he also has a green thumb) couldn't determine their species, but we knew we wanted to keep them for aesthetics and privacy. But, oh, they needed a trim.

At the end of the row, Tyler revealed something he could identify: a lilac bush. I loved lilac bushes. So fragrant! I distinctly remember the lilac bushes in the alley of my childhood home in central Minnesota. One May afternoon when I was about 14, I grudgingly performed the chore of taking out the garbage and, to my delight, discovered the aromatic flowers crowding out the scent of potato peels in the garbage can. Being the trash man that day was a gift.

That bush was spared of trimming. Please let it bloom in the spring, I prayed.

When we were done, we had piled the brush twenty feet wide and six feet high.

A few days later, Tyler alerted the fire department to our imminent bonfire. The firemen gave him the equivalent of a shrug, and Tyler burned up two years' worth of growth in a few hours. Our first before-and-after project—immensely satisfying.

9
Revelations

Amusing things one finds in a 126-year-old Methodist church:

—A 1969 map of Palestine with the footnote: "Boundaries do not necessarily carry the approval of the countries involved." Some things never change.

—A treasure trove of pots and pans abandoned by the older church ladies who had no interest in kneeling to reach all the way to the back of the bottom cupboard in the basement kitchen. We scored some great stuff, including a template for cutting a pie into exactly six equal pieces and a pristine piece of brand-name Tupperware for storing flour or sugar and labeled with a marker "UMC" (United Methodist Church, of course); I pressed this into service as a Chex Mix storage device during the holidays. Plus, I uncovered a top-quality insulated casserole carrier that some proud church lady must have mourned losing for years.

—A play telephone with a dial—who dials a phone anymore?—and a telephone book.

—A stereo and vinyl records. In the words of Ronco infomercial huckster Ron Popeil, but wait, there's more! Cassette tapes *and* CDs.

—Lights, which are not at all surprising, hidden behind doors and inside closets. But the switches were befuddling. The wiring was strange.

Dy-no-mite!

—An ancient-looking wooden box labeled TNT. I imagined how it might have found its way to the church: A railroad worker's wife (our village was once the junction of two major railroad lines) made four delicious apple pies for a church supper and opted to transport them in the handiest sturdy container.

—The owner's manual for The Excelsior UNIQUE Oil Burning Air Conditioner in the furnace room. An *oil-burning* air conditioner? A careful reading of the manual from the Excelsior Steel Furnace Company revealed the air being conditioned was probably for heat, not cooling. There was no date on the manual, but I guessed it was at least sixty years old. Excelsior Steel Furnace was founded in 1886 and, based on the existence of an operational website, National Excelsior Company was apparently still in operation as an HVAC supplier. The oil furnace in the church had been replaced at some point by gas-forced air.

What we didn't find, or at least didn't recognize as we threw them away, were the remote controls for church's ceiling fans. Hanging at least ten feet off the ground, it was impossible to simply pull a chain to start them. The caretaker told us the remotes existed, but we somehow lost them in the flurry of cleaning and organizing the first few days. I dug through a couple of garbage bags, but if they were in there, they were hidden by rotten wood and sawdust.

"ADVENT IS A SEASON of preparation."

Perhaps a church sign is dangerous in the hands of a writer. Instead of just listing the service times, a clever sign-keeper can post phrases like, "If you're looking for a sign from God, this is it" and "God answers knee-mail."

Well, the old Methodist church came with a sign.

Originally, I thought we'd eventually demo the sign, but more and more friends urged us to keep it and post messages such as, "We welcome the Hendricksons for dinner" and "Guess who turns 51!"

On the second day of cleaning it up and tearing down the crusty stuff, Tyler found the box of metal letters for the sign board.

He directed me to remove the message about the food shelf moving across town and replace it with "Merry Christmas."

The only problem: it wasn't Christmas yet. It wasn't even December.

It was the last glorious day in November, unseasonably warm enough to remove a jacket while hand trimming hedges, carrying brush and raking leaves. As a fairly regular churchgoer, I knew the beginning of Advent was coming in a few days. Advent is the run-up to Christmas, a liminal season of expectation celebrated by Christians all over the world. But to describe it only as a time of waiting sells Advent short, just as the days between Thanksgiving and December 25 are more than simply an out-of-breath sprint to be endured.

Bible readings for this time of year are about waiting and preparation and expectation. I enjoyed Advent, reminding myself it is not an empty time. It is a season of fullness. Because preparing can be just as meaningful as the celebration itself.

I posted a message on our church sign with a handy double meaning: "Advent is a season of preparation."

I could have been slogging through days of demolition and cleaning and organizing, simply wishing we could be done. But with months of work ahead of us, I'd be wishing away a significant portion of my life. I'd better be enjoying the dirty, noisy or drafty moments for what they were; anticipation should be as joy-filled as the hullabaloo of the destination.

I was inordinately pleased with my church sign message. I smiled to myself every time I drove by. One day, the former pastor of our old Methodist church stopped by when Tyler was burning brush in the back yard. She thanked him for preserving the old building, and she also made a point of telling him she liked the message in the sign.

"She got it!" I shrieked happily when Tyler told me about the encounter.

A writer never tires of the act of publication, even if it's only as public as a church sign.

DEMOLITION IS 5 PERCENT revelation and 95 percent dirty work. In those first few heady days of demolition, we were still in the revelation phase, and it was fun.

As we peeled away layers of carpeting, carpet padding, paneling and ceiling tiles, we discovered the beautiful original finishes of the church. That moment in a DIY television show when a flipper discovers hardwood floors and swoons? That's real. We did a little dance when Tyler pulled back the carpeting in the main sanctuary and found wide pine hardwood; Tyler suspected it might be Douglas fir. If we weren't so old, we would have done a breakdance when we revealed the overflow room's oak floors, the room we intended to turn into our master suite.

Under the 1970s wood paneling, beadboard—the kind that was installed a single board at a time instead of with today's monolithic sheets—lined the master suite area up to the chair rail (or, at least, where the chair rail used to be). The master room's ceiling was also narrow-slated wood. We imagined a fantastic tray ceiling with the wood revealed in the center.

But the best thing we discovered during demolition was the choir loft.

The old saying, "Man plans, God laughs" was evident. We had planned to close a week or two after we made an offer on the church, ha! That hadn't worked out. Now, our plans for the second floor were changing with every swing of the sledgehammer.

A church member told us the second floor used to be the choir loft, and as we Tyler and his hired man St. Johnny pulled down upstairs shelves and closets and walls, the balcony opened up like sunshine through the clouds. Tyler poked and prodded, and then smashed and crushed, to reveal the original, higher ceiling in the sanctuary and the huge opening into the second floor.

He was inspired.

"I have a great idea, hear me out." He described extending the balcony floor into the great room and constructing the kitchen underneath it to create more space for our master bedroom in the overflow area behind it.

An inspired concept, indeed.

For days, we had been walking around the overflow area looking for ways to incorporate the kitchen, an entry from the to-be-built garage, a guest bath, the master bedroom, the master bathroom, a walk-in closet and a main-floor laundry. It was a lot to ask of 600 square feet.

No matter how I turned it around in my dreaming mind at night or on paper during the day, I couldn't figure out how to pull it off without sacrificing a shower or a laundry room or a walk-in closet (or all three).

Tyler's concept would make room for all our creature comforts, keep the kitchen we wanted *and* fill up some of the excess space in the great room.

But the grand expansion of the second floor wasn't in the Tequila Budget. This would mean adding square footage that needed to be built, carpeted and railed. We also toyed with the idea of adding a second, more decorative stairway to the second floor. (Technically, we already had two stairways to the second floor—an interior enclosed wooden stairway and an exterior metal fire escape. The fire escape, an eyesore not required if the church was residential, would be removed and sold.)

Naturally, our taste ran toward the expensive.

The next day, Tyler made an early morning stop at a nearby spiral stairway manufacturer. They'd been making custom stairs and rails for nearly seventy years, right in our village, only blocks from the church.

Functioning spiral stairways inside and out showed off different spiral widths, spindles, treads and handrails. A spiral stairway is a custom project that must be an exact height. One does not pick a stairway off a big-box shelf and install it with an Allen wrench. Besides the height, one can choose the materials, all the decorative elements *and* if the stairs will run clockwise or counterclockwise. Immediately, our creative juices flowed. And if we're building a spiral staircase, why not also order a wrought iron balcony railing?

Being custom, neither of these design features would come cheaply.

We decided to take the wait-and-see approach to the staircase and railing. The spiral staircase manufacturer wasn't going anywhere, and neither were we.

But it was fun to dream.

WE ENCOUNTERED REMARKABLE REMINDERS of the building's age (besides the unremarkable dust). We spotted two 1969 pennies apparently lost by a carpenter when constructing the altar area. Tyler found more than one square-headed nail as he pulled things apart, and he discovered full two-by-fours (modern uniform two-by-fours are actually 1.5-by-3.5-inches in size) and a piece of one-by-eight that was fifteen feet long without a single knot, not even pin knots. Even so, it was hard to remember our church had been built before Orville and Wilbur Wright flew their first airplane.

One Sunday morning about ten days after we closed on the church, we worshiped at the Methodist church in the nearby town into which our little congregation had merged some months before, leaving behind the empty building.

Just inside the entryway in a place of honor, an old picture of our church hung on the wall. It was fascinating. It was our church, all right, but in a different world. We could see a covered wagon and hitching posts. Our trees had yet to be planted, and a railroad ran behind where a row of bushes now grow. The original entryway of our church sat just beneath the belfry. Scallop shakes decorated fluted details. This photo only fueled Tyler's desire to strip the building's aluminum siding.

While difficult to see, it looked like a stained-glass window transom was perched over the entryway.

The window we could see from the inside of the belfry was on the *outside* in this picture. We hoped to return this window and more to the structure at some point during belfry reconstruction.

The church had an active historical society, and I asked to be invited to the next meeting. An answer came in the affirmative, and I hoped to determine the exact age of our beloved little church.

Our old church in a different time.

EVEN THOUGH WE COULD have waited, we decided to buy a set of new doors for the entryway. Tyler found a deal on Craigslist we just couldn't pass up.

Earlier, while we waited to close on the church, we admired an exterior door on display at Home Depot. I knew Tyler would love it, and when I led him away from the plumbing fixtures to the front door display, I knew I was right.

We exchanged a look like a couple happening upon the perfect name for their first born.

This was it.

It was a rustic, knotty pine with an operable speakeasy door behind a grille. It looked like it belonged on a castle, which was perfect, since a man's home is his castle. And it could be special ordered as a 96-inch-tall pair. The existing entry to the church included two 80-inch-tall doors, and we knew we wanted a footprint at least as large.

Naturally, a special-order set of front doors from a big-box store exacts a king's ransom. We'd allotted something for the front entryway in the Tequila Budget, but not *that* much.

But Tyler, being Tyler, took that as a cue to snoop around architectural salvage joints and online. A couple of weeks later, someone in a nearby kingdom placed a listing on Craigslist for just such a set of doors with the title: "Remodel reject." Asking price: $1,000 less than new.

"Whaddya think?" Tyler asked.

"They're perfect," I said. The Craigslist doors even had the speakeasy portal, *and* they were arched. "We should at least go and look."

We drove ninety minutes south one Sunday after church to check 'em out.

They were indeed only slightly used and exactly what wanted. Tyler the Negotiator wrangled the owner to the ground in a metaphorical wrestling match ("We have cash. And we'll take them off your hands today") and claimed a pin; the seller accepted an offer for less than half of the Home Depot doors.

The only challenge was the "we'll take them off your hands today" promise. These were eight-foot double doors that came with the frame. They were larger than any pickup truck bed.

Fortunately, Tyler had planned for that.

He'd brought along two-by-fours, one of Tyler's many cutting devices (a cordless Skilsaw), an electric drill and a box of screws. In minutes, he'd built a frame to carry the doorframe on top of the pickup truck. Then we wrapped the doors in the biggest, most royal furniture blanket: The twelve-foot red velvet curtain that had been hanging in the front of the church.

A few bungee cords later, and we were off.

We returned safely and in one piece to the church. With a little help, we carried our entryway inside, to be installed much later during warmer and the moat had been filled (just kidding about the moat).

10
THE REPAIRER OF THE BREACH

FIVE DAYS AFTER WE closed on the church, the roofer showed up. Securing the bell tower was high on the to-do list after the seller had disclosed the roof was "rooted" and our pre-closing inspection revealed it was indeed rotted. With winter closing in fast, so was our window of opportunity.

After a couple of different bids from roofers of various talent, we decided not to hire a steeplejack, but a friend of a friend with a good reputation for flat roofs. For the purposes of clarity, a few definitions might be in order. The bell turret on our church—the ornamental feature *above* the bell chamber—appeared to be in decent condition and shingled with materials at least as new (or old) as the rest of the church roof. It was the flat roof *floor* of the bell chamber (beneath the bell) that was falling apart.

The young man with a deceivingly slight build and a long reddish beard had a name, but in my imagination, I called him Reroofer, sort of the fairytale contractor version of Rapunzel: "Reroofer, Reroofer, let down your beard!" Unlike Rapunzel, though, the roofer would not have been trapped in any castle towers; Reroofer had the agility of a monkey climbing around the belfry thirty feet off the ground.

Initially, Reroofer thought he could fix the holes in the roof in two days. After his first two hours tearing off disintegrating shingles and ancient pieces of wood, Tyler called up to him and asked him how his was work was progressing.

"It's worse than I thought."

Uh-oh.

The bell, it turns out, was three-inch thick cast iron, weighing a thousand pounds, we guessed without the benefit of a scale. Some carpenter had cobbled together a solution to the aging bell supports, and now the old fix was worse for wear.

Working mostly from the inside (which made it more bearable to watch), Reroofer transferred the weight of the bell while replacing the supporting structure with an ingenious system of straps and come-alongs (and an equally gymnastic helper on the second day of repairs). The supports were replaced with new, treated four-by-fours. When he finished, the bell hung a foot higher than before his work.

At one point that day, Reroofer rang our bell. Oh, what a beautiful sound! Full and melodious. I dreamed of ringing the bell on special familial occasions such as birthdays and anniversaries and, of course, New Year's Eve. Some grandmothers bake cookies or plant gardens with the grandkids; I wanted to be that special grandmother no one else had who offered bell-ringing responsibilities to her grandchildren.

In sharing these fanciful notions with interested listeners, I heard more than one story about kampanaphobia: the fear of bells. The phobia is triggered by a negative experience with bells.

"What will your neighbors think of you ringing your bell?"

I'd never considered the possibility that anyone wouldn't like our bell.

When I looked up the village noise ordinance, I discovered, to my dismay, it applied to residential properties, which of course is what we hoped to be rezoned as: "All noise shall be muffled or otherwise controlled as not to become objectionable due to intermittence, duration, beat frequency or shrillness." A church bell that belonged to a residence was required to abide by different rules than a church bell that belonged to a church. I prodded Tyler to discuss this with the building inspector who asked, "Well, are you planning to ring it at midnight every night?"

No, no, of course not.

It seemed the noise ordinance was enforced much like whatever rules applied to bonfires in our little village: be responsible, don't get carried away and be conscious of your neighbors.

Reroofer worked tirelessly on our bell tower for three days, fueled only by cigarettes and king-sized Snickers bars. He reinforced the framing, installed new decking and replaced the backer board and aluminum fascia. He installed a new ice-and-water shield all around, wrapped all eight pilings with shielding and built a new trapdoor.

More work—to the eight original pilings holding up the structure—was required, but that would have to wait for heavier equipment and better weather.

Reroofer finished the initial work to the belfry just in time. A thirty-mile-per-hour wind was whipping up, and the forecast called for temperatures in the teens. It was December in Wisconsin after all. When he was done, the belfry actually looked worse. Oh, it was more solid by a long shot, but aesthetically, ye olde belfry looked half-dressed without her siding. We'd agreed Reroofer would return in the spring to make the belfry pretty, but for now, we were structurally sound and waterproof (also, squirrel free).

When he climbed down and cleaned his tools, he handed Tyler a bill: $1,500.

I could have cried tears of joy.

There were many nights when rain fell on our camper's roof after we saw the holes in the roof of the belfry but before the day the church was ours. I cringed thinking of all that water flowing unimpeded into the church.

The night Reroofer made the belfry watertight, I lay in bed listening to cold, spiky drops of rain hitting the windows of our little rental house. The rain sounded like rice thrown against the windows. I turned over and smiled as I drifted back to sleep.

11
HE CUTS OFF EVERY BRANCH THAT BEARS NO FRUIT

THE DIRTY PART OF demolition began to wear us down. There's a reason home improvement television devotes five minutes or less of every show to the demolition process and usually punctuates it with crazy demolition antics. The work is necessary, but it's just plain dirty work: dust, sawdust, insulation dust and construction waste served with a side of tedium.

Tyler supervised the project and handled power tools. St. Johnny, the hired man, performed all work that required kneeling or heavy lifting, skills neither Tyler nor I relished exercising. I was assigned to menial, monotonous jobs such as removing nails from trim and flooring.

We planned to reuse as much of the church as possible. Those pieces of trim and flooring would live new lives as trim or repaired floor or accent walls in the remodeled interior. But one can't safely saw pieces of wood riddled with nails. Oh, those church builders of yore loved their nails! A single piece of hardwood flooring might have thirty nails (plus a few carpeting staples thrown in for good measure). Tyler bought a new Air Locker gun, a device powered with compressed air that niftily forced nails out from the bottom. He also dug a strange but effective device from one of his toolboxes that looked like it once was wielded by an iron welder from the Old West to move coals. I used this to yank stubborn nails from boards that could not be coaxed out by the Air Locker gun. I developed tennis elbow, but I became an expert at using these amazing tools. A few tips:

—Wear work boots. Those nails forced out with highly compressed air might pierce more decorative footwear.
—Wear eye protection. Those nails fly everywhere.
—Wear gloves. Recycled wood has splinters.
—Admire the sparks: Yes, sometimes there are sparks.
—Organize your recycled wood by type. In a five-thousand-square-foot structure, you're gonna recycle *a lot* of wood. Separate the trim, the baseboards and the flooring, or you're never gonna find the wood you want when you're ready to reuse it.

IF WE COULDN'T REPURPOSE a material ourselves, we had three ways to get rid of items we had no use for: Throw it away, give it away, sell it.

Only a few items were worth the trouble of reselling, so we opted to give away many miscellaneous objects. Unfortunately, we created a literal ton of garbage that no one could use.

Initially, we planned to use the regular garbage bins to get rid of refuse. Thirty-yard dumpsters, as it happens, are expensive. And we didn't budget for any dumpsters in the Tequila Budget. We instead deluded ourselves into thinking we'd just fill our garbage cans full every week and eventually, we'd get rid of everything.

Ha!

After the first week, it was clear the garbage would be gone about 2068.

Maybe, Tyler thought, he could just bring a few overflowing truckloads to the dump.

But the nearest dump was forty miles away.

Then he thought he could order a dumpster after the first of the year. We'd just walk around our construction debris inside the church until then.

When the walking around became wading, he knew he'd lost the good fight. Two weeks into our demolition, Tyler gave in and ordered a dumpster. A thirty-yard dumpster was delivered the next day and filled within a week. St. Johnny hauled ceiling tiles, lath and plaster to the dumpster. We identified several items for repurposing, but the basement pass-through where thousands of hot dishes and pies were served and the sanctuary communion rail where sins were forgiven found their final destinies in the dumpster.

It was difficult to write a check for almost $500 just to haul away our garbage, but we ordered another dumpster to be delivered just after the new year—such was the price of expunging the suspended ceilings, old carpeting and all that plaster lath from our landscape.

DURING THE DEMOLITION, I made several trips to Goodwill and Habitat for Humanity's Restore. Some furniture, light fixtures and even Christmas trees were our trash, but some other man's treasure.

Restore accepts construction materials and operational appliances and resells them for Habitat for Humanity's housing program. On an early trip, I tried to talk the manager into taking the built-in cabinet and accordion room divider that had sat between the sanctuary and the overflow space.

Tyler and St. Johnny loaded them into our pickup and secured them for the twenty-mile journey to a new life.

I pulled up to the drop-off just as a garbage truck pulled into the lot to empty the store's dumpster. While the truck's beep-beep-beep created background music, the Restore manager eyed my goods.

"The bad news is, we're not interested," he said. To be fair, the accordion divider had seen better days and the built-in was designed for, well, a church. "The good news is, I can try to talk to the trash guy into taking them. I'll help you move them from your truck to his."

The garbage man agreed. It being a couple of weeks before Christmas, I hurriedly dug ten bucks from my purse and profusely thanked the dump truck driver. I was sorry to be further filling a landfill, but grateful for serendipity.

Two and a half weeks after we closed on the church, St. Johnny tackled the closet I had once told Tyler I would clean out first. So many other priorities had pushed their way to the front of the line.

When we first toured the church, the single-door closet along the eave on the second floor had a hand-lettered warning: "Do not open!" Of course, I opened it. I found paint cans and a whole lot of dirty insulation.

"I think I read somewhere they had a wild animal in here. Maybe it was in there," the real estate agent said.

But Stan the squirrel found a final resting place elsewhere.

Now, St. Johnny was demolishing the whole wall; my procrastination had become his opportunity. We hoped to create storage there, maybe enclosed by short, sliding barn doors.

St. Johnny found much more than old paint (but no live animals). The single closet door led to a long space along the eave, filled with Christmas decorations. Ah, so the church had already been using the space as storage. Unfortunately, a thick layer of dust and insulation covered everything.

As usual, St. Johnny moved boxes to my sorting station, and I combed through them to determine what was garbage, what was worth donating and what was worth keeping. I tossed the tinsel, the

Easter basket stuffing and a box of Christmas manger costumes some Sunday School class in 1970 wore. Some talented mom (or moms) had turned a passel of second graders into proud shepherds watching a flock of kindergarteners by night. But the costumes had seen better days. At least three hundred dollars' worth of multi-colored Christmas lights went to the basement; at some later date, we would determine if these lights could be used to decorate the exterior of the church.

I found two manger scenes. One included a lighted plastic three-foot tall Holy Family. I couldn't bear to relegate the miniature family to the dumpster, so I situated them on the curb. On an unseasonably warm December day, only an hour went by before the driver of a passing van determined they had room at the inn.

"Hey, are you giving these away?"

"Yup," I called out from inside the church, "they're all yours."

In other manger-scene news, I picked through a cardboard stable filled with little figurines. The disintegrating barn went into the dumpster. But like their bigger relatives, I couldn't bear to toss the figurines. I brought them home, intent on at least washing them before giving them away.

As I scrubbed their faces gently in the soapy dishwater (the "gently" part came after I erased a Wise Man's face—ugh), I determined the figurines came from at least three different crèche scenes. I had three Marys, but only one baby Jesus; this evoked a memory of my little brother who repeatedly stole Baby Sweets from my Mattel Sunshine Family back in the late 1970s—babies can be *so* compelling. Still, maybe someone was missing a Mary. On the last day of the year, I used my final opportunity to claim a tax deduction for a charitable donation, and I transported my motley manger family to Goodwill. Maybe someone would find a treasure in an expressionless Wise Man, or maybe not. But at least I tried.

Some items were simply too sacred to throw away indiscriminately. But they weren't worth keeping either.

Like the flags. The American flag hanging on the flagpole was decrepit beyond salvage. We donated that one and another to the local American Legion post for proper retirement through burning. I also found a half-dozen desk flags that I donated to Goodwill. We returned the United Methodist Church flag to the nearby congregation.

Then there were the hymnals. We found boxes of them, probably a few issued by every Methodist hymnal committee in a century.

I kept four of them with the intention of making a unique light fixture for a reading nook. The rest, I gave to Goodwill in hopes someone would find a creative use for them.

And the Bibles. We unearthed more than two dozen Bibles in various conditions from falling apart to pretty nice. I kept one in excellent condition, respectfully tossed two whose bindings were disintegrating and packed up twenty-six others. Those I shipped to Christian Library International. CLI's mission is to advance Christ's light in prisons by distributing Bibles and offering Bible study. (Anyone can help CLI by collecting Bibles from fellow church members, by contributing money for shipping and by praying.)

The giving away involved a lot of trips to Goodwill and elsewhere. When volunteers offered to haul stuff away for us, well, all the better.

We found what were certainly the original French doors on the 1940's entrance stored above the back entry to the basement along with parts to pews and what looked like an old barn door that had been used as a table.

At first, we intended to put French doors on our bedroom's doorway to replace the hollow-core doors. But upon inspection, my excitement waned when we determined they could not be saved with any amount of sanding, stripping and painting. The wood was beginning to rot, and the peeling paint was probably lead-based.

We crossed our fingers that the garbage man would take them. No go. We leaned them against the back of the church while we pondered our options.

One day, a lady drove by while I was changing the church sign.

She slowed to a stop, poked her head out her car window and asked if she could have our windows.

I gave her a puzzled look. "Windows?"

"In back. The windows leaning against the building."

"Oh! Those are French doors. They're in tough shape. You should look at them before you decide to take them."

"I'll be back tomorrow morning," she said. "I'll drive my van, so I have room for them."

"OK," I said. "They're yours if you want them. Just take them, even if we're not here."

Sure enough, they disappeared the next day.

I don't know what she did with them—some sort of craft project, I hoped. But I was happy these historical doors didn't meet their end in the landfill. And that I didn't have to haul them away.

WE TRIED TO BE good stewards of our unwanted demolition waste. To avoid filling a landfill, we gave away many items, but when the opportunity presented itself, we were open to selling items. With mixed results.

I tried to sell a box of Christian books at Half Price Books. I got $2.80. I immediately invested in a $3 copy of *The Complete Idiot's Guide to the World's Religions*. I figured any woman who lived in a church should educate herself on all things spiritual.

After the second guy in a beat-up pickup truck stopped to ask if he could haul away the scrap metal we'd piled up outside next to the church, Tyler and I took it upon ourselves to see how much it was worth.

One warmish afternoon in January, Tyler and I piled all the siding Reroofer tore off the belfry and what seemed like a hundred miles of suspended ceiling grid into the back of our beat-up pickup truck and drove to a scrap metal yard about ten miles away.

We stopped for lunch because we worked up an appetite loading the truck.

We spent $14.23 on bowls of homemade soup and a shared salami club sandwich., Tyler got a dynamite apple fritter for dessert.

We proceeded to the scrap metal yard where a couple of overall-clad fellows helped us separate the more valuable aluminum siding from the steel scrap. Our booty was weighed, and they handed us a check for $30.24.

After factoring in the gas required to transport our scrap metal, we each earned roughly $7 an hour plus lunch.

This was a vast improvement compared to how we spent the next two hours. We priced bathtubs, kitchen cabinets and flooring to use on the ceiling of the second floor. Big price tags, them all.

We still hoped to sell the exterior staircase at some point. Surely *someone*—with a cutting torch or a long trailer—needed a fire escape.

For all the junk and debris we found in the church, we were delighted not to find two unwelcome guests: rot and vermin. Besides the rotted roof in the belfry, all the wood we found both hidden and exposed was astonishingly sound.

The lack of insects was another pleasant surprise. Sure, spiders and spider webs inhabited many corners, but none of those disgusting millipedes had taken up residence in the basement, and even the Asian lady beetles and box elder bugs that were infesting our nearby rental house were few and far between at the church.

As Tyler carefully removed the tin ceiling in the basement, he found three enormous wasp nests built between the exterior wall and the floor joists of the first floor. Shortly thereafter, he found another one in the false roof of the entryway. But the honeycombed structures were at least a decade old, and their creators had taken up residence elsewhere long ago.

It seems only squirrels had been unwanted squatters in ye olde Methodist church (with five extremely mature pine trees on the lot, we shouldn't have been surprised). I'd take dead squirrels over live bats any day.

Besides Stan, whose mummified remains we found in the belfry during one of the early showings, Reroofer also found squirrel carcasses in the bell tower during his reconstruction foray. And I discovered an almost perfectly preserved squirrel skeleton in a box of plastic chandelier crystals that had been stored on the second floor.

At least, I thought it was a squirrel.

I imagined her to be Stan's dearly departed mate, tempted but ultimately doomed by the packing Styrofoam in the box that would become her coffin. Her creepy beauty transfixed me. I texted a picture to my stepdaughter who, with a degree in biophysics, I thought might find it scientific. Her response? "Ewwwww!"

AFTER WEEKS OF DEMOLITION, we practiced self-therapy.

"Wow, we've made so much more progress than I thought we would."

"Well, we knew the belfry had problems. It's no surprise to us."

"You know, we can bring in an expert to discuss structural support if we need one."

"I need a break, too. Breaks are good. We can't work seven days a week."

We needed to be cheerleaders for ourselves because everywhere we looked, we were surrounded by dust and old nails, and more to do around every corner. As Tyler walked contractors through the building for quotes, more than one said, "You have quite a project here."

Anyone who's ever remodeled already knows: many contractors cannot be depended upon for anything, but least of all, encouragement.

We took to heart a battle cry uttered by master carpenter and host Ben Napier in an episode of HGTV's *Home Town,* who surely had faced mammoth home remodeling projects of his own: "That's the way the great ones all start. People doubt them. Everyone doubts them, and honestly that's how I think you become great. You prove them wrong. You prove the doubters wrong."

So yes, it was a big project. Thank you for pointing that out. We were going to persevere and invite the doubters to the open house to show it off when we were done.

I also let the church itself reassure me during those quiet moments of uncertainty. A sign left behind on what was perhaps a Sunday School room door reminded me: "Please be patient. God isn't finished with me yet."

Another message painted over the inside of the entrance, to be seen by exiting parishioners and witnessed by me every time I carried another load of tools or wood upstairs or downstairs: "Go now in peace."

A little quilted banner I found among the Christmas decorations simply said "Peace." I brought it home, washed it gently (more gently than that poor Wise Man I'd defaced) and admired the excellent stitchery. And the appliqued bell. It had a bell! This gem that reinforced these other messages found a spot back in the church.

A rock placed at the foot of the flagpole also seemed to carry a compelling message. It might have been an image of Moses with the Ten Commandments (or half of them? See? Moses was a writer, too), but it might also have been a saint or a significant Methodist figure. I think he was sticking out his tongue. I did an online reverse image search, and I learned it was a relief—that is, a sculptural technique where the sculpted elements remain attached to a solid background. I went literal with my findings, as in "relief," a feeling of reassurance and relaxation following release from anxiety or distress. Working on the church a little bit every day could be considered a relief: We had found home.

THE AREA BENEATH THE entryway steps was one of the last spaces we demolished.

Old photos revealed that the steps were not original to the church. The original entry was beneath the belfry; the current entry had been constructed in the early 1940s.

Leading to the opening beneath the carpeted wood steps, a cupboard door without a knob had been sealed with foam and painted over (maybe more than once). In other hiding places in the church, we'd found old Christmas decorations (disappointing) and a plethora of old doors (thrilling!), so Tyler and I were curious what treasures might be hidden under the steps.

He chipped away at the trim around the door, discarding pieces in all directions. "I feel like Geraldo Rivera!" he said, and I giggled.

Readers of a certain age may remember when Rivera hosted a 1986 special on *The Mystery of Al Capone's Vaults* during which he spent an hour hyping the potential discoveries of a secret vault beneath the Lexington Hotel in Chicago. When the vault was finally opened on live TV, the only things found inside were dirt and several empty bottles.

Like Rivera, our discovery was disappointing. Church members had left behind only a pile of scrap wood and a Bible comic book from 1962. The best thing was the actual cupboard door: solid beadboard.

NEAR THE END, WE measured demolition progress inch by inch. Tyler pulled up the carpeting in the main sanctuary, cut it into four big hunks, and it was all we—Tyler, St. Johnny and I—could do to drag each dusty, unwieldy piece to the dumpster. We were left with about five thousand carpet staples stretching to infinity across the floor's horizon, each one securing a piece of carpet padding to the Douglas fir hardwood flooring.

I spent hours pulling staples, carefully running my fingertips over the floor to make sure I got all of them. It wouldn't do to have any staples or nails left behind when we were ready to sand and restore the hardwood to glory.

About six weeks into the project, we'd cleared the second floor. Gone were closets under the eaves, the walls, a sweeping swath of the choir loft ceiling and the carpeting. We were down to the studs, as they say in the business. The only thing left was a gas heat stove in the corner, which could not be removed until the plumber

Carpet staples to the horizon's edge.

disconnected the gas line.

I longed to sweep (and I never longed to clean anything as more than one roommate can attest), but Tyler put me to work on other tasks; he didn't want any more dust in the air and he knew there were weeks of dust ahead of us. Still, the area that would someday soon be a bathroom, a bedroom and my office looked great. Finally, we'd uncovered the blank slate for which we were looking.

12
THE CALLING OF THE FIRST DISCIPLES

THE OVERWHELMING DUST AND debris generated by demolition made us recant our ridiculous ambition to live in the church while we took it apart. We took this as further proof that the delay in closing (which drove us to rent a house nearby) had been a blessing instead of simply frustrating.

Many evenings (or late afternoons), Tyler would walk through the back door of our rental house, remove his clothing (usually while bellowing, "Close the blinds!") and go straight into the shower. On particularly physically taxing days (like when he razed the banquet bar in the basement or the plaster in the sanctuary), he'd draw a bath. He'd summon me to bring him a beer and wash his back, which I always obliged. I had usually returned home hours before him to tend to our dog, handle some business paperwork, throw in a load of laundry and start supper, so I was in a better position to provide a little tender-loving care.

Those long showers and full tubs taught us a lesson: water is expensive in our little village. Compared to the village where we'd formerly lived, water and sewer service cost about 40 percent more.

Fortunately, we learned this utilities quirk before we invested in appliances and fixtures. Tyler immediately began online research into low-flow dishwashers, washing machines, toilets and shower heads. I'm ashamed we didn't pursue these opportunities without the stick of cost, as the carrot of being environmentally responsible should have been inspiration enough.

MODERN HOMES—AT LEAST ones on the grid—require a plethora of utility services, and our church was no exception.

We acquired accounts for natural gas and electric immediately; the church was already hooked up and the service providers only needed to know whom to bill. Lights were as easy as the flip of a switch. Then we pursued heat. Three days after we closed, an HVAC guy turned on the gas, checked for leaks and tweaked out both forced-air furnaces to make sure they worked properly. Cost: $170, a fraction of what we might have paid if there were issues. The furnaces were housed in the basement, which was sometimes wet, and we feared the furnaces might be toast (or perhaps oatmeal is a better metaphor here). But glory be, they worked.

Next up: wireless internet. The church might have been built in the 19th century, but we were living in the 21st, and we needed technology. The internet provider required the church to have a business contract (which cost more) because when we signed up, we were still zoned as a church; we would have to change that later. Tyler installed not one but two Wi-Fi-connected thermostats (because two furnaces require two thermostats).

Soon after, an unseasonably cold spell hit the southwestern Wisconsin landscape (and the rest of the Midwest), but between the body heat we generated by hard work and the furnaces, we didn't shiver inside our new home.

Our next hurdle was like parting the Red Sea. We needed something close to that miracle. You might think water service would be as easy as electricity—register your name, your credit history and your first born with the utility, and *voilà!,* power. Water in an old church is a different story.

The Methodists had been getting unmetered water for the past eighty years (or however long they had indoor plumbing). After all, the church was used just once a week plus an occasional funeral. Some former members told us a few bachelor pastors in history had lived in the church, but they must have bathed elsewhere, because the bathroom had only a toilet and a sink.

To get water, we needed a water meter. By code, only a plumber licensed in Wisconsin could install one.

This proved tricky. Tyler called at least a half dozen plumbers for this seemingly simple task. *If* they called him back (a big if), they frequently couldn't fit us in the schedule until February.

Unacceptable.

Tyler took to snapping pictures of plumbing vans he happened to drive by in the area and calling the numbers advertised on the side panels. He asked everyone he encountered for referrals.

Finally, two weeks after we closed on the church, a plumber showed up when he said he would and installed a water meter. Now the village allowed us to turn the water on, and look at that, the toilet flushed. This was all well and good, except one couldn't wash one's hands because we still didn't have a bathroom sink (and we wouldn't be getting one for many more weeks).

Plumbers weren't the only recalcitrant contractors. Tyler was the general contractor on our project, and I learned quickly (I say "I" because Tyler probably already knew) that a general contractor's primary responsibility is to dog subcontractors.

Roughly eight weeks into our project, Tyler estimated he'd called sixty different contractors for projects ranging from plumbing and electrical to concrete and storm gutters. About a third had called him back, and only about ten showed up to provide bids.

Just when Tyler lost his last shred of patience and understanding with flaky contractors, a warm January day dawned.

The effects of global warming, or climate change or whatever label you'd prefer, were causing deadly mudslides in California, but in the Midwest, we experienced an abnormal 50-degree day, We took advantage of it, and we weren't the only ones.

Tyler put me to work cleaning the garden shed behind the church and making room for construction materials we hoped to repurpose. While I wrangled about a hundred muddy garden hoses into submission, Tyler met with the parade of contractors who showed up.

First there was the concrete guy who eyeballed our proposed driveway and garage pad. When I asked Tyler later what the contractor said, he told me, "He said it was a lot of concrete."

Then a pair of HVAC experts stopped by and toured our mess. Tyler had recently pulled down the primary ductwork on the main floor in anticipation of running plumbing and electricity, and it looked like a squarish metal snake had slithered across our floor.

Meanwhile, one of Tyler's cousins gave us a gift. With an expertise in trimming trees, he offered to trim ours. He climbed the trunks of our enormous pine trees and trimmed away a forest of low-hanging branches. (We'd found an old picture of the church that showed a pine tree as a seedling; now the biggest one had a four-foot circumference and stretched upward of fifty feet.)

A contingent of window contractors showed up with a display trailer. We climbed inside—me in my muddy jeans and garden-hose tousled hair—to see life-sized windows, cut-aways that showed their construction and plenty of beautiful and covet-worthy custom shapes and designs.

As I walked down the sidewalk away from the church admiring the tree-trimmer's work, I could have sworn I saw dollar bills flying out the open windows and doors.

Ten days later, another bumper crop of contractors showed up, all in one day: Tiler, drywaller, another pair of HVAC experts, the electrician and our now-good friend, Reroofer.

We were entering Phase Two of our church conversion project: framing, utilities and mechanicals.

NOTHING IS CERTAIN BUT death and taxes, Benjamin Franklin once said. Of course, he lived before homes had indoor plumbing and electrical wiring.

But definitely taxes. They're certain.

On another unseasonably warm day in January, St. Johnny, the hired man, had just filled the back of the beat-up pickup with most of the basement ductwork. The HVAC guys had declared every bit of it incorrectly positioned for the new layout and that it needed replacement (the Tequila Budget would take a big hit for this unplanned development). Tyler and I were headed to the scrap metal recyclers for a second time.

Just as we were about to pull away from the curb, the tax assessor showed up.

I felt a little sorry for him because as he introduced himself; he looked a bit skittish, as if he wasn't always greeted warmly by homeowners. But for us, his timing was perfect since the church looked a fright near the end of demolition.

Our friends joked we should just continue to offer Sunday services to avoid paying property taxes—Tyler had a gift for gab and who minds sharing a bottle of wine with friends? Heck, we still had the collection plates. But, alas, that's not how it works.

We ended up in the assessor's visitation queue because the church had changed hands into private ownership, and we had received a building permit. He explained our property would be valued at its sale price (a good thing for us) and its condition at the first of the year (as it was uninhabitable, that was also good for us for the time being).

We invited him inside (I gathered from his response that this wasn't what usually happened) but unlike our other visitors, we didn't give him the dreams-and-quartz-countertops tour.

After a few exterior measurements, he was on his way. And so were we. Another day, another trip to the scrap yard.

One might think mail service is as inevitable as taxes, but no. At least not for a residence that formerly was a church. I don't know how the Methodists received mail, but there was no mailbox. I visited the post office no fewer than four times in eight weeks, but I still had no answer about whether we would have a mailbox on the street or at the post office. Neither snow nor rain nor heat nor gloom of night stays these couriers from the swift completion of their appointed rounds, but I guess the volume of Christmas deliveries delays answers about mailbox location.

If I couldn't get an answer during *Phase One: Demo*, maybe I'd get an answer during *Phase Two: Framing and Mechanicals*.

Demolition had revealed the bones of our 126-year-old Methodist church, and now we needed to run the veins and arteries and intestines through the structure.

Detailed planning was required to know where to put sinks and drains, electrical boxes and outlets, heating vents and cold-air returns. Tyler and I had been scheming and debating for months, and by now, we had a fairly complete plan in place, both on paper and in spray paint on the floors. By "fairly complete," I mean we would show a bidding plumber where we wanted a shower, and then he would ask us, "what kind of shower head do you want?" and we'd look at each other like, "Hmm, what kind of shower heads are there?" Or the electrician would ask, "Are you going to light your bookshelves?" and we'd look at each other and think, "What a great idea! Lighted bookshelves!"

Our floor plan had another missing piece, I learned at a regional home improvement show one weekend in January.

A home and garden show is like a chocolate chip cookie. The

boring but necessary ingredients such as vendors for basement waterproofing, excavators and roofing materials are punctuated by the chocolate chip hucksters of granite countertops, acrylic shower stalls and designer garage doors. Real DIYers like us passed on the booths populated by custom home builders, but we were impressed with innovations on otherwise boring details such as solar tubes, remote control operated shades and automatic lawnmowers.

It was at the garage door vendor booth where I learned Tyler was planning a thirty-six-foot bar along one side of the garage with a clear glass garage door opening. (Didn't I mention he was a "go big or go home" kind of guy?).

"What?!" I said, my mouth falling open. "This is the first I've heard of this!"

"Some things are on a need-to-know basis," Tyler said slyly, and resumed discussing tempered-glass door options and costs with the salesman.

Over dinner, I pressed Tyler for details on his man cave and encouraged him to draw up a detailed plan. He obliged, and I learned what he thought I needed to know. (A week later, he was forced to rethink his fantasy garage plans. Alas, the zoning setback requirement would mean a smaller garage would be necessary; a thirty-six-foot bar might not make the cut.)

In any case, we had a plan, so now we would spend weeks running plumbing, wiring and all-new ductwork for the heating and air conditioning through the exposed floors and ceilings. The work of all these skilled laborers would commit us to the floor plan and certain fixtures. We'd better know what we wanted, because once mechanicals are sealed behind drywall, changes are costly. We needed a style book and design plan to help us make good decisions. Fortunately, I'd had plenty of time to develop one.

13
FAITH IS THE ASSURANCE OF THINGS HOPED FOR

BESIDES PLAYING OFFICE AS a child, I treasured my Fashion Plates. The artsy toy from the late 1970s allowed you to design your own fashions with interchangeable plates embossed with outlines of shirts, skirts and pants. The young artist, or designer, would rub the embossed shapes to get the outlines, then color in the clothes with fashionable colored pencils. *Voilà!* A new fashion design. I was a fashion designer!

Nearly every dollar earned babysitting was saved in my fall shopping fund. I pored over magazines and catalogues, spent days shopping at malls to find the trendiest fashions and created detailed plans of my daily wardrobe to impress my rivals at school.

I grew into a 5-foot-10 woman who could pull off a wide variety of looks, and I filled every closet I ever owned to overflowing with my *fashionista* finds.

But turning 50 meant more than acquiring an AARP card—I found my muffin top and wrinkles made spending money on beautiful clothes and dressing my aging body became less satisfying. Miniskirts and sleeveless tanks and body-skimming shapes left my wardrobe.

Maybe that's why I became transfixed with dressing my home. I enjoyed the creative thrill of combining various pieces into a unique look, and when I showed it off, I didn't have to suck in my gut. I had been happy to let my husband decorate the house during my first marriage, and then with Tyler, we literally outfitted our first home in six weeks by shopping mostly at big-box stores. We were busy people then and raising a teenager took priority.

Now, as I pondered the design of our new home, I decided a vision board was in order. We had become overwhelmed by the array of options on display at Home Depot, Overstock.com, lighting stores and the architectural salvage warehouses we visited. Narrowing our options would make decision making easier when the time came. While Tyler pondered plumbing and electrical installation, I meditated on the finishing details.

I began with my tool of choice: words.

As a brand manager for a major scrapbooking company some two decades before, I had created style guides for logo use, brochure creation and scrapbook page design. These guides helped marketers and designers all over the world adhere to a coherent brand message about the company's products. I drew on that experience to write a style guide for our new house that would help Tyler and I create a home with a unified design.

First, I channeled my inner Joanna Gaines. She was the design guru behind HGTV's *Fixer Upper* who managed to infuse her modern farmhouse spaces with clean lines, airy color palettes and recycled shiplap. Her "less is more" attitude inspired me, and her home design jibed with the way I had learned to design newspaper pages back when I was a copy editor: form follows function. This principle says the shape of something (a building or a brochure or whatever) should be primarily related to its intended function or purpose. In other words, regarding house floorplans, *don't* design a ballroom for a couch potato, and *do* build bookshelves for a bibliophile.

I invested in an armload of home decorating magazines and spent hours flipping through ideas on Pinterest.

With my concepts in mind, I interviewed Tyler. After all, he was going to live here, too. A focus group is simple to assemble when there are only two people to research. I asked him, "How do you want your kitchen to look?" "How to you want to feel when you walk in the front door?" "What colors do you hate?" and "What one word would you use to describe your style?"

Then I put fingers to keyboard to create a mission statement:

> *We strive to create a comfortable sanctuary in the modern world, built solidly and maintained orderly.*

Comfort was the first adjective for a reason; we didn't want an arthouse that required ramrod posture and scared away visitors. I drew some of my inspiration from a book I read about Danish *hygge*.

"Hygge is about an atmosphere and an experience, rather than about things," writes Meik Wiking in *The Little Book of Hygge: Danish Secrets to Happy Living*. "It is about being with the people we love. A feeling of home."

Wiking wrote about the coziness factor of candles, tea, comfort food and being present in the moment. As for décor: "Anything hand-crafted—objects created out of wood, ceramics, wool, leather and so on—is *hyggeligt*…the rustic, organic surface of something imperfect or something that has been or will be affected by age appeals to the touch of hygge." That's that I wanted in our new home: *hygge*.

Sanctuary appealed to us as a good word with two meanings: churches had sanctuaries, and sanctuaries were places of peace. With this intention, I created my first mantra to carry me through the construction phase when things got tough: "We live in a church. Let's practice peace."

After living in what we repeatedly referred to as a cardboard box for a decade, we both lusted for solidity. Hollow-core doors, paper-thin walls and plain vanilla details were created for the masses; we wanted something a craftsman from a century ago would have created to persevere through a F5 tornado.

Though I was a slob to my core, I knew my husband was a Virgo who valued order. Creating an orderly home with plenty of storage and easy ways to hide away mess was key.

After researching interior designs styles on the internet and being tempted but ultimately rejecting words such as *bohemian* and *eclectic*, I settled on this summary of our style:

> *Our decorating style is*
> *rustic transitional*
> *punctuated with elements of*
> *warehouse,*
> *farmhouse,*
> *barn house and*
> *house of worship.*

Rustic transitional: Note that *transitional* is the noun, *rustic* the modifier. *Transitional* is defined as bridging contemporary and traditional design with inspiration from the industrial era, heavy emphasis on an open floor plan and leaning toward clean, straight lines but incorporating thoughtful details. *Refined* would be balanced by *raw*. The adjective *rustic* suggests elements such as exposed bricks, stone, raw steel, rough-hewn or distressed wood and metal, especially tin, aluminum and wrought iron or rusted metal.

What was *warehouse?* Think of a loft with open space, exposed steel and brick and industrial light fixtures. Add in salvaged architectural pieces, especially antique doors. What parts of warehouse did I want to avoid? Nothing cold, greasy or noisy.

I pictured *farmhouse* as an antique flea market that showed wear—

distressed wood, oversized clocks, vintage mirrors, candlesticks. Elements needed to be functional but soft and opulent. Not Mason jars, cute cows or country tchotchkes.

Converted barns had that same open space as lofts and warehouses, but barns also featured exposed wood beams, hearths, barn doors and large chunky pieces. Oh, and animals, which I would incorporate with faux animal hides. What about barns did I reject? Anything dirty. Not our aesthetic. Especially not for a Virgo.

And naturally, the inside of our home would have to reflect the outside. As a former house of worship, our house would embrace the belfry and bells of all kinds, organ and piano elements, pews, large windows, stained glass and flowing water (which recalls baptism and new beginnings). Crucifixes were OK, I decided, but not to excess; no Virgin Mary statues planted in the garden.

Our brand personality would be a balance of necessity and luxury, of industrial and homemade, of modern and classic, of masculine and feminine, leaning toward economical, casual and subdued.

I wrote down ten design rules:

1. Details matter.
2. Recycle, reuse and repurpose whenever possible.
3. Natural lighting brings the outdoors indoors.
4. Build storage into every room—two closets, two cupboards, two hooks, two nooks are better than one.
5. Accent walls create a center of focus.
6. Doors and doorways should be beckoning and give some clue as to what's behind them (think: frosted glass with the word "laundry" and design that reflects the room within).
7. Artwork should be graphic, realistic (think photographs) or abstract. Large object art and quote art—words, saying and verses—should be used liberally.
8. Flooring should be hardwood and/or tile with durable rugs made of natural fiber, jute and sisal.
9. The two rooms we spend the most time in—the kitchen and

master suite—should be most luxurious and elegant.
10. Curb appeal is worth the money. The front door sends a message. Our entryway should be functional and welcoming.

Finally, I defined our color story. Color would easily create a cohesive space, and this part of the design dossier would keep us (me) on task. When we moved from our previous home, my numerous purple home décor items appalled me. It all began with a pair of microfiber purple chairs we'd chosen for the living room that wore like steel and lasted through a redesign of the room, which included a purple wall in the kitchen. After that, I'd unconsciously chosen a purple rug, purple placemats, a purple bedspread and purple candles. Too much of a highly distinctive color!

I wanted a more neutral background for the church. Though I used words ("black and white, cream and chocolate brown, grays, light blues and aqua with occasional turquoise"), I knew actual color samples would be most useful in practice, so I cut apart a paint chip book to create a visual. The chosen chips had evocative names such as marshmallow, snowdrop, planetary silver, Havana coffee, after rain and blue mosque. A limited color palette would be most interesting with an array of textures: metal, glass, wood and fur.

We referred to this document many times as drew up our floor plan, and we referred to it many times more as we chose flooring, fixtures and furniture.

The fun was beginning.

14
REMEMBERED IN ALL GENERATIONS

OUR PURCHASE OF THE church injected the village grapevine with fresh subject matter. Unlike any other house either of us had ever owned, this one piqued the interest of a whole lot of people beyond our close friends and family.

"What's the buzz? Tell me what's a-happening," the apostles sang to Jesus in the musical *Jesus Christ Superstar*. I imagined former church members, neighbors and village officials asking the same thing over cups of coffee or bottles of beer.

No doubt about it, there was a lot more activity around the church than there had been for a year and half when the congregation and the basement food pantry left. The building had sat empty and dark, the only signs of life in the bushes and trees, which we had liberally trimmed in our first days.

The neighbors, the former pastor, a parade of contractors stopped by during those first weeks of demolition. Our friends were very interested in this latest crazy project of ours, many paying a visit just to see the dust and two-by-fours of our "before" (we couldn't even offer them a chair—or a bathroom with a door!). I'm sure they raised their eyebrows as we described our ambitious plans when all that could be seen was debris (and a whole lot of tools). But for the most part, they offered the right enthusiasm, "This is awesome!" "That will be beautiful!" "I can't wait to see it finished!"

Friends expressed interest in invitations to a housewarming party, to which I readily assented.

If any house deserved a party, it was this one.

I imagined a posh affair with tuxedoed butlers, finger sandwiches and classical music, while Tyler probably was thinking about where he could order a pig on a spit and a keg of beer, but I know both of us were looking forward to that party more than *any* of our friends.

We enjoyed the attention, I must confess. And we always welcomed a break from moving things around, tearing stuff apart or other pressing work. She was interesting, this old house, and we enjoyed talking about our grand vision. As we relished in the future, though, some visitors were pondering the past. One doesn't buy a historical landmark without buying its history.

"Old houses," author Gladys Tabor once wrote, "do not belong to people ever, not really; people belong to them." The old Methodist church had been a cultural center in our little village for more than a century. Members were baptized and exchanged wedding vows at the same altar. Funeral services were held there when they died.

Every room belonged to people from all over the region. Families were formed when couples married beneath those rafters and baptized the children they raised together. Performers found an audience and worshipped God by singing in the choir loft. The seeds of faith found soil when little children learned about Jesus in the Sunday school rooms. Women earned reputations for their seven-layer salad and pie crust in the basement kitchen where meals had been served and fellowship enjoyed. Unlike most homes—even long-standing ones—that possessed the memories of a few families, ours carried with it the feelings of generations of people.

We owned the building now, but we are only stewards of these memories. I felt responsible for honoring those who came before us, and both Tyler and I wanted to be true to at least some elements of the historical architecture even after the transformation. Everyone was complimentary and supportive. If a former church member was upset, they didn't share that disappointment with us.

During demolition, I joined the historical society meeting of the nearby congregation with whom the parishioners of our church had merged a year and half before. Tyler and I were curious about the history of the church, and I figured these ladies might have answers.

Three women were already hard at work in the parish hall when I arrived. One efficient woman was filing bulletins. Another was writing thank-you notes for donations to the church. The third, a long-time member of the congregation of our church whom Tyler and I had met earlier, greeted me warmly.

"Oh, I brought some things you might be interested in," she said. "I didn't know if you would make it here today."

As we chatted, the woman writing thank-you notes realized who I was. "Are you the woman who bought the church? The one writing about it?"

She looked at me like I was a celebrity, and I was flattered.

"Yup, that's me." I'm sure I wasn't blushing.

This friendly group directed me to interesting newspaper articles about the church and the original blueprints. Meanwhile, they continued their work. I learned that day that the best history occurs in the present, not the past. Their work to document the congregation's current activities—the pastors, weddings and funerals, baptisms and confirmations—might be best appreciated in a hundred years, just as I appreciated the work of nameless women and men who had saved blueprints and cut out newspaper articles.

Poring through the newspaper stories, I learned the Methodist congregation in my little village formed in 1859 when total membership in Methodist societies in America was growing rapidly and the U.S. Civil War was just speculation; Wisconsin had become a state only eleven years before. Services were conducted in the schoolhouse and in a building also used by Congregational and Baptist congregations.

The building Tyler and I had taken ownership of on Nov. 28, 2017, had been built in the late 1800s by a Rev. Smith, who had collected donations to purchase the lot for $300 on Sept. 29, 1891, not long after Sir Arthur Conan Doyle published his first Sherlock Holmes mystery and Benjamin Harrison was in the middle of his single term as president of the United States. The Sunday school and preaching hall (the modern-day "overflow" portion of the building) were dedicated two months later on Nov. 29, 1891, according to a history of the church recounted in a local newspaper. The building also must have included the belfry, though that wasn't specifically mentioned in the historical papers.

Our church was almost exactly 126 years old.

(The motion picture *Hostiles* playing in theaters at the time of my research mentioned a direct order from President Harrison and dramatized the struggle of Native Americans and pioneers in that era; it was difficult to imagine women wearing bonnets and men carrying shotguns and driving teams of horses to *our* church, but that was surely happening at the time.)

By 1894 (a year after inventor Whitcomb Judson debuted his "clasp locker," more popularly known as a zipper, at the Chicago World's Fair), church membership had increased to twenty-five. Since women didn't earn the right to vote in national elections until 1920, I'm guessing they only counted men. An addition—what became the sanctuary area—was built.

The 1890s became known as the Gay Nineties (history books today are quick to clarify the meaning of the word *gay* back then—an age of merriment and decadence). The era is also sometimes referred to as the Mauve Decade because chemist William Henry Perkin's aniline dye—a synthetic alternative to the expensive natural dyes in use at the time—introduced the widespread use of that color in fashion. Interestingly, what appears to be the original wall covering in the sanctuary of our church was mauve-colored paper over plaster.

This treasure graced a library wall.

The blueprints described the furnace room in the basement (the church was heated with wood at first, then coal, then fuel oil before a conversion to gas-forced air). A drawing of the cross-section revealed sixteen-inch basement walls, which already knew were quite substantial.

In the early '40s, according to the newspaper, a remodel changed the seating from east-facing to north-facing, and the new entrance—where we planned to install castle doors—had been added.

The archive included a copy of the photo Tyler and I saw hanging in the entryway where the congregation had merged and a grainy picture of the church in 1959. But we were hungry for more.

A few days later, we stopped by the local public library. There we found two more photographs of our church.

The first might have been taken when World War I began. It was labeled "M.E. Church, 19917." (Yes, there were two 9s.) The Methodist *Episcopal* Church [emphasis added] was founded in 1784; in 1939, it reunited with two breakaway Methodist denominations to form the Methodist Church, so the photo was taken before 1939 in any case. The photo showed a grand stairway that led to the front doors beneath the belfry; both the stairs and the doorway were gone in 2017. The siding flanking the window in the belfry was hung in a chevron pattern; fancy painted shingles decorated the peaks. In Phase Six or so of renovation, we hoped to return that window to the belfry and some of that interesting siding to the exterior.

The second photo hanging in the library was taken after the early 1940s. The former entrance was under the belfry with new entrances to the basement and to the sanctuary. The new sanctuary entrance had French doors (they were replaced at some point with red exterior doors); we hoped to install similar French doors inside as an entry to our master bedroom.

TYLER BECAME A LUNCHTIME regular at the village watering hole, this one built appropriately on the banks of the creek. This typical Wisconsin bar offered cold New Glarus beers, crispy fried cheese curds and a monthly meat raffle.

Like all good neighborhood taverns, people gathered to catch up on gossip, and our church had become a topic of conversation. This worked in our favor as Tyler collected the names of local contractors; the bartender/owner proved to be a great source of contractor intel.

One day when I accompanied him for lunch (chili, burgers and fries—no beer), I learned a group of women was scrapbooking in the back room.

"This place speaks my language," I marveled. In a decade of working in the marketing department for the largest scrapbooking company at the time, I'd attended easily hundreds of scrapbooking events all over the nation and the world. It was my job to attend these events with my personal photos and album and work with customers to learn what they loved, what they didn't and their ideas for making our products better.

One of the more enthusiastic scrappers struck up a conversation as we enjoyed our hot bowls of chili on a cold day, and she invited me to the monthly scrapbooking workshop.

I felt honestly welcomed to town with that simple invitation. A few days later, we'd get another one of those honest, small-town invites. We joked that we attended to church every day, but this invitation was to a *real* church service.

ONE DAY JUST AS Tyler finished showing yet another contractor around the church to coax a bid, a friendly young woman stopped by and introduced herself as the pastor of the nearby Congregational church. She welcomed Tyler to the village and invited him to have a look at some of her church's historical record.

This piqued our curiosity because our Methodist congregation and the Congregational church had been yoked from 1974 to 1985. We thought the Congregationalists might have some history of our church we hadn't yet heard.

A few days later, I had the pleasure of enjoying coffee with Pastor Jennie and a couple of friendly parishioners from the Congregational church. They showed me around, and we paid special attention to the historical details of the church (built twenty-six years before ours) and a twenty-foot-long bulletin board detailing the congregation's history.

We also investigated the written record, which provided examples of the little churches in our community that had weighed in on history's societal and political issues.

In one example, the local Congregational congregation (say that three times fast) had met in our village before they built their church and before the Civil War, which stirred controversy. A newspaper story noted: "In 1857, the American Home Missionary Society decided to withdraw aid to churches whose members were slaveholders. The society paid part of the Congregational church pastor's salary which prompted the church to go on record against the 'sin of American slavery.'"

Later, as it turns out, members of our church and the Congregational church had started a chapter of the Red Cross in our little village during World War I. Here is the story, as told in the careful handwriting of the Congregational church record:

Year of 1918

With the passing of the year 1918 our church like many others has passed through one of the greatest trials it perhaps has ever had to go through. We can proudly say we have stood the test and are now in as encouraging a position as we have been for some years.

Our pastor with the Methodist minister and a few others were instrumental in getting the Red Cross started here. As the War continued and conditions became more serious more and more people became interested in the great movement until now the village has a fine large auxiliary. In the Red Cross world our church has not failed to do its duty in giving both of time and money. …

We are all very glad we could do as much as we did in a time of great need. We have all learned the lesson of cheerful giving so in the coming year let us do our part.

In addition to a warm invitation to join the worship service, Pastor Jennie also gave me a great gift: copies of two church cookbooks, one from the Congregationalists and one created by the very congregation that had once inhabited our Methodist church. As she handed them to me, she noted the Congregationalists did this thing well: feeding people. This was clear after seeing their basement kitchen, easily four times as big as the one in our church.

Thumbing through the pages of the Methodists' book, I recognized some of the last names of former members whom we had met. This recipe book, created to honor the sesquicentennial of the congregation in 2009, was a historical gem. It included recipes from the congregation's first known church recipe book in 1912 and from one printed in 1950. One 1912 recipe for "Chicken" began with "wash and be sure to remove all feathers" and the instructions included: "Cook until tender. If it should be an aged rooster it may take two days." (I bet even the aged rooster back in 1912 was tastier than today's bland, mass-produced chickens).

An interesting recipe for Jezebel Sauce contributed by Karen Hill Krolow caught my eye. Jezebel, whose story is told in the Bible's Books of Kings, was a Phoenician princess who married an Israelite king. She did not, however, believe in his God; she worshipped Baal and forced her religion on the Israelites and ultimately died a gruesome death. It makes perfect sense that an evilly delicious sauce named for this bad girl of the Bible would be good for ham since pork was a food no-no for the Jews.

Jezebel Sauce
Ingredients
　　1 (15-ounce) can crushed pineapple, drained
　　1 (15-ounce) jar apricot preserves
　　1 tablespoon dry mustard
　　¼ cup good horseradish (German)

Instructions

Mix equal parts of pineapple and preserves, add mustard and horseradish. Serve with ham.

Another recipe in the book was the only one billed as "award winning," so I feel it would be selfish not to share it. Kathy Hill contributed the recipe for Mom Blakeman's Pound Cake, noting that it won third place at the county fair:

Pound Cake

Ingredients

2 cups sugar

1 cup butter

5 eggs

2 cups flour

Instructions

Preheat oven to 300 degrees. Cream sugar and butter until light. Add eggs—one at a time—alternately with 2 cups flour, mixing thoroughly after each addition. Use two wide loaf pans. Butter pans BOTTOM ONLY [apparently this is very important as it is in ALL CAPS], and line with two layers of wax paper. Bake one hour. After cakes are cool, remove from pans and roll in powdered sugar.

OUR DAY OF RECKONING had arrived: the rezoning hearing.

We'd been feeling out neighbors and other interested parties for weeks, trying to determine if anyone might object to rezoning the church from "park" (the tax-free designation also bestowed on churches) to residential. We paid the fee, read the notice in the paper, put on clean clothes and showed up at the planning commission meeting to observe the public hearing.

We were the only ones there, besides the members of the planning commission, of course.

This was good news, because it meant none of the neighbors objected.

A couple of the commissioners asked questions, mostly of curiosity ("Are you keeping the bell? Will you be ringing it on New Year's Eve?" "Do you plan to have off-street parking?"), and within seventeen minutes, they approved the rezoning.

Thirteen minutes later, the village board convened to consider the planning commission's recommendation. The only question we got asked: "Are you going to keep the lilac bushes?"

"Bushes? Plural?" I questioned silently.

Those unidentified bushes along the sidewalk that we aggressively had trimmed were identified by a board member as flowering bushes, known to bloom extravagantly in the spring.

"Yes, yes, all but three of them, which have to be removed for our driveway," I said.

"Replanted," Tyler corrected.

I nodded. If we could replant lilac bushes (or whatever they were), then absolutely, we would.

The village board made the planning commission's decision official: approved.

We had been added to the village tax rolls.

Which is exactly what we wanted.

News of our project reached the ears of an alert reporter at a nearby weekly newspaper, and he arranged a visit to our worksite, where the interior of the church was mostly demolished.

He arrived one cold, bright morning, and we dodged the drywallers' scaffolding in the sanctuary to show him around. I admired his wiry beard, and he mentioned he had visited the church often to cover church dinners and news of the local food bank, which operated out of our basement for a time.

"What do people in town think of your plans?" he asked me.

"Well, everyone who's talked to us has told us how happy they are we are fixing it up," I said. "But I think people who might be unhappy probably aren't telling us about it. Why? Have you heard otherwise?"

"No, no, I just heard you had big plans to improve the place."

Whew.

It was odd being interviewed, and I found myself wondering how people felt when I interviewed them twenty-some years before as a newspaper reporter. The interview was mostly painless, fun even. As with our other visitors, we regaled him with our plans until his eyes started darting around, looking for an exit. He took a few photos and beat a hasty retreat—a weekly newspaper reporter is a busy person, I knew, and other news was surely calling to him.

When the story came out, Tyler was disappointed we hadn't made the front page (I was a little relieved), but he purchased five copies of the newspaper to bring home. I was happy to see the reporter included nice comments from the former pastor and a planning commissioner who lived nearby.

The building needed expensive repairs, and the dwindling congregation could not afford them. "This is the best of all outcomes," the former pastor told the reporter.

I derived great satisfaction from clipping the story to mail to my grandmother, with whom I had been a pen pal for the better part of three decades. She was only a month shy of turning 103, and I found it apropos to share news about a century-old structure that was getting some love.

15
Therefore, do not be foolish

The final 10 percent of a project is the hardest, and this was true of our demolition phase.

The first 90 percent was no cakewalk. Sure, it was rewarding to reveal beautiful architectural elements of the church, but it required back-aching work. And then there were the suspended ceilings, plaster and lath, old carpeting, basement pass-through, walls, doorways. It amounted to two thirty-yard dumpsters worth of debris.

But that still left the ceiling of the sanctuary—the *twenty*-foot ceiling of the sanctuary.

Shortly after we'd closed on the church and realized we'd thrown out the remote controls for the ceiling fans in the sanctuary, Tyler climbed on top of a six-foot rolling baker's scaffold to install pull-chains to the fans to get them to operate. It didn't work. But Tyler did learn something: his baker's scaffold shook something awful as he fiddled with his arms above his head, and he didn't like it. Besides, a six-foot-three man on a six-foot scaffold stood still eight feet short of the top of the ceiling. (This is probably why most standard family homes don't have such high ceilings, but I didn't think of that when I fell in love with the open space.)

Tyler pondered how he might safely take apart the sanctuary ceiling and put it back together. Despite what people might have assumed about the recklessness of a pair of fifty-somethings turning a 126-year-old building into a home, Tyler was a businessman who'd heard too many horrific insurance claims to pursue a daredevil approach to construction.

THE HAZARDS OF REMODELING an old church were many, and we were warned by many well-intended bystanders.

Long before we'd closed, Tyler had already made bulk purchases of face masks and safety glasses. These came in handy as we removed millions of nails from trim and crown molding (I might be exaggerating about the number of nails, but not much). Tyler also bought work gloves for the hired man and me. One pair was Level 5 cut-resistant rated; I didn't even know such a thing existed, but I was grateful for them as we loaded and unloaded scrap metal into the pickup. All this safety equipment was *de rigueur* when Tyler and St. Johnny removed the basement's tin ceiling. Since we hoped to reuse the material again, they peeled off each piece of sharp-edged, dust-covered tin, sheet by sheet. The basement's expansive square footage seemed to gained space in our minds as they spent hours on this task. I was amazed at the debris that must have fallen from the ceiling (and elsewhere) as I went through Tyler's jacket pockets on laundry days.

As one might expect of a building constructed only twelve years after the invention of the electric light bulb, the wiring Tyler discovered in the church was a trip through time. Cloth-wrapped 12-gauge copper wire in conduit and ArmorFlex wiring was mingled with current code-approved Romex wiring. With an abundance of caution (we certainly didn't want all our hard work to burn to ashes), we replaced all of it. And the existing 100-amp circuit breaker box? It would be exchanged for a 200-amp model.

Our real estate agent sent us a seventeen-page brochure, "Protect Your Family from Lead in Your Home."

"Many houses and apartments built before 1978 have paint that contains high levels of lead," the pamphlet warned. The list of health hazards read like a drug ad in an AARP publication: lead from paint, chips and dust can cause high blood pressure, nerve disorders, muscle and joint pain, memory and concentration problems and digestive problems.

Eek.

When we finally got inside the church, we tested several surfaces. No lead.

Then more than one former parishioner in the church suggested we had a mold problem. The list of symptoms from mold allergies was worse than lead exposure: everything from runny nose and coughing to internal bleeding and death.

Tyler scoffed at this notion that we had anything more than a pedestrian mold problem, but we disposed of anything porous from the basement (where we had witnessed a water problem). One warm December day, Tyler donned his Tyvek suit, a respirator and safety goggles and power-washed the entire basement, including the furnace room that once had a coal chute.

Only a Virgo.

We also were warned we had asbestos in the walls.

If one thought lead and mold were bad, exposure to asbestos was known to cause lung cancer. And eliminating it was expensive. In fact, it was asbestos that had scared us off from the purchase of the church in Pecatonica.

On this project, however, we'd gotten such a good deal on the church, we figured if we found asbestos, we could afford to pay to remove it.

A former parishioner reassured us that only love flowed from those walls, and we believed her. But unlike some matters related to a church, this one we could test. We sent three samples to the laboratory: main floor ceiling tile, main floor wall sample and basement flooring, which looked a little suspicious to us. Within twenty-four hours, we'd learned the ceiling and walls on the main floor were mostly cellulose with no asbestos. Cause for celebration!

The avocado-green basement floor tiles, lovingly installed when avocado green was in vogue, however, were 3 percent chrysotile, a Category 1 asbestos-containing material. Category 1 was the least bad of the three types of asbestos, that is, not brittle, breaks by tearing rather than fracturing and does not easily release asbestos fibers upon breaking.

We got a reasonable quote for professional asbestos abatement, but since our structure was now privately owned, we could legally get rid of it ourselves. When we were ready to refloor the basement, we had the Tyvek suits, goggles and respirators to scrape up the flooring if we decided to go that route. But in the meantime, if we didn't disturb the floor tile, we'd be fine.

We were getting so good at these tests of safety we sprang for a few more.

The Roto-Rooter man scoped our sewer pipes, and his waterproof camera determined our pipes were as clear as a baby's arteries—no tree roots or obstacles.

Our inside plumbing was in good shape, so we had our expensive city water tested to reassure us about the quality of the pipe connecting the church from the street. The lab proclaimed our water safe. Yay! (For the price, it should be.) But we also learned it was "very hard" at 25.56 GPG (grains per gallon) and was close to the upper limit set by the Environmental Protection Agency in estimated total dissolved solids. This meant it had a lot of dirt in it). None of the "stuff" was considered a contaminant, but let's just say the water had a little too much "texture."

This meant we would be investing in a total house filtration system and a Drinkpod purification appliance. A Drinkpod was a countertop water cooler with a four-part filtration system and ultraviolet sterilization system. This appliance would become the centerpiece of our beverage bar, the section of our kitchen devoted to all things drinkable, from coffee and sparkling water to beer and wine.

We weren't done testing yet. We tested for radon in the basement. Radon is a colorless, odorless radioactive gas that is the No. 1 cause of lung cancer in nonsmokers. Our result was only 1.2 pCi/L (picocuries per liter of air), well below the EPA action level of 4 pCi/L.

Ah, deep breaths.

When we were done, we'd spent more than $300 apiece on safety equipment and safety tests. But our final test wasn't about particles and particulates. It was about structural support.

EARLY ON, TYLER SUSPECTED the opening between the sanctuary and the overflow area might need shoring up. The archway looked slightly bowed, and not in a quaint or historical way. Further evidence that something was awry: the second floor wasn't level.

Tyler had installed headers in the past, so this discovery didn't alarm him. But I, trained by HGTV remodeling shows, saw dollar signs. Many an open-floor plan had been scuttled by expensive header requirements. Though the word "header" dates to the 15th century as the name given to the king's executioner, today the word refers to a beam-like support that bridges an opening.

Initially, we considered designing the interior by ourselves. We played around with layouts using freehand drawings and rudimentary software programs. We figured plumbers and building inspectors would prevent us from doing anything stupid, like installing a toilet too close to a vanity or building a too-narrow hallway.

But Tyler knew a lot about construction, including what he didn't know, so he hired an architect with structural engineering knowledge to help him determine precisely where the structural issues lied and how to resolve them. We also needed to know how to safely construct the balcony, which hung from this same opening. (When the architect paid us a visit, he also gave the belfry a once-over and prescribed new pilings.) After much measuring and calculations and consultation, the architect recommended a new header and a bunch of other technical stuff I didn't understand. But Tyler did, and we got the design plans to help him carry it out.

After Tyler ordered the specified heavy-duty beam, I figured out why they're costly: it's not the header itself, it's the engineering required to prescribe it.

In any case, the header arrived in three parts along with a thousand other pieces of lumber (you think I'm kidding!).

Reroofer, the guru who repaired our belfry roof, helped Tyler install the new header. Reroofer walked into the sanctuary one Friday afternoon all smiles because he was about to build something. Or maybe he was just happy that day.

He pointed up and asked, "What is that?"

Coincidentally, we had another visitor: a bat, circling the ceiling of the sanctuary.

Um, where did he come from?

We went nine weeks without an interior sighting of anything alive beyond a few spiders. Reroofer repaired the belfry with much noise and commotion. No bats then.

But now, a bat had appeared out of nowhere.

Somehow, the bat got into the basement (if you know anything about the flight of bats, you know this is possible, but difficult to describe, what with all the squeezing tight of your eyes and the screaming). St. Johnny and I chased him around for a few minutes, randomly waving brooms in the air and shooing him out of window wells a couple of times, but he refused to find the exit. Suddenly, he flew into the furnace room: the dark, duct-filled furnace room with a million nooks and crannies where black bats could hide.

"Are you going in there?" St. Johnny asked me.

It was clear St. Johnny wasn't going in there.

I peeked inside. The bat wasn't flying around and wasn't in the window wells. I slammed shut the door. St. Johnny helped me secure it, and I returned upstairs to where Tyler and Reroofer were conferring about the header.

"We trapped it," I said breathlessly.

"Great," Tyler said, barely looking up from the architect's drawings. He was focusing on the bigger picture.

Then I spotted the holes in the floor of the sanctuary. The holes led to the furnace room.

Fortunately, we were surrounded by scrap wood of all shapes and sizes. I gingerly slid a couple of boards over the holes.

"Well," I said, dusting off my hands. "I guess he's the HVAC guys' problem now."

I quickly developed three suppositions to comfort me.

One, out of sight, out of mind. The bat was in the furnace room, and I wasn't.

Two, a bat, which navigates the night with echolocation, is a guide through the darkness. No one wants a bat in their house, but maybe he was a sign. A good sign. A symbol that we were on the right track.

And three, the bat was in our furnace room. He was not in our belfry.

The bat disappeared as mysteriously as he had appeared. Some days later, the HVAC guys tore apart the furnace room to prepare for the new ductwork, but the bat was gone.

A few weeks later, I noticed a quarter-size hole in one of the basement windows. Tyler chose the time-honored redneck method of repairing it with duct tape. While kneeling in the mud outside the window, he found the bat—dead on the ground. We surmised he may have escaped through the hole but succumbed to the elements once outside.

But at least he wasn't in our furnace room.

Here is the new header from the sanctuary side. The second story shows through the rebuilt loft wall above. The arched structure on the left is the front doorway, stored temporarily on the main floor.

IN EIGHT HOURS OVER two days, Tyler and Reroofer built and installed the header and then reconstructed the choir loft wall. I helped by renting a couple of heavy-duty adjustable floor jack posts and transporting them to the church—I was handy like that. When they jacked up the floor, the wood creaked and wailed, but cooperated. The second floor was suddenly a lot more level and the opening where the kitchen would be constructed was no longer saggy.

With that task completed, I could put to bed my nightmares of bathing in the upstairs tub—me in my birthday suit relaxing among a cloud of bubbles and a hundred gallons of water—and falling through the ceiling. We were structurally sound now. But we still had to demolish the twenty-foot sanctuary ceiling without killing our project foreman.

WE NEGOTIATED WITH TWO rental companies for motorized "man lifters," stalking the sellers of used scaffolding on Craigslist, briefly contemplating temporarily building out the loft floor across the entire sanctuary and me volunteering to climb scaffolding and use a hammer. Then Tyler met with a local drywaller. We planned to drywall the ceiling of the sanctuary, intending to hire out that role.

Fortunately, the drywaller was willing to not only remove the ceiling, but to rent us his scaffolding so our electrician could run wiring and Reroofer could install ceiling's faux wood. All within budget!

After all those weeks of hand wringing, in an hour our three drywallers had assembled scaffolding to reach to the ceiling and climbed aboard. They scampered up and down like children on a jungle gym. Down came the false ceiling on the balcony side of the sanctuary, the trimmed-out beams (we saved the pieces for reuse), the fiberboard paneling and the ceiling tiles of the angels.

So simple.

By the end of the day, the demolition phase of the church renovation was officially complete. Our ceiling had never looked so clean and pristine.

Tyler and I admired the scene from the safety of the floor.

16
For the Lack of Wood, the Fire Goes Out

Activity began to accelerate, as evidenced by the number of checks being written and the volume of building materials accumulating in the church.

One day, I discovered Amazon's smallest shipping box delivered to rental house. I tried to bring it inside, but I discovered abruptly I couldn't lift it.

"What is that?" I asked Tyler later. "It's as heavy as a thousand screws."

"Two thousand, actually. Two thousand nails," he replied nonchalantly.

We were embarking on a construction phase requiring at least two thousand nails.

Two days later, a Mack truck with a hydraulic forklift on the back arrived in front of the church and left behind two enormous piles of lumber on our sidewalk. In a biting twenty-mile-per-hour wind, Tyler's hired man St. Johnny and I carried in 113 two-by-fours of various lengths, thirty two-by-sixes, ten two-by-eights, thirty two-by-tens, twenty sheets of plywood and five LVLs (that would be laminated veneer lumber typically used for headers, for those of you who don't handle industrial deliveries of lumber every day).

Oh joy.

Fortunately, it wasn't snowing or raining.

We now were building instead of tearing down. This reality buoyed Tyler's spirits considerably. He and St. Johnny had toiled for many weeks in relative isolation while they had demoed the church's interior. Now Tyler could watch real progress as skilled workers improved the church rather than making it worse.

Right around that time, the gutter guys showed up to upgrade the rain gutters. Thanks to a few warm days in January, Tyler determined the occasional water in the basement was seeping through a seam on the front wall of the foundation. The way the old gutters were arranged allowed a significant portion of roof runoff to drop into one area in front of the church. Tyler suspected he would also have to excavate to improve underground drainage there, but that project could wait until spring.

In a few hours, we had new gutters. OK, we had to write a check for it, but it was immensely satisfying when someone else did the work, especially when it was twenty feet off the ground.

A few days later, as I was making the bed back at the rental house after doing laundry, Tyler called, frantic.

"What are you doing right now?"

"Um, making the bed?"

"We're out of drywall screws. You need to go get some. Three-inch drywall screws."

Now this was a task I could pull off. I had visited the nearby Home Depot so many times, I knew exactly which door to enter to find the "screws and nails" aisle.

"How many?" I asked.

"Um," he said, apparently eyeing the ceiling where the drywallers were working. "Five pounds."

Okey-dokey. Five pounds of drywall screws, coming right up.

When I arrived, screws in hand, the church sounded like a real construction zone.

Men's voices and hammers echoed in the sanctuary. St. Johnny made noise with the Air Locker pulling nails from boards in the basement. The HVAC guys moved a truckload of shiny ventilation ducting into the basement. A boom box was tuned to a rock station playing "Superstition" by Stevie Wonder, which includes the line "very superstitious, ladders 'bout to fall."

Fortunately, the drywallers were using scaffolding, not ladders.

Superstition ain't the way.

The drywallers made quick, satisfying progress on the ceiling of the sanctuary. The place took on the sheen of new construction, a nice change from demolition dust. Along with the drywall, they erected the two-by-sixes to which our faux beams would be attached.

Tyler sought out rigid polyurethane foam beams—lighter and more durable than actual wood beams and more affordable. They were advertised as "virtually indistinguishable from real wood." But seeing was believing. Ordering a couple of samples of the faux beams, like choosing any finishing details in a house, was an odyssey. The array of online options dazzled.

L beam or U beam?

Rough sawn or hand hewn (or any of eight other textures)?

How wide? How high? How long? Are endcaps needed?

What color? We knew we wanted "brown," but we could choose from among eleven shades. We finally settled on samples of pecan and antique cherry.

A couple of weeks later, our samples arrived, and Tyler stuck them on the two-by-sixes on the ceiling of the sanctuary (from the safety of the choir loft).

Remarkable. The really were virtually indistinguishable from real wood beams. They were as light as cappuccino foam, which would make them easier to install.

The beams would add just the distinction we wanted in the centerpiece of our great room: our cathedral ceilings.

After getting a look at the samples, we picked antique cherry over pecan, and Tyler's fingers flew across his keyboard getting them ordered.

About ten days later, a semi-truck slowly turned into the street in front of the church. Delivery men (and they were invariably male) frequently looked confused when they compared the address on their clipboards to the building to which they were about to deliver a bathtub, a hearth stone or faux beams. When he'd confirmed he was indeed at the right place, he opened the back of the truck to reveal a pile of boxes as long as a car, all with reinforced corners. These foam beams came packaged like crystal wine glasses; the packaging was heavier than the beams themselves. A little teamwork got the beams of assorted lengths inside the sanctuary. Now, we would sidestep them for several weeks until after all the drywall was installed.

Here's what I didn't understand about walls until I helped build some: they're three dimensional.

This should be self-evident, but it wasn't to me. A wall should be level and perpendicular to the floor and other walls. If they aren't perfectly square, you'll end up with a funhouse maze.

This feat requires skill building a house from scratch, but it's a real trick when building walls between 126-year-old floors and ceilings that may or may not be level.

Tyler took great pains to jack up the second floor to level, but "level" did not mean it was even. Every wall stud was a different length.

I helped build closet walls on the main floor by performing a role as human tool holder. "Hand me the square." "I need the level."

"Give me the power nailer." (Let's be honest, Tyler usually dispensed with pleasantries and placed orders with nouns only: "Nailer." "Level." "Hammer."). Sometimes, I was promoted to two-by-four transport specialist or measurement expert (by expert, I mean climbing the ladder and holding the zero end of the tape measure securely to the ceiling).

In this manner, we (meaning Tyler) built the walls to our walk-in closet that conveniently also supported the second floor. He and St. Johnny also installed the first of five pocket doors in our house design.

I had picked up the pocket door frame kits earlier in the week. Standing in line to pay for them, a builder behind me who looked like he had earned his experience remarked, "I hate installing pocket doors. They're a pain."

Maybe he installed pocket doors into already existing walls, because Tyler made it look easy to build one into a wide-open space.

But Day Two of wall construction was one of blood, sweat and tears.

The day began with a family crisis and progressed to a business crisis, but eventually we put out the fires and made our way to the church. Our goal was to construct the walls for the powder room, the water closet in the master bath and the wall behind the master vanity, all in the overflow area behind the kitchen so the plumber could begin roughing in plumbing.

Unlike the walls for the master bedroom closet built to the ceiling, the walls on the day's to-do list would be built for a false ceiling to accommodate the HVAC ducting and the plumbing from the second-floor bathroom. If your eyes are glazing over with the details, let me emphasize this important point: all the walls we were building needed to be as tall as the false ceiling.

We haggled about room sizes and laid down two-by-fours on the floor to outline the walls. Just as Tyler was about to measure the studs and build vertically, he decided he needed a new tool: a laser level.

We couldn't just measure down from the actual ceiling or up from the floor because each was crooked or uneven in their own unique ways. If we wanted a *level* false ceiling, we needed this crucial tool Tyler didn't already possess.

OK, it was lunch time. Let's go get lunch and drop by Home Depot. And spend more money. On another tool.

This was a battle I wouldn't win.

We dined at a Chicago hot dog joint and dropped another couple hundred at Home Depot. Driving back to the church in the pickup truck, Tyler asked me to open the laser level box (with the Fort Knox unbreakable plastic clamshell, a feat in it itself) and read the instructions.

This was not poetry or a steamy novel. This was the instructions on how to set up and use a laser level.

All I remember is this one thing: "Looking into the laser light will cause blindness."

Before returning to the worksite, Tyler dropped me off at the rental house to check on the dog, throw the washed sheets in the dryer and run some quick paperwork.

When I arrived at the church twenty minutes later, Tyler had screwed the laser level to the wall, red laser lines marking the bottom of our false ceiling.

We got back to work exchanging nouns for tools and constructing studded walls.

Not infrequently that afternoon, my sweaty Romeo (thank you, Erin Napier, for this *Home Town* description) bent over to nail a stud into the bottom plate and sprinkle a few drops of perspiration on the floor. That was the sweat in this story.

At one point, we had to reattach a top plate, which meant yanking out the nails to do it over again.

"Hold that there," Tyler directed.

I held the piece of wood at one end while he pounded out the board at the other end with a big hammer.

Blood evidence, hidden within the wall.

Bang!

The board came off and his end—complete with two angry nails sticking out of it—came down.

On his head.

"Blasted, Monica! I told you to hold it!"

Only he didn't say "blasted." And he still had the hammer in his hand. His eyes told me he wanted to use it on something other than lumber.

With his other hand he held his forehead, and blood was running down his cheek. The nails in the board had grazed his head.

"Oh my God, are you OK?"

I understood from his grumble that he was. But he was bleeding like a Halloween decoration; that's how it is with a head wound.

With no Band-Aids at the church, I held a paper towel to his forehead. "Use direct pressure to stop bleeding," echoed in my head. I held the paper towel better than the piece of wood because eventually, the scratch clotted, and we got back to work.

But not without a little blood on the top plate of the powder room wall.

You're wondering about the tears, I'll wager.

At four o'clock in the afternoon, we'd finished with the powder room and water closet walls and decided to call it a day. (Working in the church after sunset was not our style—it got dark. And we got hungry.) Before putting all the tools away, Tyler turned the laser level to the opposite wall to guide construction of the wall dividing the master bedroom from the master bath.

He gasped.

I looked where he was looking, and I gasped, too. I looked back at him, standing on the ladder, his hand on the laser level.

"How did that happen?" I asked.

No response.

The red line of the laser level clearly defined the bottom of the false ceiling. And it cut through the top window trim of the bedroom windows—at least three inches short of where it should have been to allow for full window trim and crown molding in the master bedroom.

We spent all day building the walls perfectly level. But too short.

I'm not gonna lie. Expletives were yelled in ways not befitting of a church.

WE HAD ENDURED WEEKS of dirt, dust and debris during the demolition, and when we began building walls, I realized we had weeks of sawdust ahead of us, but I believed we were done with the dirtiest of dust.

Until the plumber started work.

Following months of cat herding, Tyler collected bids from no fewer than six plumbers. When Plumber Number Six presented his handwritten bid with the flourish of enthusiasm, it seemed our search was over. "I like him," Tyler said to me as he left the room to check on some detail or another. "You?"

I smiled and nodded. This prospect spoke with reassuring authority, asked questions that indicated he had a lot of experience, and his handwritten quote signaled we wouldn't be paying for marketing. We wanted a well-plumbed house, not unsubstantiated flash.

Tyler closed the deal.

"You're hired."

As if to underscore the serendipity of our choice, St. Johnny pointed out the plumber wore a burly cross necklace. It seemed like he would fit right in.

Plumber Number Six got to work almost immediately, and we learned quickly he was the night owl to Tyler's morning lark. Tyler never met a 5:30 a.m. he didn't like, but Glimfeather earned his nickname by proving he was most productive under bright construction spotlights at 10 p.m. (or, frequently, even later).

Glimfeather was the talking owl who helped the protagonists find a kidnapped prince in *The Silver Chair,* one of C.S. Lewis's books in the "Chronicles of Narnia." Like our plumber, Glimfeather was wise, spirited and most alert after dark. Exploring the progress he made in the morning after his late-night work seemed a little like Christmas morning.

Glimfeather first jackhammered the basement floor and rerouted the sewer pipe to accommodate our new bathrooms.

The project created piles of concrete debris, and the excavation of dirt was a little off-putting. I didn't like thinking about the proximity of dirt beneath our foundation, but with holes in the floor, there was no denying it. And that sewer pipe that was supposedly in such good shape? We had a "Houston, we've got a problem" moment when Glimfeather pointed out the top of the heavily rusted pipe was disintegrating. Even the portion of pipe that wasn't being moved had to be replaced.

At the same time, February shed its wintry appearance for a few days, and a foot of snow melted under rainy skies. This time, instead of water coming in the front of the basement (where we had the gutters replaced), it seeped into the back in the furnace room. Muddy water everywhere. St. Johnny spent an entire day filling and repeatedly emptying the Shop-Vac. We moved the precious castle doors, which had found a temporary home on the floor of the basement, to higher ground.

A few nights after the rain stopped, Glimfeather sealed the dirt and new sewer pipe beneath new concrete. He then built a maze of pipes that produce the modern luxury of running water.

ONE DAY WHEN I happened by the church on the way to the post office, I witnessed the strange dance plumbers and HVAC guys must do often on custom projects.

Glimfeather had to figure out how to vent the kitchen sink drain; it had something to do with drain clogs (or preventing them, I didn't understand the details). The sink was to be situated in the middle of our kitchen island in the middle of our sanctuary. This meant it was draining and venting into the middle of our basement, and Glimfeather needed to determine where to run the pipes while avoiding the beams that supported pretty much the entire structure.

Meanwhile, the HVAC guy replaced the ductwork, much of which ran along the basement's ceiling. His work, which included more modern, streamlined ducts, required all new routing to accommodate the new rooms.

But the kitchen sink drain threatened to muck it all up.

Tyler, Glimfeather and the HVAC guy problem-solved out loud, tossing out several alternatives that each created their own problems. Tyler was adamant about maintaining the sanctity of his beams while Glimfeather was ruffled about the angle of his pipes. The HVAC guy mostly nodded and shrugged.

I literally bit my tongue because A) I knew nothing about sink vents or drains, B) I knew nothing about cold-air returns and C) no one was looking at me for direction; they were looking at Tyler. All I could think about was my stupid dream of a sink in the middle of the kitchen island and how badly I didn't want to lose this brilliant concept. I also didn't want such low ceilings in the basement that I felt claustrophobic.

Finally, the HVAC guy suggested maybe his fabricator could create a custom piece of ductwork to accommodate the drain.

Key word: custom.

Custom, means *expensive* in the renovation world. New *standard* ductwork was not in the Tequila Budget let alone *custom* ductwork.

But anything is possible if you're willing to pay for it.

In retrospect, I was surprised the dance didn't end sooner.

Of course, Tyler who sensed my agitation by the way I was pacing the basement silent but brooding, OK'ed the custom ductwork.

My kitchen design and basement airiness were saved.

For about the hundredth time, I was glad Tyler knew what he was doing and lingered at the church so he could referee these negotiations.

By now, Tyler had built the walls on the main floor and upstairs. We were ready to think about the second-floor ceiling.

Unlike the main floor's drywalled ceiling decorated with beams, we chose something with more farmhouse flavor for the upstairs, which would house a bathroom, bedroom and my office: pickled, planked plywood.

We'd seen Tyler's cousin's husband turn plain old plywood into beautiful planked flooring when we camped in their yard (was that only last year?), and we thought we could copy the idea for our ceiling.

Pickling and installing the ceiling was a multistep process that began with a good day's work ripping boards on the table saw. Tyler chose to do this with me on an otherwise quiet Saturday.

The table saw is not my favorite piece of equipment since it carried the threat of cutting off one's digits. But the boards were too big for Tyler to cut straight without help, so the foreman tagged me as his crew.

I caught on quickly when to push, when to pull and when to catch newly sawn pieces of lumber. But let me tell you, twenty pieces of plywood is a lot of 5.75-inch planks. And a half a bagel for breakfast wasn't enough to fuel the manual labor. We took a couple of water breaks, but by the end, my self-talk sounded like this (if you could have heard the whining over the whine of the saw):

"Think about sawing, not about lunch. Don't let Tyler's fingers get cut. Seventeen planks to go. Who left the front door open? Concentrate on the saw. Tyler, be careful. Don't slip in the sawdust. Don't pull too fast. Watch Tyler's fingers. Sixteen planks to go. Do I want tacos or a bratwurst for lunch? Don't think about lunch. Step over the pile of sawdust. Watch Tyler's fingers. Is that fifteen or fourteen? Keep the plank straight. Don't push too hard. Watch Tyler's fingers."

Finally, the stacks of plywood became piles of planks.

We still had days of sanding and painting and nailing ahead of us before we'd have a finished ceiling, but Step One was complete and so were Tyler's hands.

Time for lunch.

17
THE ONE WHO IS UNWILLING TO WORK SHALL NOT EAT

How does a member of the construction crew who doesn't know anything about construction contribute during a renovation project of this magnitude?

Three ways: laundry, odd jobs and errands.

Laundry probably doesn't need much explanation. Our dusty and sweaty clothes had to be washed by someone.

When it came to odd jobs, I was uniquely suited to measure for the faux beam Tyler wanted to place. I still had my own, natural-born knees and was light enough to climb the scaffolding in the great room.

Once on the scaffolding, I realized I'd left the tape measure fifteen feet below. I sat on the platform, sweating and nauseated, and now I had to put my hands in the air to catch a thrown tape measure.

I did not catch it, but Tyler had good enough aim to land it on the platform. I still had to measure for the beams. Above my head.

Let's just say we got the measurements down to the foot, not the inch. And I returned to solid ground in one piece.

Odd jobs also included communications—print this quote, find this business card, track down this phone number. Respond to the salesman working up a quote about his proposed shower base color.

Nearly every day, some guy from FedEx, UPS or USPS delivered a package, which I opened to determine the contents and then, if required urgently, delivered to the church. And someone had to crush cardboard boxes (or they'd never all fit in the recycling bin).

One day, the guy from Brown left an enormous box on our front step. By the time I opened the door open, Brown had already climbed into his truck.

"Hey, the box is open!"

"You can accept or reject. What do you want to do?"

"Um, I'm pretty sure these are one-of-a-kind leaded glass windows. They're fragile."

"Accept or reject? The box opened when I picked it up."

"Did you drop it?"

"Accept or reject, that's all I can do."

"I guess I'll have to see when I open them."

Brown drove off.

Disgusted, I carefully dragged the enormous package into the rental house and called Tyler to inform him.

"Well, open them to find out if they're broken."

Twenty minutes and five layers of cardboard, plastic, foam, bubble wrap and tape later, I still couldn't get a good enough look at the windows Tyler had found on Craigslist to determine if they were broken. (Two days later, Tyler dove deeper and determined they were. One of a kind and broken.)

And errands. I got very good at errands. If I could work Starbucks into the route, I did. Drop off another load of scrap metal? Yes. Find a glass retailer who could replace glass for the light fixtures? Sure, I'll bring him the light fixtures to see if he could do it. Need some tile samples for the shower? Home Depot, here I come.

Meanwhile, Tyler called the HVAC guys to get an ETA (again), built walls for the refrigerator and the pot filler behind the stove and directed Johnny to pick up the yard, burn brush, and check the plumber's work.

We made a good team.

18
GATHER UP THE LEFTOVER FRAGMENTS SO NOTHING WILL BE LOST

SELLING ITEMS ON CRAIGSLIST can be a pain in the neck. The picture taking and ad writing take time, but the real irritation are the looky-loos—potential buyers who ask a bunch of arcane questions about the dimensions or color or history and, after you've answered, disappear into the ether. Or the ones who send text messages riddled with spelling errors at 11 p.m. or 5 a.m. Or the jerks who show up and dicker over ten bucks.

But Craigslist is an amazing marketplace full of great deals and unique goods for buyers.

We were buyers, and Tyler was an authority. Not too many years before, Tyler turned a $500 gift into an RV we used for several years to travel the country. He bought and repaired increasingly valuable vehicles until he scored a 1983 Pace Arrow from a retiree in what was now our home state of Wisconsin. After we put thousands of miles on the 454-cubic-inch, 375-horsepower engine, he sold the old turd for a profit.

Now, when we needed nearly everything to renovate the old church, Tyler fired up his CSmart app to shop all listings for Milwaukee, Madison, Rockford and Chicago at the same time.

His first find was the magnificent castle doors he found during the demolition phase.

His next conquest: a full kitchen.

Within a couple of weeks after demolition, Tyler found a set of kitchen cabinets. They appeared to be custom-painted cabinets in the perfect color of cream we had tried and failed at least once to locate.

He placed a call to the seller and learned someone had already expressed an interest. We were second in line, but if you've ever interacted with Craigslist sellers, you know that could mean you're second in line behind a serious buyer, so you'll never hear from the seller, or it could mean you're second in line but the seller has already told four people that, or it could mean the seller is too meek to tell you it's already sold. Or it could mean the seller is just plain cruel, and they're not really selling anything.

In any case, we wrote it off. "Another one will come up," Tyler said. He was nothing if not confident.

Lo and behold, the seller called about a week later. "Still interested?"

"You bet. We'll be there tomorrow."

Tyler and I spent the next couple hours studying the ad and measuring the future kitchen space down to the half inch.

We drove the next morning to the seller's location, the showroom of a remodeling company only an hour away from the church. The kitchen had only ever been on display, never in actual use. It came complete with the kitchen sink and thousands of dollars' worth of granite countertop. The ad offered the countertop for free if we moved it at our own risk and expense.

The granite countertop looked brownish black in the pictures. I had my heart set on a light-colored Quartz countertop, but if we could get a dark granite countertop for free? Well, call me fickle then.

Our future kitchen on display.

I would be in love with dark granite.

When we saw it and ran our hands across the grayish-black countertop (even better), fantasized about washing dishes in the triple sink, and opened and soft-closed the dovetail-end drawers, our hearts melted.

It wasn't perfect, but it was darn close. And the price? We were buying the whole kit and caboodle for about 25 percent of the retail cost of the cabinets alone. Coincidentally, the remodeling firm had just sold a different display kitchen to another woman who was renovating a church into a home. It was a trend.

But what would we have to jerry-rig?

We'd need to find a 36-inch-wide stove to fill the back wall of our kitchen space, which was six inches wider than the display. But we already had an extra-wide stove vent we could switch out with the display vent.

And the little drawers in the upper cabinets—supremely bad design. Even I, a 5-foot-10 woman, could not see inside the top drawers. Those would have to be replaced, but I thought we could reuse the little drawers in the master bath vanity. To fill the space next to the stove, we could use the glass-fronted doors on the hutch at the end of the display island.

The tongue of the island stretched a bit too long for our space. We had a countertop professional disassemble, move and reassemble the countertop with a shorter tongue so it didn't protrude from beneath the balcony.

Then, we flipped the lower cabinets on either side of the sink so the wine rack would be closer to the beverage bar.

We also invested in a new matching cabinet above the refrigerator and a few doors for the island so we could use it for storage. While we were adding, we could get coordinating cabinets for the beverage bar.

Even with the changes, we were scoring a budget-saving deal on a high-quality kitchen. And we wheedled the sellers out of the stainless-steel dishwasher on display with the cabinets for half price. It was a two-drawer dishwasher designed for empty nesters; one could wash a few dishes in one drawer (which saved precious water) or a lot of dishes in both drawers. We also bought the bar stools around the island for $75 each. We were thrilled.

To start the project, Tyler shopped for a 36-inch-wide used range. We'd decided we wanted a new refrigerator, but we could live with a used stove. Craigslist came through right away: Tyler found a "luxury" Jenn-Air six-burner convection oven in stainless steel (our finish of choice). It was only eight years old.

As with the castle door deal, we drove ninety minutes south into Chicagoland, this time in lightly falling snow. We arrived at an enormous house set among several blocks of bungalows. The seller told us he added a second story when he remodeled his entire house, and now he was replacing his luxury stove with a countertop cooktop and set of double ovens.

We removed the door, knobs and burners for transport, and the seller and two young men who looked like they'd rather be playing Call of Duty or Grand Theft Auto helped us load the range into our beat-up pickup truck. We drove straight to the rental unit we'd secured a few days earlier (because our five-thousand-square-foot church wasn't big enough, I guess), and our new appliance became the first resident—on a short-term basis, we hoped.

Stove, check.

After we sprang for the rental unit, we justified buying things because we could store them away from the commotion of the church.

One morning when we were on our way to breakfast, eagle-eyed Tyler spied a raft of furniture on the boulevard a block from our rental house. We drove by slowly and stopped—the beat-up headboard looked promising.

The low profile of the headboard would be perfect on the bed we planned upstairs, where the ceilings sloped. The solid wood headboard would need paint, but the iron work added style. And it came with a footboard. And it was free!

We loaded it into the pickup and dropped it off at the rental unit. Celebrated not with *a* toast, but with toast. And eggs.

I SUPPOSE IT'S CALLED a vanity because one admires oneself in a vanity mirror. But Carly Simon might say a vanity earned its name because of its bad attitude. A vanity thinks the bathroom is all about it—it is, after all, the defining architectural design element and center of attention of a well-appointed lavatory.

I was a fan, however deadly the offense, nodding along with Al Pacino in *The Devil's Advocate* when he said, "Vanity is my favorite sin." From the lights and the mirrors to the cabinets and sinks, I couldn't wait to find vanities for the four bathrooms that sent messages like "Guests are valued here" and "This is special place."

Special, naturally, came with a price. I coveted Robern medicine cabinets—sleek ones with built-in lighting, defoggers and stereo systems—but when I priced one in the four-figure range, the look on my face was anything but flattering.

Back to planet earth where people spend only twenty minutes a day in front of the bathroom mirror. "Vanity can easily overtake wisdom," musician Julian Casablancas once said. "It usually overtakes common sense." I reminded myself that we weren't building a house in a posh suburb or a gentrified downtown locale. We were restoring a century-old church in a small town. We could not be tempted by top-end accessories or we would never recoup our investment.

I began to stress about our bathroom vanities. We needed four of them, three of them quickly. The basement vanity could be determined later, when we finished the basement (Phase, oh, Eight or so). But when we finally chose a plumber, he needed to know where to rough in the vanity faucets, and to determine that, we needed vanities.

Thanks to hours on Pinterest. I knew I wanted double sinks along a 132-inch expanse (go big or go home, remember?). Custom or semi-custom cabinets would probably be required to get matching cabinets for each sink.

After pricing custom cabinets (with price tags similarly deflating as luxury medicine cabinets), we purchased standard-dimension cabinets online. Tyler had the skills to install them, and we could incorporate those little drawers of little use in the display kitchen. If we positioned them lower in a bathroom vanity, they could house all kinds of little hygiene odds and ends. At first, I wanted light-colored upper cabinets (to go with the drawers) and navy-blue lowers, but after incorporating that shade into my beverage bar design, we went with dark brown lowers.

After buying new cabinets for the master bath, we sought to save money on vanities for the powder room and upstairs bathroom.

We scored vanity Number Two for the upstairs bathroom at a secondhand store.

My brother-in-law had once turned a dresser into a vanity for a basement bathroom, and I loved the combination of an old piece of furniture with a sleek stone countertop. I had also once converted an ugly old dresser into a beautiful credenza with several coats of paint. I couldn't use this idea in the master bathroom, because it would have been impossible to find an eleven-foot-long piece of furniture. Likewise, the wall assigned to the upstairs bathroom vanity was eight feet long—it would take a very special piece of furniture to fill that space.

One Saturday, after spending hundreds of dollars on lumber and loading it into our truck, Tyler and I arrived for a lunch date a few minutes early, so we explored the nearby secondhand store. We couldn't pass one without looking for something we might need for the old church, and here we found not one piece of furniture but two.

The first dresser was the ideal height for a vanity with an undermount sink. Tyler confirmed it would work. It even came with a forty-inch-wide mirror, and the second, taller dresser came with a thirty-inch-wide mirror.

Together, they were about twenty-five inches short of the expanse we needed to fill.

But the price was right—$185 for the pair.

Oh, they were beat up, all right. The shorter dresser had a terrible stain on the front, and the taller one was missing veneer, but I intended to paint it all anyway. Some of the intact veneer had a beautiful wood grain look I thought I might be able to preserve by painting around it. The mirrors themselves were in good condition, but the frames needed paint, too.

As I stood in front of them debating whether the work required to redeem these dressers was worth it, the proprietress sensed my interest and struck up a conversation.

"Oh, that would make a beautiful vanity," she said, describing how she'd turned other pieces of furniture into vanities. "And they're 75 percent off today."

The frugal Midwesterner in me couldn't pass up a deal that good. "Well, I could throw them away for that price," I said.

The proprietress wrinkled her nose. "Oh, you wouldn't want to do that."

"I mean I can't pass up such a good deal," I said. "But what do you think I could put between them to fill the space? A basket maybe?"

"Hmm, let me think about that," the proprietress said.

Lunch included chewing on this dilemma. I mean, I had to figure out how to make the $46.25 deal work. I couldn't pass this up. And then suddenly I knew: If I removed the mirror from the taller vanity, it would fit perfectly under the sloping eave on the second story, and then I could create a little makeup space—complete with mirror—between the two pieces of furniture.

I returned to the secondhand store with a less money than we paid for lunch and asked the proprietress to hold them until we could return with an empty truck. A few days later, we added the beat-up dressers to the rental unit. Soon, the HVAC guys would be done haunting the basement so I could paint.

This left the guest half-bath, aka the powder room. The vanity in there would be most used by guests, so the pressure was on.

Earlier, long before we closed on the church, Tyler got an amazing deal on a modern-looking faucet that I was trying to work into my vision for the powder room vanity. But I didn't think it was tall enough for a vessel sink, and I wasn't sure if I would have the time and energy to repurpose another piece of furniture for an undermount sink.

I was stymied.

I jotted down a detailed design plan for the upstairs bathroom.

In the way the universe delivers what one needs exactly when one needs it, Tyler and I visited a nearby plumbing wholesaler to select master bathroom fixtures.

On display was a white vanity, the ensemble completed from head to toe with the countertop, sink, brand-name faucet and even the mirror. It was distinctive in its indistinctiveness; it would look dynamite against an accent wall, maybe an accent wall of reclaimed wood from a church, for instance. And it was on sale for 70 percent off. I pulled Tyler's tape measure out of his jacket pocket.

"It's 37 inches wide," I said. "Didn't we just build the powder room to be 37 inches wide?"

Sure enough, we did.

While we were there, we bought power-flushing toilets for all three bathrooms.

Boom. Powder room, done.

FANS WERE A BONE of contention in our house. Tyler loved the white noise and breeze created by ceiling fans, but I preferred the still air often accused of feeling like a coffin. I conceded, however, that the sanctuary probably needed fans to move air around the twenty-foot high space.

The church came with standard functioning ceiling fans, but Tyler wanted bigger ones, more along the lines of jet engine turbines. The ones he found, I loved for the design. The blades were sleek. The finish was described as "distressed koa with tea stain finish" (koa is a large Hawaiian forest tree), and it closely matched the color of the beams we planned for the ceiling.

With five 62-inch blades, one fan would move 8,200 cubic feet of air per minute. Tyler bought two. (Drawing on a little tenth-grade geometry, I figured the sanctuary had a volume of 16,400 cubic feet, so both fans together would move all the air in one minute; Tyler would be in heaven.)

As for a deal, he saved $100 off retail when he located one for sale online in an open box.

Both fans arrived within days of each other and, like our other deals, they went to the rental unit to await installation.

ONE SATURDAY WHILE JUNKING, we found a pair of leaded glass windows we couldn't do without. Every other antique store we'd happened across sold stained-glass windows in all kinds of strange rectangles, decorated with gaudy oranges and red glass, and almost always as singles. Nothing was quite right.

We looked for a matched pair we could install on either side of the balcony doorway. This way, they would be interior windows and we wouldn't have to worry about weather-proofing leaded glass. The windows would add decoration to the balcony wall while adding natural light from the second story to the great room.

"Our" windows sat in a well-curated antique shop less than ten miles from the church. The leaded glass seemed so much classier to me than so many stained-glass windows we had seen; they fit our aesthetic perfectly.

The next weekend, Tyler built a frame for transport from waste lumber accumulated at the church. When we picked up the windows, he sealed the custom-built frame on the sidewalk in front of the store, and then we added them to our collection in the rental unit to await installation with so many other pieces we had collected.

Another task on our long to-do list. But we had another open window distracting us.

19
THE LOST IS FOUND

FEW PEOPLE GO THROUGH life without hearing the old maxim, "When God closes a door, he always opens a window." It's the line a friend uses to impart hope in the face of loss, which appears on the scene in every life.

This was the case in the old Methodist church, too—literally if not metaphorically. The religious center door closed, and the window as a home opened. Even more granularly, we needed to seal off one of the doorways. Instead of opening a window, though, we created a new doorway.

The doorway on the outs was the main floor's side entry. While we were keeping the exterior entrance that opened to the basement, the three steps up into the main floor would become part of our master bedroom that allowed us to incorporate another window into the boudoir. Tyler would have to weave in a new oak floor over the steps, but we salvaged flooring from the other side of the room where we were installing the master shower. When he poked around into the stairway above the departing entrance, he discovered where the center-stringer board for the stairs was cracked, which explained the stairway's unevenness. It needed to be replaced.

Ghostly faces? Or holes for hooks?

Just inside that entrance, one could see a peculiar row of nail holes in the beadboard. It didn't take much imagination to realize those holes were for coat hooks, where generations of Sunday School kids hung their jackets. I hoped to keep that beadboard and add more along the new wall where the door was removed. I weighed whether to use wood putty in the holes or keep that little tribute to what the room used to be.

Meanwhile, we planned to build a door in the north wall to the garage in an area Tyler called the mudroom. Since it was February, and the garage wouldn't be built for months, installing the door would just involve a little spray paint and imagination. But in April, Tyler and one of his skilled laborers installed the actual door, a modern piece with a little leaded glass detail. At this point, it still led to nowhere, but now the drywallers could work around it.

As in our renovation project, February brought closing and

opening doors in real life, too.

Our aging miniature schnauzer, the poopy puppy who walked with me to the church that first evening after the closing, died.

Back then, in late November, we knew our beloved dog who had lived with us for ten years and traveled all over the country probably wouldn't make it to live in the church with us. She had been ill all autumn, and the veterinarian ultimately diagnosed lung cancer. We had been keeping her comfortable for months when she finally passed away the day after Valentine's Day.

Even if she couldn't live long enough to run the steps of the church and sniff every corner, I had hoped she could hang on long enough so we could bury her in the yard. But she died when the ground was frozen, and I had no interest in keeping her body around long enough to wait for the spring thaw.

The day I watched her leave this earth as peacefully as she could, given her poor health, I left the veterinary clinic empty handed and broken hearted.

I cried hot, angry tears while I gathered up every last dog toy, treat and dog coat crowding the corners of the rental house to dump in the garbage. I thought this would help me forget her adorable tail wag, distinctive miniature schnauzer beard and stinky breath I had come to love.

It didn't work, of course.

Every morning as lay in bed planning my day, I would think fleetingly of walking the dog who no longer existed. Every day at two o'clock, I would unnecessarily remember to give my sweet, absent dog her epilepsy pill. Every time I returned to the rental house after an errand to the church, I would look at a shaft of sunshine coming through the French doors and wish I could see my pretty dog standing up in her bed, looking expectantly at me.

A door had closed.

But God was on duty. A window opened.

Our granddaughter was born. She was a week overdue, but she

arrived late one afternoon in a swirl of snowflakes like Elsa from "Frozen." She was perfect. We became frequent guests at the nearby house of my stepdaughter and son-in-law where their obsession with burp rags and diapers matched ours with two-by-fours and floor plans. Nearly every day, our phones would light up with an adorable pink-punctuated picture. Our granddaughter was a beautiful distraction from the gap created by the dog's demise and from the overwhelming amount of work represented by the church. As any parent or grandparent knows, it's hard to think about much else when one is holding a crying or contented baby—she simply demands all your attention.

About a month later, a neighbor and former member of the church who had already gifted me with photos and a box of vintage Christmas cards picturing the church called me over to her house. "I have something for you," she said when I arrived.

She handed me a tiny wooden chair.

"These used to be the Sunday school chairs in the area in the church you're turning into your bedroom," she said. "I have vivid memories of these chairs in a circle in that room."

The Sunday school room, of course, was the room where we were removing the doorway, the one where there once was a row of coat hooks. She knew very well her gift would someday soon be the perfect-sized seat in the church for my new granddaughter.

20
THE GOOD SAMARITAN

SHOWERS, AS IT TURNS out, are expensive. We planned to have three of them in the church, one on every floor.

Even while discussing the Tequila Budget, we agreed we wouldn't tile our own showers. We were happy to do demolition, sand the wood floors, install our own kitchen cabinets, but tiling? Forget it.

Tyler and I had attempted a tiling project in our former home, replacing the carpeting (yuck!) in the master bathroom. It turned out OK, but it was difficult work and perfect corners were tricky to accomplish. Perhaps ironically, Tyler was not a tiler. For the church, we knew an expert needed to install the tiling.

Acrylic showers we saw at a home show intrigued us—no seams to leak, easy to clean and long-lasting. But the quoted price tag—$19,050 plus plumbing and fixtures for all three—taught us they cost as much or more than tiling. The bottom line forced us to confront our means and the end. How much was beauty worth?

We made compromises. We eliminated custom showers on the second floor and in the basement; we could go with fiberglass surrounds for those showers—only our guests would be using them anyway. We also relegated the basement shower to Phase Eight; we first needed to get the main floor habitable.

Tyler asked the acrylic shower guy for a quote on the master bathroom shower only: still $8,728 plus plumbing and fixtures.

Uff-da.

The shower posed two insurmountable hurdles. It was extra-large, so we couldn't go with a standard insert. And we wanted to maintain an openness that demanded two glass walls. "Extra-large"—and especially "extra-large glass"—were pricey.

OK, let's get another quote, this time for tile. We approached a well-known area remodeler who sent a knowledgeable and efficient estimator. He asked informed questions, performed detailed measurements amidst our dusty church and returned a professional, detailed quote: $12,500 plus fixtures and plumbing.

Oh, boy.

Well, unless we left out a toilet and sinks, such a beautiful shower was still more than we budgeted for the entire master bath in the Tequila Budget.

This was a problem.

While shopping for cabinets, Tyler spied a do-it-yourself shower option that wouldn't require us to tile. The material for the shower walls came in full sheets that could be cut to size.

Price for this do-it-yourself option? $7,414 plus plumbing and fixtures.

Well, we were getting warmer, I guess.

Then I experienced another one of those moments of serendipity that had blessed us throughout this project.

I went to the post office to ask about whether we were the getting a mailbox or post office box. I had already been there four times without hearing a clear answer.

As we stepped into line, a man who held open the door for me motioned to let me cut in before him.

"No, go ahead," I said.

But he was a gentleman of the generation when etiquette demanded ladies first (let's be honest, he looked to be my age). I accepted his offer.

I explained my problem to the man behind the counter, beginning with this description that had become familiar to my lips: "I bought the old Methodist church, and we're turning it into our home." Etc., etc.

During a pause in our conversation, the gentleman behind me asked, "You're remodeling a church?"

"Yup, we are." I smiled.

"Do you need any help?" he asked.

"Yes! You know anyone?"

"Yeah, me," he said. "I'm a master carpenter. And I do other things."

"Do you know any tilers?"

"Yes, I do tiling."

"Do you have a card?"

He fished a card out of his pocket. By now I was ignoring the postal employee. I read the card, and an old Paul Simon song floated into my head.

"Al? Can I call you Al? Do you have time now? My husband is at the church. He handles all the contractors. You could go talk to him now."

"Sure," You-Can-Call-Me-Al said. "Where's the church?"

And the polite gentleman went to the church, introduced himself to Tyler—You-Can-Call-Me-Al—and told him, yes, he could tile a shower for us. He did it all the time.

Meanwhile, I nailed down an answer about our mail. We would get a box at the post office, not a mailbox.

After a back and forth over a week or two, we agreed to provide all the materials per You-Can-Call-Me-Al's specs, and he would perform the work to be paid by the hour.

Still, we would have to buy a custom glass door and have it installed. This meant visiting another contractor. One lead led to another, but after I defined my wishes with a glass expert, he sent me a quote. Besides the door, another half wall was included, which was more affordable than two glass walls but still lux.

During these negotiations, we saw a *Fixer Upper* episode in which the shower door had a cut-out in the glass instead of the handle. Very trendy. I inquired about this, and by gum, the glass expert could do such a thing. For a price, of course.

In the end, we would have nearly exactly the master shower we'd envisioned: extra-large and airy.

The only do-it-yourself part would be the shopping.

You-Can-Call-My-Al suggested buying tile at a big-box store because if he ran short, it would be easy to get more. If, on the other hand, we found something special-order from Spain, well, then we might have problems. Also, big-box tile was affordable and efficient.

I went to Home Depot (again) and made like Christina from "Flip or Flop." I juggled samples and settled on three: one for the floor of the shower, one for the walls, and one as an accent. I brought one of each home to the rental house to sell Tyler the salesman on them. Tyler agreed to my vision.

"Off the shelf" should mean easy to get, but that proved untrue for one tile option. Our nearest Home Depot did not have enough of the shower floor tile, so I ordered the twenty-four tiles we needed from the warehouse to arrive Monday.

They didn't arrive Monday. And it didn't arrive the following Monday either ("Two weeks!"). By now, You-Can-Call-Me-Al was assembling the foundation and waterproofing the shower. He couldn't begin tiling until he had the shower floor tile. The entire project nearly ground to a standstill because the warehouse couldn't deliver on the promise.

Tyler bawled out the store manager, who ultimately offered us a 20-percent discount on another choice of tile. But we didn't want another choice. Some pointed questioning led us to discover nearby Home Depots carried the tile, but none had the quantity we needed.

A brief trip to Minnesota to visit family during a rare spring blizzard offered up an answer. I visited four Home Depots in the Twin Cities metro area to piece together enough square footage to keep You-Can-Call-Me-Al in tile for the duration of the project.

Our timeline was saved by mass production and suburban convenience.

THOSE CUTE SHOWER NICHES HGTV house flippers construct look so pretty when the house is staged with candlelight and floral arrangements. When put into use, though, those niches are an eyesore filled with mismatched face wash and deep conditioners.

In the initial design of our custom shower, we intended to hide our extra-large shower niche in the corner. At least our shampoo would be mostly obscured to looky-loos poking their heads inside our master bath to get a look.

But then we discovered the pre-engineered insets wouldn't fit between the studs on that wall. You-Can-Call-Me-Al offered to create a custom niche, which sounded reasonable until Tyler discovered the inserts would fit neatly in the glass-door wall. Even better, our niche would be visible only from inside the shower. Ta-da! No more ugly shampoo cluttering the impressive view of the shower.

Happy accident.

ALL TOLD, OUR EXTRA-LARGE master shower would cost about $7,000 in materials and labor plus plumbing and fixtures.

Ah, the fixtures.

I wanted a rainfall showerhead. I naively believed that's how they were sold: showerhead, rainfall; quantity: One.

Um, no.

One needs valves. They're the parts you can't see, but without them, you don't have water pressure or temperature control. Then you need something called "valve trim." This is the knob that turns on the water.

Then you need the shower head. But sometimes you might also need a shower head arm and a shower head flange.

Naturally, each of these parts has its own price.

Oh, and you're not done yet. Now you must choose a style. And don't forget the finish: brass, copper, bronze, chrome—and not so fast—would you like that in polished, brushed or matte?

Tyler chose a distinctive Kohler bathtub faucet for the upstairs bath, but we went with the "contractor special" for the shower. For the master bathroom, we considered Kohler, a manufacturer based here in Wisconsin. In the end, we went with Moen polished chrome fixtures. Brass is new and trendy, but I hated brass. Polished chrome would look clean and durable, and its popularity meant it would be easy to find accessories and other fixtures.

The bathroom fixtures in the rental house were brass, and apologies to brass fans, they were ugly, not retro, not trendy. The whole room was a lesson in how not to finish a bathroom. We had been living in the little rental house for four months. It was cozy and infinitely cleaner than the church-in-renovation (despite my poor housekeeping). As we obsessed about the finishing details in the church, I couldn't help but notice all the little mistakes in our rental.

Case in point: the bathroom. This tiny room was a mess of poor design and even worse execution.

As we planned our own bathrooms in the church, we hoped to avoid similarly poor workmanship. Instead of simply tolerating an ugly bathroom with brass fixtures for a few months, we'd be living with our new bathrooms long term. If they reflected poor workmanship, we'd only have ourselves to blame.

But nothing could be as bad as the contractors' bucket.

Shortly after Glimfeather, the plumber, began work, the only piece of operational plumbing—the basement toilet—was decommissioned to move around pipes or drains or vents or something.

But like other bodily functions, pee happens. The parade of contractors through the church were exclusively men, so Tyler could get away with establishing a five-gallon bucket in the basement back entryway as a temporary urinal. Who needs a porta-potty when you've got a bucket?

I, of course, opted out. Way out. I wouldn't even volunteer to empty the thing. But I also had to plan my coffee consumption and work breaks to make trips back to the rental house to relieve myself when necessary.

For a month, the guys carried on with nary a complaint (guys are like that).

As Glimfeather wrapped up his work, the original toilet—in all its porcelain glory and running water—was reinstalled in the basement bathroom. This still lacked an operational vanity sink and a door, but still—a toilet! Applause—with unwashed hands—erupted in the crowd.

MEANWHILE, TYLER ORDERED THE fiberglass shower surround and corner tub for the upstairs bathroom from two different big-box retailers (each cost roughly $1,000, which goes to show how much less cookie-cutter options are than custom ones). We needed to have these before we constructed the walls because they both were too large to get through the doorway. Fortunately, when they arrived by delivery truck, the odd assortment of contractors onsite at the time helped haul them upstairs.

We (by "we," I mean mostly Tyler) built the walls for the bathroom on the second floor. Like our other bathrooms, this one featured a pocket door.

ONE AFTERNOON WHEN I arrived at the church after a day filled with exciting errands like picking up rough-in valves for Glimfeather the plumber and more paint for the drywallers who were making like Michelangelo and painting the cathedral ceiling, Tyler put me to work handing him tools for the construction of a form to contain the floor-leveling compound in which the upstairs shower stall would be nestled.

Tyler built sides for the form; the bottom was simply the century-old pine flooring. Leveling compound is like concrete, only soupier. After adding water to the dusty compound, Tyler poured the goop into the form.

Immediately, we could hear the dripping.

"Is it leaking?" Tyler said, then more urgently when it was clear it was indeed leaking, *"Where* is it leaking?"

I ran down the steps and looked in horror at the rainfall of gray, pasty soup dripping through the floor, through the form, through the shower drain hole.

"Everywhere!"

One of the HVAC guys, who had been working in the basement, appeared out of nowhere to rescue a big roll of aluminum foil bubble wrap covered in pasty drips of leveling compound. "What is that?"

"Leveling compound," I answered.

"Well, it's leveling all the way to the basement."

I shoved a tray and a bucket in place to catch drops.

"Get back up here!" Tyler bellowed.

He'd filled in a couple of the holes, but we'd lost so much compound through the cracks, we needed more to fill the form. Tyler began mixing again. "Hand me bottles of water."

We didn't have running water in the church yet. The first batch of soup was mixed with a jug of water collected that morning at the rental house.

Tyler mixed up another batch of soup and dumped it in the form. "Is it still dripping?"

I ran downstairs again to look even though we both could hear it. "Yup."

But the waterfall had slowed to a trickle.

When Tyler came downstairs, I asked, "Did you know that was going to happen?"

"Well, they're old floors. There's bound to be a few holes."

"It was pretty holey."

"Well, that's right. We live in a church. It's a holy floor."

21
A WHOLE HEAVENLY ARMY

OUR NUMBER ONE DESIGN rule was "details matter," and this was most important starting at the top: the ceilings. The high ceiling in the sanctuary—our future great room—drew us to be interested in a church. They needed to be grand, not just good. We accomplished a host of finishing details during these weeks, but the ceilings are where the finishing work began.

First, drywall. Drywall, for the uninitiated, is a panel made of gypsum plaster pressed between thick sheets of paper. In modern homes, drywall is rarely seen but it literally surrounds us, concealed with paint or wallpaper or paneling inside our walls and ceilings. In the 1950s, it began replacing the traditional lath and plaster as a speedier alternative. Our sanctuary ceiling required new drywall to replace the old fiberboard tiles.

Drywall comes in four-by-twelve-foot sheets, and the drywallers chose to get it into the church with a boom truck through the upstairs windows. Instead of half-inch, Tyler chose five-eighths-inch drywall for the sanctuary ceiling because it was stiffer, heavier and laid flatter.

The sanctuary ceiling, half drywalled.

At one point, St. Johnny and I moved a few pieces out of the way, and it was like, well, hitting a brick wall.

But the unwieldiness of these large sheets of drywall didn't deter the team, even as they navigated scaffolding fifteen-feet high and higher. Mudding the seams came next, and in a matter of a few days, they had performed their magic.

Next up, paint. As with the drywall, the team was nothing if not efficient with a sprayer and an enormous roller. When I walked into the sanctuary to check their progress, it was like walking into fog; the process created an astonishing number of airborne particulates. Hours later, a fine white dust covered everything in the room.

How much paint is required to paint a church ceiling? Now we knew. We purchased ten gallons of primer and ten gallons of white paint. I couldn't even lift the buckets! Then, two days later, I picked up two *more* gallons of paint so the drywallers could finish the job. Twenty-two gallons. That's a lot of paint.

❖

THE GRAND PLAN TO open the choir loft required Tyler to construct a balcony for the loft to open up *to*.

This project began with two steps. To clear the edge of the sanctuary ceiling, we needed two steps down from the second story onto the balcony. For the most part, Tyler worked from underneath the two steps, standing on a ladder.

Now he was ready to build the balcony.

The HVAC guys had no idea when they woke up that morning that they'd be carpenters for a few minutes that day.

Once the header supporting the second floor was installed, Tyler built the archway upon which the floor joists of the balcony would rest. He enlisted the help of the HVAC guys to raise the arch. (Witnessing this, it reminded me of an old-fashioned barn raising—it takes a village to build a balcony). Then Tyler—with St. Johnny's muscle—nailed great big two-by-tens into place. Pretty soon, he had a pergola built above what would become our kitchen.

Putting a layer of plywood over the floor joists was easy—after the first piece. I was glad I didn't watch Tyler straddling floor joists nine feet off the floor to juggle that first piece of plywood and nail it.

To wrap up the balcony, Tyler built cross joists from the pergola to the north and south walls of the church. These were narrower than the center part of the balcony to clear the spiral stairway on the north side and the front window on the south. Tyler planned a dramatic scallop and swoop to soften the balcony's edges. You-Can-Call-Me-Al was an even better carpenter than a tiler. Picking up in execution where Tyler's grand plans left off, he built the most graceful sweeps constructed of wood you've ever seen.

"Aren't you impressed that I built that balcony basically by myself?" Tyler asked me a few days later. He knew very well his knowledge of construction and ability to carry out the plan impressed me. He asked this question out loud because after all he had built throughout his life, even *he* was impressed.

Now we could not just imagine but actually *see* all the square footage we had added with this balcony. It was magnificent. We had essentially added a second living room; one would be able to watch the big-screen TV on the main floor from the balcony. Tyler described the dream recliner he wanted to situate there in all its roomy, reclining leather glory.

But the drawback of all that square footage was all that square footage. We had planned to save a lot of money on flooring by restoring the Douglas fir, oak and pine floors throughout the rest of the main floor and second story. But there was no restoring the plywood flooring on the balcony.

A trip to a flooring store yielded one word when the salesman announced the price per square foot of the carpeting we liked: "Ouch!"

OK, well we could put off that decision (and expense) for a while. Clearly, we would have to shop around. A big-box retailer was summoned to measure and provide a quote, maybe install the ethereal loop-pile carpeting in a creamy white with light gray lattice pattern we saw displayed on an endcap. It was called "Snowflake." I was reminded of a quip from humorist Erma Bombeck: "All of us have moments in our lives that test our courage. Taking children into a house with white carpet is one of them."

"Do we dare install white carpeting?" I asked, polling family members with chunks of Snowflake, Moon Dust and Hammerhead.

"The Hammerhead is safer," my son-in-law said.

But everyone else voted for creamy white.

We returned to the local manufacturer to fantasize about a spiral staircase. The proprietress offered to let us mix-and-match her overstock railing spindles in the back room. We pawed through a half-dozen dusty boxes (imagine the blackness of dust in an iron welding joint), and we were rewarded with enough forty-two-inch spindles to create a traditional wrought-iron railing with a hint of upscale details. The proprietor also visited to measure and discuss details of the stairway, which would take eight to twelve weeks to fabricate.

Now Tyler paid attention to the other ceilings. The master bath required a false ceiling. The hallway to the master bedroom required a false ceiling. The master bedroom required a tray ceiling. The master bedroom's ceiling vexed Tyler because of the unlevel floor and existing ceiling. Tyler persevered, as always, and made it work in a way Tim Gunn of "Project Runway" would have approved. In the recessed area of the tray ceiling, we installed a ceiling fan.

The entryway required reconstruction to remove all the cross beams in the false ceiling. We would drywall the actual ceiling with only two or three cross beams. Tyler also removed the last ancient wasp nest that clung to the church.

Among other details above our heads, Tyler created an archway for the open doorway from the master bedroom to the master bath, and he rebuilt the hopelessly crooked back stairway to the second floor.

WE DREAMED OF SECOND-FLOOR skylights. Our Number Three

design rule was "Natural lighting brings the outdoors indoors." We had discovered a novel skylight that transmitted light from the roof to a main floor kitchen with a series of reflective surfaces inside a tube. We later learned these tubular daylighting devices can also include a bathroom vent and a solar-powered nightlight, which would be perfect for our upstairs bathroom.

Tyler hurried to install the pickled plywood planks on the upstairs ceiling, and the skylight installer arrived bright and early one Monday to install one tube in the bathroom and another one (without the vent and nightlight) in the adjacent area that would someday house my office.

The tubular skylights generated an amazing amount of natural light upstairs, just what we imagined. And, we learned we could get a tax rebate for using energy-efficient lighting. Score!

BEFORE SEALING UP CEILINGS and walls, I installed insulation.

The pink stuff.

This job required no expertise, only perseverance. I was selected.

I suited up in Tyvek, safety goggles, gloves and safety glasses, and set to work on the first area requiring insulation: the attic eaves.

It was like wrestling with Tyler if my king-sized husband were cotton candy—the insulation was bigger than I was, and there was no way I was gonna win this fight. I resisted, I poked, and I punched when called for, and, eventually, I got the pink rolls stuffed between the studs.

The worst part was the height of the attic eaves—exactly short enough that I couldn't stand and tall enough that I couldn't reach the top while kneeling. My quadriceps were not up to the challenge.

After wrestling with insulation for two days and thinking I was finished, I learned properly installed insulation requires a vapor barrier. I spent an afternoon wrestling with plastic to cover the insulation and a staple gun (one of the few power tools I operated).

When I finished, I was reminded of a mantra that circulated in the scrapbooking circles I once traveled. Scrapbookers rarely lack raw material because life and the photos one takes while living life keep happening. It can become overwhelming if one agonizes about every single detail on every single scrapbook page so sometimes scrapbookers power through an imperfectly decorated page just to move on to the next. Done is better than perfect.

TYLER LOOMED OVER THE bed at 5:50 on a Saturday morning. "Home Depot opens in ten minutes. Time to get out of bed!"

Did I mention Tyler was an early riser?

I complied. Fortunately, Starbucks is on the way to Home Depot, and Tyler deigned to stop. At least I could sip coffee.

We proceeded to Home Depot where I watched him walk the insulation aisle, checking packages.

"This is the one! Grab that cart."

We took only one pink loaf of blow-in insulation back to the tool rental desk.

"How many packages come on a pallet?"

"Eighteen."

"I'll take two pallets."

No kidding. That earned us the bulk discount, but we still invested four figures in insulation.

Two pallets of insulation did not both fit into the back of the truck. I drove one pallet back to the church and went right back to Home Depot for the second.

Just about the time Tyler had cut in half all thirty-six loaves of insulation in our front yard, Reroofer arrived.

Reroofer didn't know he would be installing insulation, but he was game for anything (he must have had his coffee, too).

A neat, enormous pile of insulation, awaiting installation.

The assembly line began. Reroofer climbed into the space between the sanctuary ceiling and roof with one end of the hose, while I fed insulation a half loaf at a time into the blower outside the front door. Tyler more than once reassured me that Reroofer was upright and ambulatory inside the attic rather than being buried by pink insulation. "He's fine! Now get back out there and mind the blower!".

I found the job strangely satisfying. As the blower consumed half-loaf after half-loaf, the enormous pile of pink insulation slowly but consistently disappeared.

Four hours later, we were done.

Or at least I was.

I went home to shower.

The proof was in the pudding, in this case, in a late-spring blizzard. Thanks to all that insulation keeping the heat inside, our house was the last one in the neighborhood with snow on the north roof.

But Reroofer, our agile roof walker, wasn't finished yet that afternoon before the blizzard. With an uncharacteristic daylight handoff from Glimfeather the plumber, Reroofer threaded the soil vent pipe through the roof and repaired the roof hole created when we removed the portable gas heater (and accompanying stove pipe) from the second floor.

A soil vent pipe, for people who only use bathrooms but don't know how they work, has nothing to do with soil. It runs vertically from the underground drainage system to the roof. The vent allows odors from waste to be released into the atmosphere. By placing it above roof-gutter level, no one's the wiser about the stink of your poop.

For what wouldn't be the first time, Tyler sent Reroofer up there with a can of black spray paint. I don't have to remind you that details matter, and who wants a white pipe sticking out of the roof when one could have a black pipe? Not Tyler, the Virgo, who had already spray-painted the exterior vents for the dryer and stove white to match the siding.

Reroofer's work was impeccable; when he was done, the roof looked as good as new.

A week or so later, the HVAC guys threaded a flue-vent liner through the chimney to prepare the fireplace would install in the sanctuary-cum-great room. Before ascending the ladder to straddle the highest peak on the roof, Tyler handed the appointed HVAC guy a can of heat-resistant black spray paint with explicit directions to paint the vent at the top of the chimney.

"What did the HVAC guy say?" I asked later.

Tyler said, "I think he was surprised I had heat-proof black spray paint on hand."

TYLER WAS A MAN with a mission to build his home solidly. As with many efforts in his life, that meant cooking for eight when only two people were eating dinner.

Our doors would, of course, be solid wood, not hollow core. The church came with several solid wood doors, so this wasn't difficult to achieve.

As for drywall, only five-eighths inch would do. In his opinion, standard half-inch drywall did not hang flat or stand up to wear.

Insulation, for all its cotton candy fluff, was another way we built solidly. Besides the attic eaves I insulated and the blow-in insulation Reroofer sprayed in the roof, I spent days rolling the pink stuff between wall studs to keep out the cold, protect pipes and provide a sound barrier to shield us from the outside world. I imagined us living in a muffled pink cloud bank.

Tyler even thought about the church's connective elements.

Glue, for example, is a connectivity pansy. If one's house is glued together, the Big Bad Wolf could blow it down even the morning after a bender that involved copious amounts of cigarettes and whiskey. Nails ... well now you're talking power in terms of connecting solid surfaces. But if you really want two surfaces to stay together, you use screws.

The big daddy of connective devices is the TimberLok, a coarse-threaded screw, usually used on larger timbers (as the name implies). In most cases, these expensive babies are not sold by the case; one buys them in a box of twenty. Tyler used TimberLoks in the kitchen header, in the columns holding up the balcony and in whatever warped pieces of lumber he encountered to straighten them out. If a tornado hit the church, we might lose the roof to Kansas, but the two-foot thick foundation and the balcony would remain attached to the *terra firma*.

And then there was the blocking.

At the end of framing, Tyler spent long, boring days nailing blocking between the wall studs and ceiling joists. Blocking creates the sort of solid structures that resist barroom brawls.

More than once, Tyler returned to Home Depot to buy more lumber. "I can't believe we used all that wood," he'd mutter.

22
A LIGHT UNTO MY PATH

BENJAMIN FRANKLIN PROVED LIGHTNING was electrical by flying a kite in a thunderstorm in 1752, but it wasn't until 1879 that Thomas Edison invented the electric light bulb.

Our Methodist church was built twelve years later. Electricity surely didn't light our church until at least the 1930s when President Franklin D. Roosevelt created the initiative to build the national electrical grid that brought electricity to rural America.

Perhaps the church was lighted with gas at some point, but we couldn't tell. We found evidence of early 20th century knob-and-tube wiring and cloth-covered wiring behind some of the walls, but none of it was operational. The remaining wiring consisted of a mix of flexible armored tube copper wire, modern Romex and a little conduit.

Tyler discovered the flaky operational wiring when he connected innumerable power tools to various outlets. The outlets that provided dependable power soon were favored, and extension cords were employed when electricity was needed in far-flung church locales.

To be safe, Tyler decided to rewire the whole church, no matter how old or new(ish) the wiring. Our electrician had worked on the church, so he knew the electrical system faults in a contemporary way and the antique parts in a knob-and-tube way. By the time the HVAC guys finally finished and Glimfeather the plumber had nearly completed his work, our walls had been framed. Our electrician could now go to work.

Of course, the electrician needed direction. Where to put outlets? Where to switch the lights? Which kind of lights? How many?

Welcome to a world of arcane terminology such as amps and volts, poles and pucks, cables and circuits, cans and dimmers, GFI and GFCI.

From an interior decorating standpoint, Tyler and I could often agree. I liked his choice for the balcony shape, and he approved of my ideas for a tile rug in front of the kitchen sink. We were simpatico about our great room sectional, the kitchen cabinets and the bathroom layout.

But we could not agree on lighting.

It wasn't even light fixtures we argued about—it was the very existence of lighting!

Tyler liked subdued, indirect lighting in all circumstances.

I liked direct, high-wattage lighting in most circumstances.

I attributed this to our eye color. He had blue eyes, and mine are brown. I thought his eyes let in more light than mine. Our preferences also might reflect our leisure habits. He likes to nap. I like to read. These activities required different kinds of lighting.

In any case, we needed to find ways around this profoundly different lighting philosophy. In many cases, we chose dimmable lights. In other cases, I simply lost the battle.

The sanctuary lighting, for example: I would have installed recessed can lights throughout. Instead, I got none.

As easy as it was to choose an electrician, our differing lighting preferences made it hard to give him direction. This resulted in our first real fight about the church. I couldn't believe I had to describe exactly how many and where the can lights in the kitchen would be. And Tyler couldn't believe I didn't realize the electrician required such specific direction.

I hated the decision-making pressure. I had to think about how we would use each room, which appliances we'd use, how I was going to situate the furniture and lamps and whether the ceiling light would hug the ceiling or hang as a pendant.

After negotiating with Tyler, I created electrical maps of every room. I was the only one who consulted them, but at least I could direct the electrician (who wrote notes in Sharpie pen on the wall studs).

SOME LIGHT FIXTURES WERE the recycle-reuse-repurpose variety, but we still needed a few new ones.

The existing exterior lights were functional but sadly plain. And too small for my taste. The new lights would frame the castle doors, so we chose a contemporary castle mash-up stylistically, and Tyler found a matching set on eBay.

The fixture included seeded glass, which roughed up the design just enough to qualify as rustic. We would employ this design for interior light fixtures, too.

In another delivery snafu, one light box arrived with a distinctive rattle. The round glass—impossible to replace—lay as a pile of shards in the bottom of the box. Fortunately, the seller offered a quick refund and Tyler bought another immediately. Like our other finds, the lights went to the ever-more-crowded storage unit.

Lighting is the type of detail one only notices when paying attention. Suddenly, I was shopping for light fixtures, and I realized most lighting is so boring. When I saw interesting lighting, it deserved to be admired. More than once while we shopped in a building supplies department, I wandered the aisles gazing up at all the flamboyant lighting options until I got a kink in my neck.

One day, we stopped at a nearby lighting store. All light fixtures, all the time. The knowledgeable owner showed off trendy options, affordable options and distinctive options plus all the options we could get in every option: More sockets? A different finish? Bigger? And look at how different lightbulbs change the look of a fixture! When he didn't have the actual light fixture to show me, he pulled out inches-thick catalogues with more looks.

I marveled at his command of the vast inventory.

"I'm a bit of a lighting savant," he said sheepishly.

I became paralyzed with too many options. He directed me to his website, where I found *more* options. But there I could do searches by type, size and finish. Still, I couldn't pull the trigger until consulting with the Lighting Savant, so I made an appointment back at the store where he shepherded me to what I finally decided were the *right* options.

For the front entryway, I chose a big, airy chandelier of which Joanna Gaines of *Fixer Upper* would approve.

For the kitchen island, I found a trio of vintage industrial pendants with seeded glass.

While I could have chosen the exact same lights for all the bathrooms, I decided instead to customize each to the space. This wasn't a hotel we were outfitting after all.

The first lights that caught my eye in the Lighting Savant's showroom I chose for the powder room—the big, clear glass bells were distinctive without calling undo attention to themselves.

For the master bath, I wanted narrow up-and-down lights in polished chrome to install between the three arched mirrors I planned above each sink and the make-up area. (To be fair, I *really* wanted lighted, mirrored medicine cabinets, but we shelved that idea when I looked up the prices. Still, the ones I chose were the most expensive light fixtures of all the new ones we bought.)

Upstairs, I planned a full-on farmhouse feel, and this was the bathroom where I planned to paint a pair of old dressers for the vanity. For the vanity lights, I chose country-inspired glass in industrial polished chrome. The result had a whiff of the nautical, which I found satisfying. Our son-in-law was a sailor, and our granddaughter's playhouse would set under one of the eaves up there, so why not embrace a bit of nautical?

My new lights would be delivered in two to four weeks. Next, I devoted my attention to recycling light fixtures we had found. At first glance, some had more potential than others.

During demolition, I ran across a quartet of ugly, spider-like lighting fixtures. They were ugly to me because I disliked brass. (I heard brass fixtures were coming back, but I can't endorse that trend). I relegated these fixtures to the donation pile. Tyler stopped me. I didn't understand why at the time, but he obviously saw something in them I didn't.

During those early days of clean-up, I found two banker's boxes filled with plastic crystals. These might make Christmas decorations, I thought. Perhaps they somehow hung on a Christmas tree-like icicles. I packed them away while I figured out how to use them later.

As we discussed how to run electrical wiring, Tyler and I browsed the lighting displays at big-box stores. We were trying to determine which rooms would have can lighting, where we might put sconces and whether to put light kits on the ceiling fans. The electrician would need to know these nuances when he ran wiring through ceilings and walls.

In the lighting department, I was inexplicably drawn to crystal chandeliers.

I was being stupid. We didn't have a ballroom, and I didn't spend a lot of time in floor-length gowns ordering around servants. "Chandelier" wasn't in the rustic transitional design plan.

But. Chandeliers are so lovely! Ethereal even. Evocative of heaven. Belonged in a church!

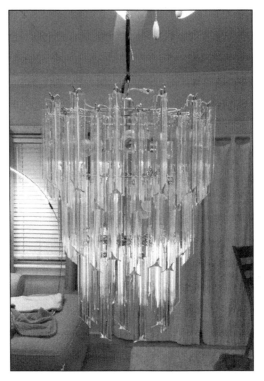

The whole was greater than
the brass and plastic parts.

(I can justify anything.)

I thought maybe I could use those Christmas icicles I found in some sort of chicken cage or tin can to create a rustic chandelier. (You've heard that definition of creativity that suggests putting two opposite things together in a new way? A tin can chandelier would be the dictionary picture for that).

I found a modern light fixture like this at Menards. I was not delusional; it was an actual thing.

But before making this Frankenstein light fixture, I tried using my icicles on the brass light fixtures that I had found and almost gave away. Couldn't hurt to try, I thought.

Poof! Magic happened! The crystals were made for the light

fixtures. Whodathunkit? (You knew this was coming, right?) Beautiful! Two of them would be perfect lighting for the nightstands in our bedroom.

OK, they were still brass, but I could remedy that.

Ever hear of spray paint? It's magic, too. A few years back, Tyler and I turned sofa legs into the coolest curtain rod finials with spray paint.

I also used spray paint to bring another set of light fixtures into my rustic transitional design scheme.

The lights we chose to hang in the sanctuary, our new great room, would feel right at home because they had hung there while illuminating church services, baptisms and weddings for a least a decade, maybe a generation or two.

The former pastor had purchased the light fixtures when the congregation moved out sixteen months before we bought the church. She told us a member had donated them, so they held sentimental value. When she met us, she offered to sell them back to us for a song, to which we readily assented once we saw them. The design melded into a union of traditional and modern that hinted at religiosity without overt evangelism. The cross on all four sides of the square fixture has a curved geometric design. Both Tyler and I felt honored we could recycle these light fixtures and hang them where they were meant to be.

They needed a little work, and I was the right woman for the job.

I disassembled them, sanded the surfaces, spray painted them hammered black (I tried a few parts in hammered bronze and rejected the two-tone look) and then hauled them all to the glass expert—the same one who would later installed our glass shower door—to replace the dingy shades with seeded glass. After he worked his magic, they sparkled.

We hired an associate of the Lighting Savant to rewire them and weave the wiring through the chains from which they would hang from the ceiling. These chains had been left empty and dangling from the ceiling when we took over. More than one member of the peanut gallery observed they were heavy enough to pull a car. Well, we were "building solidly" per our mission statement, weren't we? These light fixtures would *never* fall! He considerably shortened two of the chains so the lights could hang over the balcony.

One of the sanctuary lights, post reconstruction.

These chandeliers excited me. I could hardly wait for the day they would shine from the sanctuary's beams.

While we were paying homage to the church's historical features, Tyler relocated the milk glass ceiling lights he found during demolition to the "Hall of History."

We maintained the only hallway that existed in the church. The fifteen-foot-long hall, which led from the sanctuary to the back stairway up to the second floor, included a closet and the doorway to what would become our bedroom. With its new high ceiling, Tyler imagined we could hang pictures of the church throughout history on its expansive walls. Thus, the Hall of History name.

He found three milk glass lights of various shapes during the demolition and several rusted canopies. (The Lighting Savant taught me this term; a "light canopy" is the lamp part used to cover ceiling electrical boxes). Though the orbs didn't match, Tyler thought it would be a nice tip of the hat to history by put them to work in the Hall of History. Once again, I spray painted to combat the rust and create a uniform element for the disparate orbs. I chose satin black to stand out against the white ceiling.

And the screws to secure the orbs in the canopies? Thanks be to Home Depot, I found a whole array of options to replace the badly rusted ones. Would it surprise you to learn I chose brass? Indeed, bright brass would be the discrete accent to set off the black-and-white fixture. Details mattered.

23
THE GARDEN OF EDEN

A LATE-SPRING SNOWSTORM left inches of heavy, wet snow behind in Old Man Winter's ridiculously long wake. When spring finally arrived, so did Phase Three of our renovation: Drywall, Paint & Flooring.

Long, sunshiny days swept away months of gray skies. Slivers of green poked through dirty snow. Though strange to hear, birds sang as I tramped over snowy sidewalks no one bothered to shovel because people knew it would melt soon enough; I shed my fleece scarf as I inhaled the frosty morning air on my way from the rental house to the church. Spring is my favorite season, and ever-widening sidewalks were as distinctive a turning point to me as robins. Growing up, I walked to school in north-central Minnesota; in winter, it was a slippery trudge in boots. But in springtime, I could skip over clean concrete in my Nike tennies.

Before the snowstorm, Tyler noted the maple tree in our front yard dripping sap like bereft woman. In a future post-construction spring, he planned to tap the tree for sweet syrup. Leafy green perennials in every corner of the yard toughed out the white stuff. It looked like we'd have blooms of some sort soon. Tyler's hired man, St. Johnny, spread a load of mulch around trees and over the flower bed once tended by members of the church.

Soon, we would have to mow. Tyler snapped up a deal on eBay for a riding lawnmower he intended to teach me to use. I preferred the push variety, and I scoffed that we'd have any yard left after he poured concrete for the driveway and garage, but I couldn't complain too long. The practically new mower was a good deal, and we picked it up from the seller who lived less than forty minutes away.

Our renovation phases didn't always have clearly defined beginnings and endings. The demolition phase clearly began the day we purchased the church, but it continued into the mechanicals phase and beyond as we discovered new walls, windows and cubbies that required dismantling and replacement.

Similarly, the drywall, paint and flooring phase began as soon as the drywallers finished removing the sanctuary ceiling. They immediately drywalled and painted it, and the ceiling simply overlooked all the work being done during the framing and mechanicals phase.

We treasured a clear marker at the end of framing and mechanicals. The building inspector officially OK'd our rough-in. Approval! This was necessary to proceed with covering the studded walls that contained all the precious and expensive—but unimaginative—plumbing, wiring and HVAC ducting. Finally, the dirty demolition phase and boring mechanicals phase were behind us.

As we neared the end of the framing and mechanicals phase of construction, Tyler worked through box four of nails for his air-powered nail gun. Each box, you might recall, had two-thousand nails.

And two-by-fours? He estimated we'd used at least one-hundred-and-fifty to build walls and ceilings. The framing and mechanicals phase had dragged on nearly twelve weeks, four weeks longer than demolition, which had felt like it would never end. We were excited for the phase that signaled the most dramatic physical changes in the church. So excited, in fact, we couldn't sleep (well, that may have been just a symptom of middle age, but you get the picture). A building really begins taking shape when Sheetrocked walls cover the studded ones.

Besides nails, lumber and lassitude, Tyler's belt showed the measure of the effort we'd put into our construction project.

During the first three months, he tightened his belt by about a notch a month. By the fourth month, he had to bore a new notch in his belt, and that was apparently still not enough. One day, he had one hand on his nail gun and the other on a ceiling joist to hold it in place while he secured it. In front of an audience of St. Johnny, the carpenter helper, our electrician and an HVAC guy, his pants fell to his ankles.

He ho-ho-hoed his way through a situation that would have mortified anyone else, but thank goodness he was wearing his new, snugly fitting underwear.

Another measure of our effort? Splinters and gloves.

Tyler picked wooden splinters out of his digits nearly every night as he sat on the couch decompressing from another long day. I wasn't so rugged; I wore gloves.

Tyler had purchased a big box of cotton brown jersey gloves for me and his hired man to use. They were handy (get it? Handy gloves?) but too big for my slender (some might say boney) fingers. During demolition, I'd run across a pair of work gloves marked with "DCE." The only DCE this Lutheran had ever heard of was the Director of Christian Education, so I imagined the Methodist DCE had left them behind. They fit perfectly, so I commandeered them.

Four months and countless nails, pieces of wood and rolls of insulation later, the seams began splitting. I never had worn out a pair of work gloves. Before the church, I'd never even *owned* a pair of work gloves. I never gardened, and my hobby involved using writing utensils, not hammers. When more of my fingertips were bare than protected, I held up my threadbare DCE gloves and complained to the foreman that I needed a new pair "like these." Two days later, Tyler returned home from Home Depot with not one, not two but three pairs of work gloves surprisingly like my DCE gloves.

I would never complain about my work gloves again.

TYLER INSTALLED THE FRONT doors before the drywall was installed. Remember? The doors for the man's home that is his castle? The doors we purchased months ago were stored in the basement, awaiting their final home. Initially, we thought we'd wait until everything else was finished. But Tyler thought it better to let the drywallers work around the castle doors, rather than pull apart their careful work later only to redo it.

We couldn't fit the enormous arched door frame through the basement door, so it had been moved around the sanctuary fifteen times while various contractors worked around it. Now Tyler pulled off the exterior siding on the front entryway, and You-Can-Call-Me-Al (our tiler) helped him slide the door frame into place. Tyler's hired man, St. Johnny, helped hang the heavy doors in the frame, and You-Can-Call-Me-Al performed the required cosmetic surgery so they would swing smoothly.

All winter and early spring, the only evidence of any activity inside the church was the string of pickup trucks parked outside of it. Now, the whole world could see a hint of the transformation in store for the rest of the structure.

Our rustic castle doors with operational speakeasy portals were absolutely the perfect doors for the church. Even before we put back the siding and installed the exterior lights or even door handles, we earned compliments from friends and passing strangers on this exceeding public design choice.

They made me so happy.

A man's home is his castle.

FRIENDS IN GREAT BRITAIN who were coincidentally renovating their kitchen remarked on the differences in English drywall terminology. In Wisconsin, *drywall* came in panels made of gypsum plaster pressed between thick sheets of paper. In Great Britain, a *dry wall* was a wall of stones without mud in between them. Brits, my friend informed me, use either wet-plaster brick or block external walls; plasterboard—the equivalent of drywall panels—is used on internal stud walls. I was reminded of the old days when I visited London frequently for work, stuffing my luggage in the *boot* (that is, the trunk) and dining on lunches of prawn sandwiches garnished with rocket (shrimp sandwiches with a side of arugula).

Day One of drywall was delivery day. Tyler removed windows on the first and second floors, and two fully equipped guys pulled five tons of drywall from a flatbed truck into the church in a couple of hours.

We got rid of two thirty-yard dumpsters full of extra weight, and now we were replacing that load and then some. The drywall proved so heavy it was dangerous. The delivery guys wired stacks of four-by-twelve-foot sheets against the walls of the church with little warning clips: "Warning! DRYWALL IS HEAVY! Attempting to move may cause injury or death."

Not that I needed another reminder of the weight of construction materials. There is a reason you don't see old ladies with no upper body strength working in the construction industry. I struggled to lift pretty much everything. (Except insulation. That was easy to lift. Hard to manipulate.) Lumber was heavy. Five-gallon buckets of paint were heavy. Tile was *really* heavy. Sledgehammers? Solid-wood doors? Drywall? Rebar? Brick? Well-constructed cabinets? All of it reminded me how little strength I had *ever*, let alone now in my fifties. Before our construction project, I puffed up my chest when I was able to open a bottle of spaghetti sauce by myself. I wasn't built for this.

Day Two of drywall was less efficient than simple delivery. Our drywaller had subcontracted our job to another team. When they arrived, they discovered the job was at a 126-year-old, not-perfectly straight church that required five-eighths inch-and-therefore-heavier drywall.

The dour-faced subcontractors left in their pickup truck with nary a word.

I saw them driving away as I walked up to the church. Only I didn't know they were *our* workers.

"Where are the drywallers?" I asked Tyler, who was busying himself with one of the other thousand details requiring attention.

"They left."

"Are they coming back?"

"I don't know," he said.

Well, they didn't come back.

After regrouping with Tyler and explaining what the B Team didn't tell use before departing, our drywaller agreed to use his A Team. These were the same men who'd had so skillfully finished our sanctuary ceiling, but it would take longer. Despite hearing echoes of "Two weeks! Two weeks!" in my ears, we readily agreed.

The A Team began (on Day Three) in the master bath so our tiler, You-Can-Call-Me-Al, could put down his saw and pick up his spatula again to get back to tiling.

The drywall concealed all our sins: crooked pipes, ugly studs, awkwardly stapled insulation plus dirt and sawdust. White sheets occasionally interrupted with "5/8" CP LITE-WEIGHT FIRE-RATED" print covered everything. Even before mudding the seams, the new drywall made actual rooms out our wooden studs. People warned us our rooms would feel smaller, but I didn't feel that way at all. Our rooms finally felt like rooms.

In completing the bathroom, the new Sheetrock sealed up our shortcut. The linen closet—an awkward eighteen-inch-square chunk of space between the mudroom, the walk-in-closet and the bathrooms—lost its status as a doorway and became what it was designed for—a closet.

After five days of hanging drywall in all the rooms on the main floor and second story, the A Team taping and mudded the seams, which nicely finished all the edges.

Our wall work was nothing on the scale of God's and it was taking a lot longer than six days. But in the words of Genesis, we saw everything that we had made, and behold, it was very good.

AS THE WALLS TOOK shape, my parents who lived in Minnesota visited.

I almost always brought home A's from school, but showing my parents around the church proved better than any report card. Finally, they could see in three dimensions all we had been describing these many months.

The day after walking through our future home the first time, I asked my parents what they thought.

"Well," my mother said, "we think you've come a long way in five months. But you have a long way to go."

My seventy-something father was an avid woodworker who had contributed beautiful built-in bookshelves to both of my last two houses. (Alas, the bookcases are still there, even if I'm not.) So naturally, he lent a hand to the church reconstruction project.

Tyler wanted materials tougher than the drywall wrapping the two pillars that held up the balcony. Those posts stood in a high-traffic area near barstools that may get backed into the posts on exuberant occasions. Dad agreed to wrap the pillars with vinyl board (think of the material in PVC pipes, only flat). He and I traipsed around Home Depot to find the right stuff and delivered it to the church, where Dad spent one morning measuring twice and cutting once to make our pillars look as clean and nearly finished as our walls.

Mom, Dad and I also visited the impressive showroom where I found the Lighting Savant's distinctive light fixtures. Mom and Dad needed both advice and pendant fixtures for their kitchen. They found both—the Lighting Savant was just as helpful to them as he had been to me.

A successful visit all the way around.

WHILE THE DRYWALLERS DID their thing inside the church, Tyler got busy outside. Finally, the weather made the Great Outdoors inviting again, and Tyler began work on his Garage of Dreams.

In the way that other phases overlapped one another, *Phase Six:*

The Garage necessarily overlapped *Phase Three: Drywall, Paint & Flooring* for two reasons. First, nice spring weather was finally upon us. Second, it was becoming increasingly apparent we weren't couldn't move into the church when we elected to wrap up our lease on the nearby rental house. We needed to return to the camper, which we preferred to park on the cement slab of our future driveway and garage rather than a muddy yard.

This wasn't an entirely unwelcome development given the nice weather. Recall that we were forced to move out of the camper in mid-November only because of snow and the imminent threat of freezing sewage pipes. On the other hand, it would have been convenient to move directly from the rental house into the church. But without the luxuries of finished flooring, countertops and closet racks in the church, we elected to take up residence in the camper.

When deciding to purchase this church, the size of the lot appealed to us as much as the location. No churches came with attached garages, and some small churches offered no place to build a garage. When we contemplated the church in Pecatonica, Illinois, the garage we planned would have taken up all the open lot. Though there was no parking lot or off-street parking with our 126-year-old Methodist church, the structure itself was built on the front of a long triangular lot, which left lots of land for a garage with space left for a garden and other green space.

For several weeks, Tyler had been pacing and tracing the outline of his garage and driveway, collecting bids, consulting with the building inspector on setbacks and footings, and pricing creature comforts (such as urinals and the method of garage heating). Bids on outsourcing all the work ran high, so with his eye on the Tequila Budget, Tyler took on some parts of the project himself. He was ready to break ground.

Or at least break concrete.

The first step in his grand garage plan was to break up part of the concrete stairway from the basement. The original straight stairway required a turn so it could be situated completely inside the future garage. The top four steps had to go.

Tyler jack-hammered through several feet of concrete. St. Johnny earned his pay that day, hauling away the heavy chunks and digging a four-foot-deep hole to accommodate a new mid-stairway landing.

Tyler came home from the church that day in a state of exhaustion. After months of demolition and wall construction, he admitted that was only a warm-up. "I haven't worked that hard in years," he said at the end of jackhammer day as he flopped on the couch, soon to be sleeping.

After the surgery on the stairway, it was time to dig footings for the garage.

In the case of our garage, footings meant a hundred feet of walls deep enough to reach beyond the frost line—four feet deep. A concrete pad wasn't enough since our garage would be attached to a structure with an existing basement. To dig these deep trenches, Tyler rented a mini-excavator and hired a friend of a friend who could manipulate the excavator with precision. The trenches—three sides of the garage—were completed in a day.

My role that day was errand girl. I went to Subway to get lunch for the hungry workers. I worked harder the next day when I used pruning snips, an implement like a manual hedge trimmer, to clip a hundred years of pine roots obstructing the trenches. The excavator had cut through a lot of roots, but it wouldn't do to have *any* obstructions when we were ready to pour concrete. I squatted in the mud to cut roots two feet below the yard's surface, and then I moved rebar from the borrowed flatbed trailer to the yard. Rebar is heavy, at least for old ladies, so I carried two pieces at a time and walked them rather than trying to lift ten pieces at a time.

That was my contribution to the garage.

Meanwhile, Tyler used the excavator to dig up bushes. Running an excavator is like playing a video game; the controls affect both the excavator itself and the operation of the scoop, depending upon how you turn them. He maybe couldn't have dug a precise trench, but with practice to activate his muscle memory, he dug up arborvitae roots like a pro in no time. Tyler first learned to operate a backhoe to save money when he dug his own septic system for his old tobacco farm decades ago. Necessity is the mother of invention (or something like that).

Tyler and I had been married nearly ten years, but I learned new things about him all the time during this renovation. I didn't know he knew how to run an excavator until I saw him, sweaty and concentrating, behind the controls. Such a skill just doesn't come up in everyday conversation. Fortunately for our budget, my Renaissance Man was saving us money in every phase of this undertaking.

The next day, the building inspector dropped by so we could prove we really dug four-feet-deep footings. (Apparently some people prevaricate regarding this detail, which is why the inspector makes an appearance before the cement mixer does).

A cement mixer rumbled into our yard to pour eighteen yards of concrete into the trenches. Next, we employed an experienced concrete finisher and his crew to fill in the basement windows with concrete block and build wooden forms for the cement pad's concrete walls. A few days later, the concrete mixer dropped by again and left behind eight-and-a-half yards of concrete.

By now, the yard was a muddy mess, and continued rain intermittently interrupted our progress. Between the heavy machinery and the patchy spring showers, our lawn looked like a pig pen with apparently random concrete walls sticking out.

Amid the spring showers came a hailstorm for the ages. A squall rolled through about 9 o'clock one evening; it sounded like a guy with a baseball bat pounding on the flat roof of our rental house. Tyler went outside to determine the damage and brought back a jagged lemon-sized piece of ice, one of many.

The next morning, we found holes as big as my fist in the west-side window screens of the rental house. Twigs and branches covered the yard.

Our vehicles were pockmarked with tiny dents. An assessment of the church property revealed hail damage to the west side of the cargo trailer and, alas, the church.

During the next few weeks, no fewer than a dozen roofing and siding contractors visited us, offering to repair the hail damage and work with our insurance. Scores of neighbors enlisted their help. Soon we wouldn't be the only property in town with hammer-wielding contractors making improvements.

THE RAIN HAD TURNED our yard into a staging area for a mud pie maker. Slippery black dirt, piles of reddish clay and stacks of wood cluttered what might otherwise be a bucolic scene.

Tyler bought four yards of 100 percent organic, sterilized composted cow manure that he dumped in a burial-mound-like fashion next to the flagpole.

Ah, *more* mud.

Then Tyler planted two cherry tomatoes, four beefsteak tomatoes, four pepper plants, four cucumbers plus basil and mint.

He also picked up marigolds and salvia, which he planted in the church sign planter.

He reveled in his gardening. While living in a camper. he missed growing plants and picking vegetables and, most of all, eating fresh produce he grew himself.

Some greenery in our yard didn't require planting, only discovering.

Tyler claimed as ours a raspberry plant growing on the edge of our property bordering the dumpster area for the nearby rental properties. This, he would baby until he could coax it into producing berries. Near the front of the property, the congregation had left behind a garden plot featuring a vast array of perennial greenery, including a beautiful yellow tulip and a daffodil.

Tulips are my favorite spring flower. Picking them only spoiled their beauty so they were best enjoyed *in situ*, which served to inspire many spring walks. Predictably, the tulip blooms wilted in a few days.

Not quite as ephemeral, but still fleeting and worth appreciating in their time, was the lilac bush on the corner of the property. I had prayed the lilacs would bloom when Tyler trimmed all the bushes in the fall. Indeed, spring brought woolly purple blossoms, intoxicatingly fragrant.

The yard was a muddy mess, but she wore a mighty pretty corsage.

24
THE HOUSE ON THE ROCK

OUR CHURCH RENOVATION PROJECT started to look like the list of traditional gifts one should give a spouse for wedding anniversaries. The paper year was celebrated when we dumped a ton of it during the demolition. We'd observed the precious metals years by replumbing and rewiring the church. And wood? Tyler and crew handled innumerable two-by-fours in building walls and ceilings. We'd skipped over the crystal and china years to land squarely in the anniversary years celebrated with stone.

Sheetrock, for example. It was the brand name for our drywall. Sheet*rock*. And what's concrete anyway? Concrete was a substance created from gravel and cement that dries rock hard. We'd poured yards for the foundation walls of our garage and would pour many yards more. Speaking of gravel, Tyler spent two days using his cousin's dump truck to haul load after load of gravel from a nearby gravel pit for the base of the garage foundation.

We couldn't build our home solidly without stone. What's more solid than stone? It was bricks, after all, that stymied the huffing, puffing Big Bad Wolf. A sixteen-inch-thick foundation of field stones formed our church's foundation.

Now, as we executed the interior design of Church Sweet Home, varieties of stone played important roles. Our first stone decisions involved the fireplace.

Somehow, we managed to neglect the fireplace in our Tequila Budget. It might have been the tequila we drank at the time, but we were probably more drunk with excitement in those first heady days of dreaming about buying a church.

Of course, we needed a fireplace. It wasn't a bad-news budget-breaker like redoing all the heating and cooling ductwork. And it wasn't one of those great ideas we added to the project midstream like the balcony. Nope, we just forgot about the centerpiece of our great room as we planned our great room. Duh.

Unfortunately for the budget, a fireplace isn't like register covers (another one of those things we neglected to consider when we were figuring our figures). A fireplace costs big bucks, and we weren't likely to find the gargantuan one we wanted on Craigslist.

So the Tequila Budget took another hit when we shopped for a fireplace.

Maybe we'd burn the budget at some point.

In the fireplace.

Once again, Tyler rejected a forty-inch-wide fireplace since a forty-*eight*-inch-wide one was available. This *was* the centerpiece of the biggest room in the house, after all. Tyler ordered his enormous gas fireplace online to be delivered directly to the church. Oh, just wait. We planned to put a TV above the mantel. We wouldn't be stingy with the size of that either.

In full, the chase of the fireplace would be seven feet wide. As we pondered the design, we considered putting it in the corner of the great room or along the east wall but ultimately sided with symmetry. The fireplace would be located where the altar once was; appropriate perhaps, given that Pagans used altars to burn sacrifices. Though we toyed with shorter options, our "go big or go home" philosophy drove us to build the chase to the ceiling, even though it was vented to the exterior chimney. This meant investing in two-hundred square feet of stone.

While shopping for rigid polyurethane foam beams, Tyler found faux stone in the same material. We ordered a sample, hoping to be as impressed as we were with the polyurethane beams. It would not be fun to heft actual stone to the top of the chase, but the faux stone was horrible. The edges weren't as crisp as real stone would be, and the material bubbled. Unlike the beams, guests would be able to walk right up to it and inspect its faux-ness. Back to the drawing board.

Faux stone. No way.

Natural stone, though, was substantially more expensive and would require the skills of a bricklayer.

Hmm.

Maybe we could afford manufactured stone, which is made of pigmented cement baked in molds. Though certainly not as light as high-density polymer, veneer stone weighs about half of its natural stone counterpart. Tyler had experience installing this type of product, so while he would need help, he wouldn't need an artisan mortar man.

Our lead drywaller suggested a stone vendor a half-hour away. The store that sat amid nondescript industrial park buildings barely had a sign, but inside we found a small showroom and an upright display of the brand of manufactured stone we had in mind. I pulled samples off the display, and we were impressed with how it mimicked the look of natural stone.

We selected a sedate gray ledge stone and held our breaths while the salesman calculated the math on our square footage.

His number sealed the deal. We had found our fireplace veneer.

You know how when you're looking for something, you tend to find it everywhere? In that way serendipity works, we happened upon a fireplace store on the way home from the manufactured stone showroom. The young salesman was well informed about all things fire (including some envy-worthy outdoor grills we'd like to own at some point), and he was happy to show us heavy-duty manufactured wood fireplace mantels. Unfortunately, the longest one he offered measured six feet; we needed seven. And his price was appalling.

Tyler asked around for barn beams he could repurpose into a mantel, but he met with little success. We weren't the only people who aspired to a rustic look, making barn wood beams all the rage, and "all the rage" means pricy.

Tyler returned to Craigslist, and before long, a real barn beam turned up. The seller was asking only about a quarter of what we would have paid for the too-short manufactured beam.

But he lived in downtown Chicago. Ninety minutes of high-volume traffic away.

My kind of town, Chicago is, if you're content to ride the "L," the city rail system. Or flag down a rude taxi driver. Or take your chances with Uber. If you're driving a car, it's a video game of narrow one-way streets filled with parked cars and obnoxious jaywalkers who pop out of nowhere in the middle of the block.

And driving a nineteen-foot extended cab pickup through Chicago's residential streets only amps up the stress.

Well, the seller lived on a street like that.

But we managed to connect with him in front of his brownstone where we double-parked briefly, and he showed us to the alley behind his house. As he flipped open his garage door, the barn wood beam inside seemed to glow. I swear I could hear the sort of cinematic music set to Bo Derek's beach scene in the movie *10* (am I dating myself?).

This hand-hewn barn-wood beam was perfect.

Eight feet long and eleven inches square, this beam could have been a model for an authentic-looking manufactured wood mantel. Because it was as authentic as it gets, it even sported a rusty nail.

The seller told us he personally removed the beam from the peak of a 122-year-old barn near Dyersville, Iowa, and transported it to Chicago to use part of it in his house. If Dyersville sounds familiar, it's because *Field of Dreams* was filmed there amid America's most iconic cornfields.

"What do you think?" Tyler asked me in a tone of voice he used when he didn't want to show the seller how much he really wanted it.

"Sure, if that's the look you're going for," I equivocated.

"Will you take $200?" Tyler asked the seller. He only asked this so he could say he tried.

"$275. Firm. You won't find another beam like that for less than three times the price."

The seller knew his product.

"Pay the man," Tyler told me.

Now we had to get the beam home. It weighed two hundred pounds if it weighed an ounce.

Fortunately, the seller was willing to help. He and Tyler wrangled it into the back of the truck (tailgate down), and we secured it with a tie-down. But let's be honest: if the beam was going to fall from the truck when we were driving seventy-five on the interstate, no puny ratchet strap was going to stop it. We would have just kept going.

As we drove away through the narrow alley, our perfect fireplace mantel in tow, Tyler marveled at his exquisite find.

"Kinda crazy though," Tyler mused. "I thought I'd find one way out in the country, and I ended up finding one in downtown Chicago."

Besides sweat equity, one last piece was required to complete the fireplace.

Before we started shopping, the fireplace was all one piece in my mind: the fireplace. I didn't understand that a fireplace consisted of a firebox, the chase, the mantel and the hearth, and other parts, too, that I couldn't describe, let alone name. All priced separately, of course. Building a fireplace was like choosing an SUV's upgrades. Long ago, when I purchased a Dodge Durango SUV, the salesman

**Tyler standing proudly in front
of the skeleton of his fireplace.**

asked me if I wanted a back seat. A back seat? Of course, I wanted a back seat! Durangos come without back seats?!

Of course, we wanted a hearth for our fireplace. Historically, hearths are associated with home and family because a hearth serves as the main source of heat in a home and where meals were cooked. We wouldn't have embers popping out of the fire, but without a hearth, a modern fireplace looks unfinished.

I had no idea where one purchased hearths. Oh! The fireplace store. Of course. But Tyler led us to a landscaping store located on the fringe of our little village. Modern Pinterest-worthy backyard patios feature fireplaces, so our landscaping supply firm did indeed sell, and deliver, hearths. And not just to the front door, but inside to the back of the great room. This was important because we chose a seven-foot-long solid slab of Indiana limestone. Like every other construction material, it was heavy as heck.

Limestone, if you'll recall ninth-grade geology, is formed of calcium carbonate, deposited over millions of years as marine fossils decomposed at the bottom of a shallow sea; in this case, one that once covered the American Midwest. Because of Chicago's proximity to Indiana, limestone was used extensively to rebuild the Windy City after the Great Chicago Fire, which occurred two decades before our little Methodist church was constructed. The Pentagon, the Empire State Building, the new Yankee Stadium in the Bronx and churches, university structures and courthouses across the country feature Indiana limestone in their exteriors.

And now we had a piece of it in our living room.

We had one thing in mind when shopping for countertops: remnants.

Sure, I dreamed of quartz countertops early on when anything I could dream was valid, but we knew laminate was out of the question. No one on HGTV installed laminate countertops.

Quartz, of course, doesn't come cheap. But we lucked out when we bought the display kitchen that offered the granite countertop for "free," noting we would be extricating it at our own risk. Free is good, especially for granite, so we paid a pro to remove and store it for a tiny fraction of its retail price.

That left us with a long list of other countertops to procure: The beverage bar off the kitchen, the master bathroom vanity and the upstairs bathroom vanity. We chose quartz for the curbs on the master shower.

Do you see dollar signs yet?

We could have chosen a single sheet of granite or quartz and used it throughout the house, but in another bit of locational luck, a custom countertop dealer had a retail shop only four blocks away. Driving by the establishment revealed a *lot* of *lovely* leftovers.

I determined to find remnants for all our stone needs that would save us a little money and, I believed, add some interest to our home. We weren't doing a California flip house, after all, and we didn't want a slick, matchy-matchy look.

Shopping the stacks of stone in the countertop shop's backlot was like shopping in a high-end purse retailer—*everything* looked good. But choosing remnants for the bathroom vanities was straightforward. I knew I wanted light and clean, so I zeroed in on anything white. Because we chose to insert makeup nooks at a slightly lower elevation than the counters in both vanities, we didn't require long remnants, which were a rare commodity in the piles of odds and ends.

For the upstairs vanity—the repurposed dressers painted in light aqua and dark gray—I choose a white quartz with gray veining called Bianco Gioia, Italian for white joy.

The master vanity had dark wood lowers and cream-colored upper cabinets, so I found two similar looking white quartz pieces sprinkled with brown called Soprano and Clarino.

The kitchen beverage bar was tricky. The cabinets were a different color than the main kitchen, so we wanted something light colored but also someplace to prepare coffee, which is known to stain countertops. I really would have loved something with blue in it, but none were to be found. None of the suitably colored remnants I saw in the backlot were big enough. We resigned ourselves to acquiring a quote on a half sheet of quartz. We shopped the sample rack inside and found a quartz called Intermezzo, a creamy cross between beige and gray with threads of black to create a crackle effect. (Intermezzo, musically, is a short connecting instrumental piece in an opera, so the quartz—between dark and light—was aptly named.) I borrowed the sample to compare it to the cabinets in our rental unit and determined it was "It." When I returned it to the countertop shop, the upbeat salesman (who had seen our display kitchen when his firm disassembled the granite) underscored my choice.

"That's perfect!" he confirmed. And then what he said thrilled me: "And we have a couple of remnants of that."

Apparently, I had overlooked them when I was shopping the back lot. He just knew his inventory better than I did.

Our custom shower needed a curb, for which we wanted quartz. A shower curb is the threshold and door frame where the glass door hangs. Normally, homeowners choose the same material for the curb as they do for the vanity, but we didn't have that luxury with our remnants. But in the backlot stacks, I found an oddly shaped remnant of Cambria quartz in Torquay, described in Cambria's material materials as "an instant classic, Torquay offers a beautiful marble-like appearance that's both posh and continental, much like this English Riviera town itself." The copywriter had me at "marble-like." Is posh transitional? I decided it was. The remnant I found would yield the pieces we needed to complement the shower tile.

To learn how much money we saved by using quartz remnants, we acquired a quote for a new piece of quartz on the beverage bar, a space of roughly eighteen square feet, that came to $2,353, measured, fabricated and installed. The remnant we chose for that space came to $928. And by shopping remnants, I took advantage of an opportunity of selecting a stone I would never be able to afford if I were buying entire sheets of it.

MEANWHILE, THE CONCRETE FINISHERS worked on Tyler's Garage Mahal, or at least its foundation.

With the footings poured, the concrete artists built the new back steps before pouring the foundation. Tyler, you recall, jackhammered the top of the existing concrete steps to the basement for a new landing and new top steps. The finishers performed meticulously. When they completed their work, these *pièces de résistance* were the straightest, most level steps in the entire church.

While mighty fine, this stairway wouldn't be complete until we had a walkway over the basement entry so we could exit from the main-floor back door. Tyler considered building a wooden walkway over the basement landing, but he decided he wanted something shallower so people using the back steps could avoid dinging their heads on the way down. He needed a steel walkway to accomplish this structural feat.

As luck would have it, we drove by the back door of a workmanlike shop the next morning. Tyler pulled to an immediate stop when he saw a black leather apron-clad man taking a breather in the doorway. His toothy, graying dog, menacing but beautiful, growled at us.

"What do you do here?" Tyler asked. It was just a question, but coming out of Tyler's mouth, it sounded like a demand.

The guy stared at him for a moment, perplexed and maybe a little irked to be grilled by a passerby when he just wanted to enjoy a lull in the early spring morning.

"Whaddya mean?"

"I mean, what kind of work do you do here?"

"Fabrication," the guy answered, still not impressed with being questioned.

"Perfect." Tyler threw the truck into park and exited, greeting the dog with a "Hey, boy!"

I watched as Tyler explained he needed someone to build a steel platform for a walkway in our church. Like the dog who appreciated Tyler's scratch behind the ears, the apron-clad man seemed to soften when he realized Tyler could be a customer.

"Sure, just stop by when you have some dimensions with you," the guy said as Tyler departed.

Maybe every little village I've ever lived in has had a steel fabricator in town like the blacksmiths of old, and I just didn't know it because I never had need for one. But I found this encounter to be another stroke of serendipity. When Tyler climbed back into the pickup so pleased that he'd found a fabricator only four blocks from the church, I just looked at him, amazed.

THE FOOTINGS HAD BEEN poured. Untold loads of gravel hauled in. The steps formed.

After a couple of rain delays, it was time to pour the garage's foundation.

Tyler was so excited that day, he got up even earlier than normal. He couldn't wait for me to provide breakfast; he left before I got out of bed and pressed McDonald's into service.

Tyler had ordered six-and-a-half-bag-mix concrete, the importance of which, like nuances of five-eighths-inch drywall versus half-inch drywall, escaped me. More cement bags added to the mix means more strength, and the better it performs when exposed to freeze-thaw cycles. Something about how the finishers finished the edges of the concrete also pleased Tyler.

All I knew was that it looked mighty smooth and flat when the day was done, which is all you can ask for in a good floor.

THE EASIEST STONE TO install at the church was the decorative rock we used to border the exterior.

The existing gravel was old, tired and indistinct. Tyler wanted to freshen the look, so he took me to the nearby landscaping supply store to browse the options. In the past, we might have used fresh mulch next to the foundation, but when we did that with the first house we owned together, it just invited bugs inside. We relegated the mulch to the perimeter of the church property to insulate the roots of the bushes.

Until that morning, I had no idea there were so many different gravels, rocks and crushed stones with which to decorate a yard. Like so many things in my life, I just wasn't paying attention. We could choose from every shade of gray and brown, plus a few blues and reds, in every size from pea gravel to boulders.

We were drawn to the grey slate with its rocks shaped to skip across a pond. It glittered in the sun with dozens of shades of grey. I liked the cool, blue hue that I was pleased to discover later coordinated perfectly with the new color of the church foundation.

We also chose edge stones. Tyler and hired man St. Johnny sweated it out to place the stones and spread the slate.

When they were done, it rocked.

25
Formed out of Dirt

As OUR OWN CONSTRUCTION project consumed us, we were blithely unaware of another occurring right across the street.

Sure, we could see something was happening at the elementary school, but to our uninitiated and self-centered eyes, it was just another remodel or addition or whatever it was, *just steer clear of our construction vehicles, we're doing important work over here!*

Of course, school construction projects are major community affairs, given they are publicly financed and ultimately house a precious commodity: children. Whatever was going on over there was a big deal to everyone but us.

I learned later from local folks that the only original part of the school that was left—built in 1908—was razed just a few months before we moved to town. (Imagine the circus surrounding that! We filled two dumpsters; the school probably filled fifty). The construction workers we saw were working to replace the decrepit structure. Locals we spoke with were a bit nostalgic about the demolished building. First the school got torn down, then somebody purchased the old church with plans to do who knows what to it.

Just as we chipped away, little by little, on our renovation, the school district made steady progress on theirs. By springtime, we could see workers paving a parking lot, surely a sign they were nearly done. A monument of sorts containing what looked like the old school bell was erected. Ah, another historic bell. This one had probably been used to begin many schooldays long ago. The district was paying tribute to what had gone before, just as we were.

The school bell, for display only.

The monument described the original school, built in the 1800s, which burned down on November 18, 1907. (Among the historical treasures Tyler unearthed is a photo of the burning school with our church in the background.) The bell on display came from the original building. The pillars flanking the monument were from the school that was rebuilt in 1908. Some of the brick pavers encircling the bell and monument commemorated family names, teachers, students, and even custodians—built by nostalgic patrons who remembered the old building fondly.

As I returned home after an afternoon of cuddling with our new granddaughter, I checked in with Tyler. He was breathlessly excited on the other end of the line.

"Oh boy, did I ever score this afternoon! What a score! Come straight to the church and find out what I scored!"

Apparently, he scored. Something.

I began conjuring up what could thrill him so. Recently, a former member of the church who visited us and she gifted us a watercolor painting of the church that had come into her possession. It was beautiful and meaningful, and we would certainly hang it in the Hall of History. Did some other interested party drop off something equally significant? Or maybe he found something in the church. Another member mentioned losing a class ring in the church yard—did he find it when he was digging around? Alas, no class ring turned up, but maybe Tyler found something else—a piece of jewelry? A time capsule? Gosh, he sounded so enthusiastic. Maybe he came into money from some unknown benefactor. What could it be?

As I pulled up in front of the church, a semi-truck blocked the street. The back of the truck was filled with dirt, and some unknown foreman was directing the driver to dump his load.

In our yard.

I began getting the picture that it wasn't jewelry Tyler found.

As I exited my truck, I heard the foreman telling Tyler he had two more loads. Did he want them?

"Yes! I'll take all the dirt you've got!" Tyler told him.

The semi-truck and the foreman left the scene. Tyler, sipping a beer, regaled me with the story of his score.

That morning, Tyler was knee-deep (quite literally) in his garage foundation construction project. He noticed an enormous backhoe digging a hole in the heretofore green yard of the elementary school. Huh, it had looked like the construction workers over there were wrapping things up, and now they were turning new soil.

Naturally, Tyler didn't let curiosity gnaw at him. He walked over and was told they were building a turn-around for trucks that delivered lunch to the school.

"What are you doing with all that black dirt?" Tyler asked. It was rich, beautiful black dirt (if dirt can be beautiful—apparently, the blacker the dirt, the more organic matter and nutrients are in it).

"Haul it away, I guess," the foreman told him.

Tyler offered to let them haul it one block. Straight to the church. The foreman couldn't refuse. Rather than pay a driver to haul it an hour away, he could niftily dump it a block away.

"We'd pay $600 a load for black soil of that quality," Tyler told me when I expressed disappointment that his score turned out to be … dirt. Only a gardener could appreciate the value of dirt; I was not a gardener.

Well, we were the proud new owners of four semi-loads of black dirt, enough for a king-sized berm.

"The timing is perfect," he continued. "I've got a grader right now to move it around."

Indeed, he did. His cousin had lent his to us for our garage project.

Lucky us.

26
YOUR SILVER AND GOLD MULTIPLY

ALL THE SCREEN TIME Americans have accumulated over the years has had a toxic impact not only on our attention spans but in our landfills.

We inherited—or bought, I guess—an old tube television when we acquired the church. It sat in the basement in all its bloated 1980s glory; who knew if it worked anymore. We planned sleek flat-screen televisions in our new space, and even if the old TV worked, it didn't work for us. It reminded me a college art project in which we students removed the tube screens from old console televisions and created dioramas inside that made high-minded cultural statements of one sort of another. We recycled and learned something at the same time. Win-win.

That was 1987. The television landscape had changed in thirty years.

All the locations that accepted our old housewares, such as Goodwill and Restore, wanted nothing to do with old electronics. Old televisions were as desirable as old cassette tapes. Ancient technology.

OK, so we'd recycle it. I checked around.

Would the garbage man take it away? Nope.

How about the scrap metal yard where we'd hauled several truckloads of heating ducts, aluminum siding and copper-studded hunks of metal? We would leave there with enough jingle in our pockets for lunch. Alas, no. A big sign declared "No TVs."

I recalled recycling electronics in the past at Best Buy. Would the big-box store take our TV?

Sure. For a price: Twenty-five dollars to recycle one old TV.

Wow.

Old television sets are filled with toxic components such as lead, mercury, flame retardants, cadmium, beryllium and other terms not heard since eighth-grade chemistry. The value of the good stuff—platinum, gold, silver and copper—doesn't outweigh the trouble of responsibly getting rid of the bad. It's a huge problem when people upgrade their computers and TVs more often than they observe leap year. Think about how many television sets you've owned in your lifetime. Where are they now? The landfill?

I wasn't the only one struggling to dump a TV. Once I realized how difficult it was to get rid of an old TV, I began seeing them everywhere. One of our neighbors left eight—eight!—televisions and computer monitors on the curb for four months, through drifting snow and falling rain. We wrinkled our noses in disgust every time we drove by. Then we left for a getaway one weekend, and when we returned, they were gone.

Other folks in town had less obvious eyesores in their yards. A TV here, a couple there. Our rental house had a TV in the dungeon-like basement. I fantasized about playing the village TV fairy—taking all of them away and paying the reverse ransom to get rid of them.

Though troubled by the problem of excess and the resulting detritus, I was too cheap to play fairy.

We didn't have the space to keep even one junk TV in the basement of the church, and we had too much pride to leave it sitting on the curb indefinitely. I sacrificed a lunch one day and ponied up the cash to let Best Buy take the dinosaur TV off our hands.

Part of me felt morally superior for getting rid of the old TV responsibly. And part of me felt guilty for coveting the flashy flat-screen models on display.

UNLIKE OUTMODED TECHNOLOGY, WE discovered some old things never lose their value.

Take old safes, for example.

We had been shopping for ideas to furnish the church—or "chome," as my sister wanted me to call it. "It's not a church anymore, it's your home," she implored.

"I don't live in it yet," I said.

"You should at least start using some transition noun. Like, "hurch." No, chome. Call it a chome."

In any case, Tyler and I ticked off the furniture we'd already purchased for the chome: sectional sofa, barstools, china cabinet, dining room table. "We still need nightstands for the master bedroom," I said.

Nothing we saw inspired us, but apparently, the problem percolated inside Tyler's mind. Somewhere, somehow, my creative husband got an idea that we should use old bank vaults for nightstands, and he started shopping for a pair, on Craigslist, of course. I loved the idea—a pair of distressed antique safes would be the perfect foil for the sleek chandeliers I planned for lights flanking the bed.

One day, an antique safe was advertised for sale about seventy miles north of us. He offered only one safe, but Tyler believed another one would turn up at some point and that we should look at this one while it was available.

Tyler and I took a circuitous route the following Saturday

morning through Wisconsin's heartland, dodging bike racers part of the time (Wisconsin, I had come to realize is big into B things—beer, bratwurst, bicyclers—plus cheese and Friday fish fries). After navigating a long, curvy country road, we were greeted by the seller and a flock of fluffy chickens in the seller's yard.

The chickens scattered, and the seller led us to the advertised safe, tucked behind a bunch of other miscellaneous items—including the unattached door to a walk-in safe—on an outdoor patio.

The impressive antique safe stood about four feet tall. Too big.

I was crestfallen. A three-hour round-trip drive for nothing. "This is too big," I said. "We were looking for something we could use for nightstands."

"A smaller safe? How big?" the seller asked.

I pantomimed a box roughly two feet tall.

"I might have something like that," he said. "I'm sort of a safe collector."

He led us to his house and through a sitting room where two safes performed duties as end tables.

"Yes, those exactly!" I said, pointing.

"They're not for sale."

Me: crestfallen again.

"But I have a couple more that might work."

Me: interest piqued again.

Clearly, this guy was something of a safe aficionado. How could we be so lucky to connect with a genuine safe collector with not one safe but several?

We followed him through the sitting room and into the attached garage, where he pointed out three safes tucked behind and under various garage items. Two were very similar black safes dating to the early 20th century—the stuff of matching provincial nightstands. *And,* he was willing to part with them.

We struck a deal after a bit of dickering (but not too much—the seller knew the combinations to the locks, which makes them more valuable. Repurposing a safe as a nightstand may have been inventive but it wasn't cheap.)

But now we had to load them into our pickup. The safes weighed four hundred pounds each—the hinges could be manipulated when the safe was open to remove the hand-painted door, the seller told us, and one of those weighed one hundred pounds.

Naturally, a safe collector would happen to own a front-end loader.

He rolled them out of the garage on their perfectly burnished rusty wheels and then fetched his front-end loader. Before he loaded the safes, though, he knelt in his driveway in front of them to show me how the combination locks worked, safecracker style.

One of them was empty, but the other one held a couple of bags of coins (quarters? gold doubloons?) and several hundred dollars in bills.

"Good thing I checked!" he said, trotting his booty inside. Yes, indeed.

He rolled the safes into the front-end loader's bucket and lifted them gingerly into the back of our pickup, no muscle required.

It wouldn't be so easy for us on the other end. Those antique safes might have been almost as difficult to get into the church as the old TV was to get rid of.

Fortunately, Tyler's clever creativity extended from bedroom design to the transport of safes. He built a temporary bridge out of the leftover wood from the garage foundation forms to roll the safes from the back of the pickup directly into the main floor of our church/chome.

The safes would require a bit of clean up, but *voilà*, distinctive and functional rustic nightstands were ours.

27
TRAMPLING DOWN THE WAVES OF THE SEA

As the lilacs faded and May transformed into June, activity flourished inside, outside and around our Church Sweet Home project.

The conversations between Tyler and me sounded more like a corporate project manager's Monday morning update meeting than a conversation between husband and wife.

"I need an update on how much we've spent on the garage so far."

"Do you know when the drywallers are coming today?"

"When are you going to pick up that replacement siding?"

"When will you have a few minutes to look at that bathroom vanity with me?"

"Find the fireplace receipt—I need to return those parts."

"I need the key to the rental unit so I can drop off the lights."

"Listen to this voicemail from the carpet guy, and let's discuss."

"What did the spiral stairway proprietress say about the timeline?"

"Did You-Can-Call-Me-Al finish grouting the shower today?"

"Remind me to buy window wells tomorrow."

"Have you heard from the guy who's supposed to measure the shower?"

"Did you pay the concrete company?"

"You need to get back to the spiral stairway manufacturer about the stairway railing material."

"Did the carpet guy call you back?"

We were spinning like tops, just trying to keep our equilibrium.

It seemed nothing was getting accomplished, but this big project had many moving parts. In fact, we were ticking off several to-do list items. If we had been remodeling only the bathroom or building only a garage, these "little" tasks would have been big steps to completion. They only *seemed* small in the face of the mountain of all we had yet to get done.

OUR A TEAM OF drywallers was equal parts dedicated and talented. Day after day, the drywallers hung heavy sheets of drywall, mudded the seams and then sanded it all down before priming the walls and painting the ceilings. On some in-between days, huge fans circulated the air to dry surfaces.

One afternoon I showed up to find the chief of the A team taking a break on our front porch (also known as the public sidewalk, seeing as our front door opened nearly onto the street). He took in the fresh air, joking around with Tyler.

As I joined the conversation and looked into his eyes, I came to understand the current phase of the project: ceiling paint. A thin film of paint dusted the chief. His normally dark eyelashes were alabaster. As he laughed and blinked, he looked alien.

Thank goodness for our drywallers. Just as promised, and right on time, they completed their work. When they were done, the interior never looked so neat and clean. *Now* we were getting somewhere.

MEANWHILE, OUR CONCRETE FINISHERS completed their careful work on our driveway. Like our dramatically swooping balcony, our driveway incorporated graceful curves; vehicles would be turned in from the street and curved around to enter the garage. The concrete finishers made the wood forms obey and figured out how to jigsaw the seams. When they were done, they accomplished the twin goals of smooth conveyance and proper water drainage.

While he had the concrete mixer's attention, Tyler had him pour the air conditioning pad. I've enjoyed air-conditioned homes through my adult life, but this would be one of those details to which I'd never paid attention. But not Tyler; he preferred concrete pads to the pre-fab plastic ones, and I didn't even realize an air conditioner requires a pad at all.

The last day of elementary school across the street created an uncharacteristic parking jam. The streets around our church were lined with cars owned by parents marking the day by picnicking with their children on school grounds. Interestingly, people recognized our new driveway as "real," even though it was closed to entry by yellow caution tape. Relieved to find a spot, I slipped into the opening to block our driveway with the beat-up pickup after an errand.

Tyler, meanwhile, was self-conscious of his construction mess. With the driveway poured and hardening in the summer sun, Tyler borrowed a skid loader to landscape the piles of dirt created by the driveway project. He fashioned a low berm that lined the driveway and protected the roots of the ancient pines in the backyard. We'd designed the project to spare all our trees.

Though it would take a few weeks to grow, he spread grass seed over the dirt. Soon we would again have a bona fide lawn.

Tyler also chose to install window wells around the basement windows on that side of the church so he could spread around all that fabulous black dirt he'd collected from the school and divert drainage water away from the foundation.

Now all we needed was the garage itself, which we had scheduled as an autumn project. In the meantime, Tyler erected our thrift-store patio set on the garage foundation. He conducted many a contractor and wife meetings there while enjoying a cup of coffee or a beer. That patio table we'd scored for $40 became a confessional of sorts for our scruffy group of contractors, some of whom who shared stories of addiction, imprisonment, health problems and love gone alarmingly and heartbreakingly wrong. Other general contractors might not be privy to such intimacies, but other general contractors didn't own a church and celebrate quitting time with beer.

While we collected our wits on the patio at the end of another workday, Tyler walked the garage foundation and described his planned layout. Pantomiming doors and windows, he would build shelving there, his tool chests would go here, the beer fridge would go over there, and so on. As he dreamed of his mancave, my heart fluttered just to see him so happy.

I would feel that embodiment of excitement again a few days later when the drywall team and You-Can-Call-Me-Al joined forces to install the faux beams in the sanctuary (a.k.a. the great room). I couldn't bear to hang around during that day, listening to debates about angles and watching the men teeter on scaffolding, but when Tyler and I surveyed their work, I could barely speak.

Finally, our home was beginning to look like I imagined it would when we first toured the church eight months before. Even without light fixtures and fans, our fake beams looked finished and majestic. The beams were everything I'd hoped they'd be.

WITH THE DRYWALL UP and the driveway complete, Tyler returned his attention to the church interior. It was time to install another beam: the two-hundred-pound barn-beam mantelpiece he'd found on Craigslist. Unlike the polyurethane foam beams on the ceiling, this project required a heavy-duty approach to fastening it.

Tyler determined the optimal height of the mantel by researching the firebox manufacturer's recommendations. The beam was combustible wood, after all. Then he enlisted You-Can-Call-Me-Al's carpentry skills; this was no one-man job.

First, they reinforced the mounting area behind what would be the stone by installing two four-by-sixes stacked on top of each other as a mounting plate. Then they drilled holes in the backer plate for eight ten-inch lag bolts.

As he handled the beam, Tyler admired it. The Iowa barn that housed the beam was 122 years old, according to the seller, but the beam itself could have predated our 126-year-old church. Either the steam-powered sawmill hadn't been invented yet or it wasn't available, so the beam had been hand-hewn from a red oak log with a broad ax.

Because the thick beam was eleven inches square, Tyler cut it to length with a chainsaw—inside the church. In any other circumstance, a chainsaw wielded inside a building was the stuff of horror movies, but in this case, it was simply convenient.

You-Can-Call-Me-Al and Tyler created temporary wooden brackets to prop up the beam in which they predrilled holes for the lag bolts. Once they secured the mantelpiece in place, You-Can-Call-Me-Al tested their work by standing on it, eight feet above the ground. Al might be described as wiry, but still, this was a good test.

Built solidly, indeed.

LIKE SO MANY OTHER elements of house construction, doors do not come completed.

Take the fireplace, for instance. We bought a fireplace, which was just the firebox. We also needed to purchase stone for the chase. And a hearth. And a mantelpiece.

Or a shower. Once you find a shower head, you also need the handle. And the trim parts.

Find cabinets you love, and you still must invest in hardware.

So it is with doors. Our front doors were a steal on Craigslist, but they came without doorknobs. Or locks.

The options available at the big-box home improvement store were too mass-market for our distinctive castle doors. Tyler did what he does best and took to eBay, where he found wrought-iron hasps and handles.

My dad, an accomplished carpenter who wasn't afraid to work with expensive wood, noticed we hadn't yet installed doorknobs. He remarked, "Better measure six times and cut once on *that* project." Our impressive doors were heavy solid wood; Tyler had only one chance to get the handles right.

But we couldn't continue to open the doors with the tiny handles for the speak-easy portals as we took to doing early on, so Tyler did what he had to with his chance and installed the distinctive handles and locks. Cutting once.

The heavy wrought-iron hasps, installed at eye- and knee-level, produced a delightful Quasimodo sound effect. When someone knocked, he or she would hear me shifting the hasps inside, one at a time, like a deformed bell ringer preparing to open an ancient castle door. "You rang?"

WHILE THE DRYWALLERS WORKED upstairs and the concrete finishers labored outside, I holed up in the basement with creative projects that would find life in *Phase Four: Cabinets*.

The kitchen backsplash, for instance, presented a problem. I wanted something rustic, so glittery glass tile was out. Subway tile? Too boring. I also wanted a backsplash that would coordinate with both the cream-colored kitchen cabinets and the navy beverage bar cabinets.

Nothing was quite right until I found Paramount Flooring's porcelain tile in Havana, inspired by the cement tiles that lined patios, walkways, walls and floors in 1950's Cuba. To puzzle out the backsplash, I ordered four boxes of tile in Sugar Cane (white), Havana Sky (blue), Old Havana Blend (mixed colors) and Deco Mix (square decorative tiles).

One quiet Sunday afternoon, Tyler's cousin and her husband visited. Her husband helped Tyler pull the old sidewalk pieces out of our driveway; the concrete finishers would pour new sidewalk when they finished the driveway. Tyler's cousin had similar taste in décor, and while the men worked outside, she helped me lay tile on the basement floor to see how the pieces might look as a backsplash. The Sugar Cane tiles carried the day. I figured I'd use a few random Havana Sky pieces to add interest and tie in the blue. The decorative square tiles would be the ideal accent above the stove in a style similar to one I saw on DIY Network (I want to give proper credit here, but I can't remember if it was *Stone House Revival, Barnwood Builders* or *Barn Sweet Home*—clearly I was watching an inordinate amount of HGTV and DIY Network).

One more decision, made.

AMID EVERYTHING ELSE, I painted the dresser that would ultimately become the upstairs bathroom vanity. Tyler set up a "paint parlor" in a corner of the basement for this type of work. A few weeks later, on the recommendation of a friend, I spent an evening learning about the wonders of mineral paint, which required only one or, at most, two coats for furniture projects like I was attempting. But at this point, I was using latex paint: four coats of Sunken Pool, two coats of distressed Adirondack Blue and then three coats of clear polyurethane. Plus, I sanded between every coat. Each coat required only about a half hour to apply, but patience and diligence was required to get drying time between coats.

One evening early during the garage foundation project, I sat alone in the basement trying to squeeze in a coat of paint before I couldn't see any more in the gathering twilight. Usually, I caught a few minutes of public radio on my phone while meditating on my brushstrokes. But that night, I just absorbed the silence of the church.

Until I heard a creepy creak. A door—somewhere—opened. Or closed.

Crrreeeeeeeeeeeeeak.

It sounded just like a boogeyman opening a door with ax or chainsaw in hand in a horror movie. Tyler stored his tools in the basement just feet away from my paint station. If the boogeyman had arrived empty-handed, he wouldn't go wanting for an implement of terror for long.

Buddhist monk Matthieu Ricard once said, "When hearing a door creak, the optimist thinks it's opening, and the pessimist thinks it's closing." I didn't know which camp I was in.

"Who goes there?" I called out loud.

No answer.

Maybe my imagination was getting the better of me. It was rare that I spent time alone in the church. Usually I was there during the day when Tyler, at the very least, was working and often, several other men. I remembered how I'd scoffed early on about churches being haunted. Maybe my disbelief had ticked someone—or something—off.

Crrreeeeeeeeeeeeeak.

OK, this was real. It was *not* my imagination. I joined the camp of optimists and assumed this was a spirit with whom I could negotiate.

"I'm a good guy," I said out loud. "Let's be friends. We can both live here peacefully. I want to fix things up, not tear things down."

I began brushing paint faster.

Crrreeeeeeecceeeeak. Thud.

The thud drew my attention to the windows at the back of the church.

In the thickening darkness, a phantom didn't appear. I saw the back door to the church, swaying in the breeze. And creaking. Because Tyler had recently jackhammered the back steps and cut out part of the wall, the door latched into thin air, swinging to and fro and occasionally slamming shut.

This discovery made me laugh out loud.

It was not a ghost.

That's the creepy door, the one by the back window.

It was the wind.

A few weeks later, Tyler eliminated the creepy creak by building a proper back egress. The steel fabricator with the beautiful-but-menacing dog completed his work on the steel bridge. When my twenty-something adored stepson paid us a visit, Tyler took advantage of his upper-body strength. They hauled the steel bridge into place, and Tyler built a floor and interim railings from scrap wood. This created a proper, if temporary, back entry to the main floor while eliminating both the latch-less swinging door and the accompanying creak.

We replaced a functional but unlockable storm door with a new back door. If ghosts intended to get in (or out), they'd better have a key.

As I FINISHED MY last coats of polyurethane on the vanity, I pondered knobs. Initially, I had intended to reuse the original wooden knobs because they matched the veneer I had preserved for the top drawers. But with 90 percent of the wood painted, I considered painting the knobs, too.

I took to Facebook to poll my friends, creative thinkers with good taste. One of them suggested vintage glass or crystal knobs, and others seconded. It was a great idea I hadn't even considered.

On my next visit to Home Depot, I found a suitable glass knob. Cost: $6. I needed 18 knobs, so this meant I would be spending more on knobs than I did for the whole second-hand dresser set! The look of the single knob inspired a visit to eBay, where I found a mismatched lot of vintage crystal knobs—enough for the dressers—for only $25. Sold.

Unfortunately, I discovered after applying the last coat of polyurethane that I had used too heavy a hand on the drawer edges. Some of them no longer closed. Another round of aggressive sanding fixed that.

Still, I didn't mind expending the effort. Including the quartz countertop, my eight-foot custom vanity cost only $1,020.86. And it looked like a million bucks.

Some people can see the beauty trapped in ugly things, and some people simply do not. The Facebook advice was just another example of the community rooting us on and helping us bring to fruition our vision.

28
A STAIRWAY RESTING ON THE EARTH, WITH ITS TOP REACHING TO HEAVEN

AMONG THE BENEFITS OF living a mile away from the spiral stairs' manufacturer is seeing—in person—the (excuse the pun) step-by-step construction of our stairway.

After we visited the manufacturer when Tyler first uncovered the balcony in January, the proprietress had befriended us. She invited us over whenever an artisan asked a question about some element of masterpiece that would someday grace our great room. The spiral was constructed in total at the manufacturer facility, to be delivered whole.

We determined the height and diameter of the spiral stairway with careful measurements in March. Then April saw us pawing through the proprietress' leftover balusters to cut costs on our stairway. Balusters are the columns that support the rail. We selected a 4:1 mix of industrial-hammered balusters and traditional basket balusters.

Then we chose a newel—the post at the foot of the flight of stairs. We selected a giant-sized basket baluster. (In the case of a spiral stairway, the pillar supporting the staircase may also be called a newel.)

Treads? We went with the industrial diamond plate.

Clockwise or counterclockwise spiral? Ours would be clockwise going up.

Paint color? Black. This, we decided in May.

Railing? We waffled, first selecting a smooth vinyl cover for the flat rail, but at the last minute in early June, we chose the flat-steel handrail.

Our engineering-minded spiral proprietress also helped Tyler determine proper basement floor support for the steel structure that would weigh about eight-hundred pounds.

Finally, we worked through every detail, and delivery day the first week in June arrived.

To be clear, delivery day was delivery *only*. The installation was our responsibility. The spiral stairs proprietress suggested we needed one guy for every hundred pounds of stairway, meaning Tyler plus seven guys. I could help, but I counted as only a half a guy (which was a pretty accurate assessment of my strength).

Accumulating seven guys willing to lift a spiral stairway in a village to which we hadn't even officially moved sounded like a tough sell only to me. Tyler drafted his hired man St. Johnny, our tiler/master carpenter You-Can-Call-Me-Al, the carpenter helper, three drywallers plus a very large man invited by one of the drywallers. Then there was me, a half-lifter. The proprietress and two of her men unofficially pitched in.

Ten guys and two women. And a little grunting.

This should be easy, I thought.

We first removed the stairs from the trailer, which we accomplished reasonably easily.

A spiral stairway with a diameter of six-foot-three would be considered larger than normal (ironically, my husband at six-foot-three was also considered larger than normal). This size spiral would need to be literally screwed into the church twice, because we had one exterior doorway and another at the top of the great room's entryway steps. Fortunately, both were double doorways. The proprietress and her head man had performed this feat hundreds of times, and they were confident it could be done—with a little grunting.

Their record was seventeen minutes from trailer to securing the bolts to the floor.

We began spiraling in our stairway bottom first. The top of the spiral had a landing that would be secured to the balcony, making the top even bigger than the rest.

After several minutes of turning, grunting and shaving off edges of the exterior wooden doorway, we learned bottom first wouldn't work

We backed it out. Most of us huffed and puffed in the middle-of-the-day sunshine while You-And-Call-Me-Al removed the doors from their hinges in both doorways.

At this point in the installation, I was reminded of the story in the Gospel of Mark about the father who brought his child to Jesus to have him cast out the spirit that afflicted the mute child with convulsions. "If you believe, all things are possible to him who believes," Jesus told the father, to which the father replied, "Lord, I believe! Help my unbelief!" Jesus followed through and cast out the unclean spirit.

I expressed my skepticism to the proprietress.

"Oh, we can get it in there," the ever-optimistic proprietress said.

"I believe!" I said. "Help my unbelief!"

She laughed.

The proprietress' head man suggested we turn the spiral stairway around in the front yard to spiral it in top first. Much grunting ensured, but before long, our spiral was completely screwed inside our entryway. One doorway down, one to go. Experience made the second doorway easier, and gruntingly, the spiral was inside the sanctuary of the church.

We (or more accurately, the men, because I was spent) lugged the spiral across the room and, after one last round of grunting, tipped the spiral upright.

She (our stylish spiral presented as a she) was bolted in place, and within minutes, Tyler and I climbed to the balcony on the steps of our spiral. Total installation time, including false start: Forty-four minutes. Not a record, but a competent average.

She was beautiful with all her black-hammered spindles punctuated by her elegant basket balusters. She fit the corner of the great room perfectly, both in size and style.

Tyler and I posed for a picture standing at the top of the steps in all our sweaty glory. We couldn't stop smiling.

Us, at the pinnacle of success.

29
PLAGUES OF PHARAOH

THERE COMES A TIME in every mountain climb when exhaustion sets in and the craggy cliffs appear insurmountable. The ascent feels endless.

That time came for us when the days were literally the longest days of the year. They felt endless.

Our time of trial began innocently enough. With a few raindrops.

What's a few raindrops? Into every life a little rain must fall. We'd already survived a spring hailstorm for the ages.

The summer rain accumulated into a flood.

Early on during demolition, water flooded the basement, a symptom of improper drainage and aging storm gutters. We replaced the gutters and thought we fixed the problem. Then a winter rainstorm came, and the furnace room got wet. Building a garage foundation should fix that, we thought.

But when the summer rain came, we hadn't finished moving around all our fabulous dirt and instead of draining away from the foundation, the water drained right into the basement on the east side.

And by the gas meter on the north side.

After a very long day of sanding floors, Tyler discovered lakes of water in the basement, one of them threatening my newly painted bathroom vanities. It was late, but through the dim light, we slopped through the basement water, moving valuable items to dry ground.

The water near the vanities ran blood red.

Students of the Old Testament may recall that during Pharaoh's first plague, the water turned to blood.

This wasn't a good sign.

The red water was because of my stupidity, not God's wrath (at least, I don't think so). I'd used the red velvet curtain that had once hung behind the altar of the church as a drop cloth, and as water puddled in the basement, the curtain soaked it up, dyeing it red. Why I was protecting the ancient basement floor that would be replaced anyway from paint drips, I still don't know.

While Tyler squeegeed the water into the basement drains, I gathered the curtain in a tub and lugged it outside. Sheets of rain continued to fall, and I nearly did, too, as I navigated the muddy yard to toss the tub away. I'm sorry the distinguished curtain that hung for so many years in the church and then served as splendid furniture blanket and drop cloth met such a lowly end, but it did.

That was Monday.

Rain continued to fall off and on all week. If it wasn't raining, the skies were gray. The days that were supposed to provide the most hours of sunlight all year were only long days of gray.

Tuesday, Tyler pulled the upper kitchen cabinets from the storage unit, or at least the ones he could find. (Please don't ask me why he mounted cabinets before we finished the flooring or painting—the foreman didn't have the same sense of construction phases as I did.) Somehow, he'd lost the glass-fronted doors in the labyrinth of stored construction materials. The kitchen cabinets we snagged from the remodeling company had been disassembled for transport, and they looked like a lost civilization in the storage unit—the second storage unit we'd acquired to store all our finds. We had tucked away the glass-fronted doors somewhere on one of the units to keep them safe. Now we couldn't find them at all.

I finally found the well-hidden glass door fronts wrapped in furniture blankets in the back of one of the rental units.

Wednesday, we unpacked the new upper cabinets to fill in kitchen gaps. After removing six layers of packing, we discovered we'd ordered custom cabinets in the wrong color.

Phooey.

Instead of being mounted, they would have to be exchanged. We hadn't saved any time by ordering them weeks ago; in fact, they cost us money to store them.

Double phooey.

Thursday, we determined the luxury crown molding for our kitchen cabinets was wide—too wide if we wanted to have a standard distance between the bottom of our upper cabinets and the countertops. Oh, we could order shorter upper cabinets, of course, for a price. Or we could go with narrower cheap-looking molding. What we couldn't do was change the height of the support beam that dictated the height of the kitchen ceiling. After some breathless waiting, the building inspector informed us that the standard distance was simply preference, not required by code. We could tighten it up a bit if we wanted to. We chose a non-standard distance between the countertop and cabinets to keep the luxury crown molding.

Friday, Tyler assembled the ceiling fans for the great room. He discovered the fan he'd scored on an open-box deal no longer had the necessary screws for assembly. He carefully salvaged the one leftover screw from the box in which the brand-new fan arrived, and he drove to the hardware store to purchase duplicates.

Only he dropped the screw in the crevice of the truck console.

If you've ever shaken my husband's baseball-mitt hand, you know it's not built for salvaging tiny screws from narrow openings.

He talked a clerk at the hardware store into lending him a magnet.

"We don't usually loan tools," she said, as she reluctantly handed it over.

He fished the rebellious screw from its hiding place and bought twenty news ones. Just in case he dropped another one in a crack somewhere.

At this point on Friday afternoon, I began feeling a tickle in my throat, signaling a cold was coming (par for the course of this frustrating week), but the rain had finally stopped. Tyler called our electrician, who wasn't otherwise engaged (serendipity), and he agreed to install one of the fans before we called it a day.

The electrician completed his work, and Tyler called me into the sanctuary of the church.

When I walked into the great room, I felt like a mountain climber cresting a hill. The view of the summit—so much closer than it was at the bottom—was amazing.

The fan was majestic. Artistically designed. The perfect color.

After a long week, things were looking up.

Our electrician agreed to come back the next day—a Saturday—to install sanctuary lights, the ones the former pastor had sold to us for practically nothing and that I had repainted and rewired. They had new LED Edison bulbs and were ready to go. This time in the rental unit, I put my hands on them immediately. I briefly thought I'd misplaced the assembly screws, but they were right there in the bottom of the box.

Our electrician ascended his ladder to perform his magic (again, I couldn't watch the high work), and Tyler called me into the sanctuary.

Our great room ceiling was complete—drywall, paint, beams, fans and lights. It had been months of effort and required the expertise of dozens of men (and one woman). We'd busted the Tequila Budget, but not by that much. Tyler and I sat in the two rolling chairs he'd situated in the room for just this occasion to ponder our work.

We were immediate fans of our fan.

As we leaned way back in the chairs, we marveled at how finished and coordinated everything looked. Our terrible, horrible, no good, very bad week was over. We couldn't yet watch TV or dine or even do dishes in our "chome," but we didn't want to leave yet either. Finally, it was very good.

30
TOWER OF BABEL

GOOGLE "DECISION PARALYSIS," AND you'll find 11,900,000 results. If Google didn't prioritize the online references for you, oh paralyzed one, you might never learn what the phrase means. But Wikipedia's definition rises to the top, and you learn decision paralysis is a common modern-world problem when one is faced with too many detailed options. The perfectionist is caught up in finding the one right one. Soon, over-analysis prevents *any* option from being taken.

We'd been choosing from among a million different options for months—granite or quartz? Pecan beams or antique cherry? Polished chrome or brushed nickel? Now we were presented with decisions that affected the look of the entire church-cum-house, and we would have to look at them every day: wall paint and trim. Decision paralysis had set in.

Way back in the autumn, when I'd created my project design template, I'd chosen a limited palette of about eight colors to guide my choices, but anyone who's considered painting their trim beige knows there are about a hundred different shades of beige from unbleached silk to khaki.

In any other house I'd owned, I (or my husband) painted every room a different color. Isn't that what everyone does? But in every other house I'd owned, paint color was usually the most distinctive design feature. In the church, I had all kinds of distinctive features vying for attention—etched windows, high ceilings, a dramatic spiral stairway, original wood floors. I decided I didn't need a bunch of different paint colors muddying up the canvas. For painting, I'd settled on creamy beige trim and medium-gray walls. *All* the trim. And *all* the walls. I wanted to paint every room in the same colors to create a cohesive backdrop to everything else going on. Now I'm not sayin' I didn't vacillate about this decision, especially when it came to choosing which shades of creamy beige and medium gray.

A trio of girlfriends came to have a look at the church (and catch up, too—we did talk about subjects other than the one that obsessed me). While they were there, I pulled paint chips I had been pondering back at the rental house into the great room for the first time. I simultaneously realized that not only would I have to coordinate trim and wall colors with the ceiling color I already had, I needed to think about my kitchen cabinets, which came in two colors. And my fireplace stone. And the floor stain.

Yes, I confess to creamy-beige-and-medium-gray dreams in the form of tiny paint chips in a vacuum far removed from the church. Probably not wise. As soon as I held my creamy beige up to the off-white kitchen cabinets, I realized my creamy beige was yellow.

Blech! Yellow was *not* in the design scheme. Oh, how narrow the line between creamy beige and yellow!

As my friends and I chatted over tiny chips in the natural afternoon light, I realized every choice would look different in morning light. And under cloudy skies. And in artificial light (which the Lighting Savant taught me came in shades of kelvin).

Did I really want to paint the whole house in the same colors? The sanctuary trim was originally creamy beige. Did I really want that everywhere? Did I really want medium gray walls?

My resolve dissolved.

My friends urged me to get some paint samples and paint big swatches of the colors on the trim and walls of the church and look at them at different times of day. After they left, I was at the nearby big-box store choosing paint samples in a half-dozen colors. And that evening, when all was quiet and Tyler had already gone to bed, I burned the last half hour of natural summer daylight painting those samples on trim and walls all around the great room.

One of the samples I chose for the trim—Casual Khaki—turned out not to be just like the trim color already in the church, it was exactly the same shade of creamy beige.

I'm still not sure if that was serendipity or my subconscious, but I liked it. Tyler did, too, when he saw the color in the early morning light.

For my medium gray, I narrowed my choices to Loft Space and Silver Bullet. Loft Space was the early contender, but it wasn't quite right.

I continued to overanalyze, and I found a picture on Behr's blog of a room with different colors on the trim and wainscoting. Well, we had beadboard wainscoting around the entire perimeter of the great room and master bedroom. Maybe we needed a third color, too. Maybe this was the answer.

I needed to finalize decisions soon because Tyler planned to hire a painter. He didn't trust me to cut in the wall lines to the ceiling, and he didn't have time to do it himself. Time to call in a pro.

LITERALLY THE NEXT DAY, Tyler gathered You-Can-Call-Me-Al and me in the great room to measure trim. I was to take notes, but the conversation was immediately over my head. I knew what a baseboard was, and I understood we needed wood around the windows and doors, but after that, I was lost. You-Can-Call-Me-Al threw around words like "casing" and "chair stops" and measurements like "five-and-a-quarter topped with one-and-seven-sixteenths."

"Wait, huh? What am I writing down?" I asked.

Tyler threw up his hands.

You-Can-Call-Me-Al, with his people-pleaser mediation skills, suggested we call his Trim Guy.

Before Tyler could say "What's his number?" You-Can-Call-Me-Al dialed his cell and left a message for Trim Guy.

A few hours later, Trim Guy stood in our great room with thick books of trim descriptions and a clipboard.

Fortunately, the sanctuary came with a lot of beautiful trim. The window casing was five inches wide, and a bold chair rail topped the beadboard wainscoting. The narrow original baseboard, however, had been long since removed. The casing on the main door didn't match the window casing; it must have been a newer addition.

Tyler and Trim Guy talked about the differences between primed fiberboard and Gesso-coated pine while I flipped through a book that looked like a shapes primer for toddlers. It was filled with backbands, bar rails, base caps, bases, brick mold, casings, casing blocks, chair rails, crowns, crown backers, dentil molds (dentil molds?! Shouldn't those be part of a dentist's offerings?), jambs, mantel mold, mulls, panel molds, rope molding, specialty millwork, stops, and tongue-and-vee groove. That would be everything from B to V. Every bit of it came in different sizes and thicknesses.

Uff-da.

No wonder I didn't know what to write down.

Fortunately, Trim Guy read hand signals. I talked with my hands and pointed around the room, and he figured out what we needed, including flexible matching trim we could use around the round top of our front door in the entryway. How clever! Who knew such a thing existed? Trim Guy knew, *and* he knew what it was called. He proceeded to walk the entire church, making measurements.

Then he sent us a quote, which looked like Sanskrit. Except for the bottom line. Which was infinitely understandable.

One line read this way:

> 520   LF   18136-OG-B 4-1/4" CASING
> FIRST FLOOR   1.520   790.40

How do you even know if you're getting the stuff you want?

The bottom line was an eye-popper. The first digit was a 5. Like so many other construction materials, we weren't just buying "trim," we were buying casing and fascia and crown molding and baseboard and chair rails and something called "pop." Every piece was priced by the foot. (And that didn't count the two boxes of nails we needed.)

Last fall, when we were enjoying tequila and jotting dream numbers on notebook paper when we first saw the church, we didn't budget for trim. And even if we had, we probably wouldn't have budgeted $5,000.

But we had to have trim. And big-box basic maple trim wouldn't do the job in the vision we had for the church.

We squirmed and harrumphed and eventually called Trim Guy to place an order for 2216-CB fascia and 24136-A-CR crown and a bunch of other inscrutable stuff.

FORTUNATELY, WE SAVED A lot of scrap trim and wood during demolition, and at least some of it could be recycled in a beautiful and money-saving way. And by using what we had, it required very little decision-making and no paint.

When Tyler took apart the basement ceiling to save the tin plates, all of it was nailed in place with tongue-and-groove planks. The church builders of old may have used leftover pieces from elsewhere in the church or another location altogether because though it matched in shape, it came in a rainbow of painted and unpainted colors. We saved the planks and moved them around the basement and then the deteriorating toolshed out back and now finally, we could put them to use—as accent walls, the modern method of featuring one wall in a room for an aesthetic purpose. One of our ten design rules required putting an accent wall in nearly every room.

First up: the powder room.

The rustic reused wood was a nice backdrop for the sleek lighting and vanity mirror.

Without sanding, treating or even cleaning the tongue-and-groove boards, Tyler nailed the shortest and most uniquely colored boards to the south wall. Our sleek, pure white vanity and mirror set would stand out. The rustic backdrop with only a coat of polyurethane to finish it added miles of character to the 21-square-foot room.

Then he tackled the half-wall in the master bedroom where our king bed and the bank-safe nightstands would ultimately be placed.

For our former house, we bought an enormous bedroom set featuring a grand four-poster bed with marble accents that looked a little like a throne (we got a deal on the floor model). The whole set was so big, I didn't move it once in the decade we lived there, and we sold it when we moved because we figured we'd never again have a bedroom big enough. This left us without a headboard in the church for our king mattress, and I decided I wanted something nonstandard: The *whole wall* would become our headboard.

During construction, Tyler and my stepson built a half wall, like the one featured in "The Downtown Loft Challenge" episode of *Fixer Upper*. Joanna Gaines created an accent wall with white oak planks and a narrow shelf, and then she set artwork, a few books and a candle on the shelf above the bed. Instead of white oak, we used the reclaimed basement ceiling boards—a mix of the white, gray and black ones—to decorate the lower half. During a fall antiquing trip, Tyler and I found a set of old arched church windows without glass; that's the artwork we would display on the shelf.

Tyler used some of the miscellaneous beadboard we salvaged in the church to finish a closet wall so it would coordinate with the original beadboard wainscoting in the room. It wasn't an exact match, but among all our decisions this was easy—the beadboard was free. Once trimmed, with chair rail and painted with the rest, it would look dynamite.

31
DOWN ONTO THE FLOOR

I USED TO BELIEVE no shower felt better than the one I took after a thirty-hour trans-Pacific plane flight.

At one point in my marketing career, I took such flights regularly. I began the trip, usually before dawn, wrangling a huge suitcase and heavy computer bag. I'd drive or take a shuttle to the airport. Stand in lines, handle dirty money (all cash is dirty, even someone who's not a Virgo knows), touch doorknobs and hand rails already touched by the thousands of other members of unwashed humanity, dine off filthy seatback trays, drool on myself as I tried to sleep, change planes at least twice, usually four times (because there were no direct flights from St. Cloud, Minnesota, United States of America to Mount Ku-ring-gai, New South Wales, Australia), wait in the sunshine for another shuttle or cab to my hotel, stand in line to check in and finally arrive at my destination a day and half after I began. If I could summon the energy, I took a shower before anything. Oh, that shower was sweet, washing away hours of exhausting traveling and disgusting germs, and I exited the shower a new woman.

I used to believe that shower was the best ever.

Until I sanded wood floors.

No shower feels as good as the one a rehabber takes after sanding 126-year-old wood floors for a few hours on the second story of an old church in 90-degree temps.

Sanding hardwood is hard work. To the elbow grease, add a flurry of sawdust and you have your good reason to hire out the work.

But we didn't. We hired out the duct work, the electrical, the plumbing, the drywall and the painting, but sanding didn't require any particular expertise, only numerous trips to the big-box rental desk, attention to detail and a willingness to endure a *lot* of dust. It's the job you often see novices attempt on DIY Network's "First Time Flippers"; viewers see about ninety seconds of effort, even though the rehabbers probably spent weeks working. Though the investment in time is big, the investment in cash is small, and the return is potentially huge. Everyone likes the sound of "original wood floors."

And so, we found ourselves sanding floors in the old church during cold days in February and hot days in June.

Fundamentally, sanding is "granular demolition." Despite labeling it the "flooring phase," the truth was we were still tearing up the flooring seven months after we purchased the church. Removing the layers of flooring and gunk covering the original wood floors began to feel as if it would never end. During the official demo phase, we peeled back the old carpeting and padding that was two decades old if it was a day. Then there were the thousands of carpet staples and hundreds of nails covering every square foot of the sanctuary.

Next came pieces of tin.

Tyler found dozens of dinky pieces nailed all over the sanctuary floor. Someone had meticulously cut the tin to size, nailed each corner and added nails every two inches when the piece was bigger. Tyler removed them to discover they covered little divots and other dings.

In the room's back corner, he found a much larger hunk of tin. When he peeled it up, he discovered a time capsule of sorts: several copies of what appeared to be religious newspapers for young people—*Dew Drops* and *Young People's Weekly*—filled with serialized stories and articles of advice. He was amazed to see they dated to the 1920s.

He theorized the back story to this strange find: A teenage boy—maybe the minister's son—was tasked with covering the dings before it was covered with something (tile? carpet?). When he got to the place where perhaps the wood stove smokestack once snaked through the floor, he stashed a pile of Sunday school newspapers for posterity with the unspoken message, "I was here."

At this point, we were finally down to the mastic-covered wood, and sanding commenced.

IT WAS STILL WINTER that first day. The morning dawned with five inches of heart attack snow on the ground and an early-morning wake-up call.

The day before, Tyler learned from Home Depot that floor sanders are rented first-come, first-served. But he asked the guy at the rental desk if he could call that night to confirm a floor sander was available when the store closed, which would indicate if one might be available the following morning. The guy agreed to call Tyler, but Tyler didn't actually expect him to, given our experience with flaky contractors and our inexperience with the folks employed at the local Home Depot. But indeed, at 8:15 p.m., the guy called and confirmed that not one but two floor sanders would be available.

So Tyler woke up, made coffee, picked up the floor sander, grabbed breakfast at Starbucks and returned to our rental house by seven o'clock, where I groggily brushed my teeth and made coffee.

"Mission accomplished?" I asked.

"Yup! Today's the day we take the top layer of grunge off the floor."

He was excited. I was just waking up.

I got dressed while he ran the snowblower over the sidewalk in front of our rental house. We'd sold our enormous high-powered snowblower a year before when we embarked for a life on the road, never dreaming we'd be living again in the snowy Midwest so soon.

But lucky us: Among the strange and varied items the congregation left behind was a little snowblower. It didn't work, but Tool-Time Tyler was never deterred by such details. He fiddled with some element or another of the small engine, filled it with gas, and *voila*, we were the proud owners of a snowblower again.

The winter so far had called more often for a shovel than a blower, but that morning's snow was deep and heavy. When we were ready to head to the church, we loaded the little snowblower alongside the big floor sander in the back of the truck. The first task was clearing the sidewalks over there.

Blowing snow, as it happens, is like sanding floors—move slowly, walk in a straight line, generate snowdrifts (or sawdust drifts). I didn't appreciate shoveling all that much, but I looked back over a well-shoveled sidewalk with satisfaction.

With foot traffic from a parade of contractors looming, we weren't interested in finishing the hardwood floors just yet, but Tyler took the opportunity presented by the wide-open spaces to sand off the top layer of glue and mastic with a drum-type floor sander and 24-grit sandpaper.

Talk about satisfaction! Our 126-year old Douglas fir flooring in the main sanctuary was beautiful under all that gunk. Some people might object to the knots and seams, but the rustic transitional design scheme was perfect for us.

SANDING IS A LITTLE like driving across North Dakota. At first, you're impressed with the everlasting undulating landscape, but it's not long before you realize the points of interest that are too few and far between.

I didn't realize it then, but the floor sanding had only just begun. There was this first step with a drum sander and 24-grit paper on a diagonal to remove the mastic and level the wood. Then two passes with a drum sander, one with 24-grit sandpaper and another with 36-grit paper with the grain.

Have you ever seen 24-grit sandpaper? I hadn't. I'd only used the relatively even sheets of sandpaper to smooth edges and surfaces on furniture I painted. How cute. Twenty-four-grit sandpaper is the wicked sumo wrestler of finishing materials—it looked like it had gravel on it and if you got in its way, you'd be flattened.

At this point, I used a floor edger to sand right up to the walls in the sanctuary; this step required the operator to kneel, and since I still had my natural joints, I was elected. Then someone (usually Tyler, but sometimes St. Johnny) used the orbital sander with 60-grit sandpaper going with the grain.

On ordinary wood floors, one might be finished sanding. But we didn't have ordinary wood floors; we had 126-year-old wood floors. Over the course of a century, the floor had settled everywhere except where the beams in the basement supported the structure. This left narrow grooves in the sanctuary floor that remained untouched by the stand-up sanders. Seated on a rolling flat cart low to the floor, Tyler used a belt sander and a hand-held oscillating sander to smooth out those grooves.

The final pass was with an orbital sander and 80-grit sandpaper.

Of course, vacuuming was required after each sanding step.

And that was just the sanctuary floor. We had to do the whole thing all over again in the master suite (with maple flooring, which is much harder than pine), in the Hall of History and on the second floor. In total, we eventually finished about 2,200 square feet of wood floors.

TYLER AND I AGREED we'd do activities other than work on the church on weekends—shopping, chores, socializing, resting—but the pressure of finishing the floors ate away at our best intentions. We couldn't install cabinets until we finished the floors, and we couldn't install countertops until we had cabinets, and we couldn't have sinks until we had countertops, and we couldn't have running water until we had sinks.

One Saturday morning in June, I agreed to sand floors for four hours. If we returned the sander within four hours, we paid less than using it all day. It seemed a good way to get an unappealing chore out of the way first and then enjoy the rest of the day. Plus, we figured to be done before the hottest temperatures of the day, predicted to be in the nineties.

We got out of bed at 5:30 a.m. and rewarded ourselves with breakfast at a diner, which was a cook short and fighting problems with its electronic ordering system. A thirty-minute treat turned into seventy-five minutes of Chinese water torture. We didn't get the sanders rented and into service until eight o'clock.

We donned ventilators, safety glasses and ear protection. Tyler used the orbital sander on the second floor, and I used the edger. I couldn't control the sander's power with my limited core strength. I had to leave one knee on the ground and use my other leg and both arms to propel it where I wanted it to go. I probably looked like a middle-aged spider struggling to control a panicked fly.

The center of the floor looked good after the previous sandings, but the edges remained thick with mastic. No sooner would I install a new sanding disk than it would become gummed up with glue, unable to remove any more layers. So it was up to retrieve another disk, then down on my knees to install it and proceed a few more inches along the floor's edge.

No sound could be heard above the buzz of one sander, let alone two. So there was no music, no conversation, only attention to detail.

I took as few breaks as possible, besides the disk replacement, with the intention of finishing the edges upstairs and then tackling the Hall of History and the mud room on the main floor before returning the sanders. But I ran out of sanding disks before I got downstairs. And Tyler ran out of energy.

Still, we had to drag the sanders down the stairs, blow clean the devices, hoist them into the truck and haul them back to the rental desk by 11:30. All in searing high-noon heat and humidity. The pancakes and eggs we had during our extra-long breakfast break provided just enough fuel to meet our deadline. As we climbed back into the truck, Tyler asked, "where to for lunch?"

Tyler had no shame, apparently, but we looked a fright. Sweaty, covered in sawdust, my hair all askew from wearing a ventilator and ear muffs all morning.

"I'm not going anywhere for lunch," I said. "I'm going home to take a shower!"

Tyler obliged my vanity, and I indulged in the best shower of my entire life.

After our showers, we were so exhausted we fell back into bed (we got up early, remember) and napped. It was one of those glorious naps during which you sleep so hard that when you wake, you are still paralyzed with slumber. I lay there for a few minutes savoring my job-well-done accomplishment. Tyler roused, and we determined a late lunch at the nearby Mexican joint would satisfy our hunger most quickly. When I tried to get out of bed, I realized my lower back ached not a little I-know-I-worked-hard-today ache, but a big I-think-I've-hurt-myself ache.

"Oh, my back hurts," I said.

"Oh, my back always hurts," my compassionate husband said.

I got out of bed, dressed with some trouble and made it to the Mexican joint. But I couldn't bend over or babysit for a week because I didn't trust myself to be able to pick up my granddaughter. My husband quickly realized I was not suffering from run-of-the-mill back pain and handled sanding duties solo for a long while after that. It took three weeks for my back to return to normal operation. I determined it wasn't the work of sanding that hurt my back but the effort of lugging the super-heavy industrial sander up the steps. This underscored the safety reminder every manual laborer since the age of Doan's Pills learns: lift with the legs, not the back.

SANDING FLOORS WAS TOO physically difficult to perform two days in a row (at least for fifty-somethings). So on "rest" days, Tyler, St. Johnny and I accomplished other duties: cleaning up the basement and sorting wood, buying windows and ceiling fans, building feature walls, pickling wood planks for the second floor ceiling, buying *more* sandpaper and a thousand and one other tasks.

Eventually though, the end—meaning clean raw wood—was in sight. Curious and relieved to be nearing the end of sanding, I added up how much we'd spent on sandpaper, and I was surprised to figure out we'd spent *hundreds* of dollars on sandpaper—nearly a hundred dollars more on sandpaper than on renting the sanders.

Which firmly establishes sanders as the printers of the home improvement world (how much more is spent on print cartridges than the printers!).

NOW THAT THE RAW wood finally showed through, it was time to fill some of the seams. On newer wood floors, polyurethane alone would do just fine, but as our floors aged, some seams had widened.

Tyler inspected literally every inch of flooring. Ever the Virgo perfectionist, he was a harsh task master. Near the end of the sanding, he directed me to remove all the dried water putty in the seams of the master suite's maple flooring. Putty had been used as some point to fill some of the wider seams, and it appeared white against all the wood. Still "wide" was less than an eighth of an inch. Leaning on my knees while seated on a rolling office chair, I used chisels and tiny screwdrivers to pry the plaster from every seam in those two rooms.

Instead of using water putty, Tyler used a trick he'd learned on an earlier project. He mixed the last layer of sawdust (which was little bits of wood, not that horrible glue and varnish) with clear polyurethane and squeegeed the goop over the floors (maple sawdust mix on the maple floors, pine sawdust mix on the pine floors, and never the twain shall meet). Some had to be sanded off again, but the seams were therefore filled with a sawdust mixture that was essentially the same as the planks.

For the very worst seam on the second floor, more than a quarter inch in width, Tyler stuffed twine before filling it with sawdusty polyurethane. It couldn't be hidden, so we went with the theory that it added character.

Our next hurdle was stain. Fortunately, choosing a stain color proved to be much easier than choosing paint colors for the trim and walls. We went without stain on the maple in the master suite and on the pine on the second floor. A couple of coats of clear polyurethane was all we needed to show off the hardwood.

In the sanctuary-slash-great-room, we had a lot going on already. Between the ceiling beams, the fireplace and the kitchen cabinets, the floor played only a supporting role. Plus, its rustic patina didn't need any more attention called to it. We chose a Driftwood stain tinged with a hint of green; this would tone down the red in the Douglas fir planks to create a neutral backdrop.

After days of sanding, we spent days applying stain and polyurethane. The hardest part was enduring the odor. Do you remember the pungent odor of school hallways the day the janitors applied shiny vanish to the gymnasium floors? Sort of a chemical stench crossed with a tobacco barn? The church stunk to high heaven, but it lasted only a day or two. Tyler's obsession with industrial-sized fans played in our favor. He threw open the doors and invited in the fresh summer air.

A feud between Minwax and Home Depot over which big-box retailer could have exclusivity on the Minwax brand proved to be a windfall for us. One day when Tyler was renting a floor sander yet again, he spied an endcap display offering polyurethane for half price. He bought every can.

THE FLOOR OF THE Hall of History presented a unique challenge. The Hall of History, you'll remember, was fifteen-foot-long and led from the sanctuary to the back stairway where we imagined we could hang pictures of the church throughout history on its expansive walls.

But, oh, the floor. The pine planks were certainly original to the 1891 construction of that portion of the church and had once been part of the entryway. Count how many feet crossed that threshold on the way to Sunday school or worship services! Imagine the Sunday best shoes worn by parents holding newly baptized babies or couples freshly married! Several repairs and patches in the flooring were evident. Besides ground-in dirt, it was covered in paint of various colors—yellow, red and aqua—and sported huge gashes, divots and seams. One had to squint hard to see the potential.

We considered an affordable wood-like tile or perhaps carpeting, but we hesitated spending good money on a hallway floor that would most certainly be mostly covered by a rug runner. Tyler tried sanding it, only to reveal its history (appropriate to the Hall of History) and even it out.

The finished product wasn't exactly attractive (or perfectly level), but we had found the character we hoped. With new thresholds and baseboards, the rustic floor might be described by a forgiving critic as charming.

32
WORKERS IN THE VINEYARD

WE JUGGLED ENOUGH AS summer inched on that new projects occurred in a steady rhythm every day.

The carpet guy measured the balcony. The railings guy, too. The glass guy measured for our shower door because the quartz guys finally installed the curbs on the shower! And while the glass guy was there, he measured for new entryway window screens and glass for the sanctuary windows. Trim Guy measured for trim. Two different painters eyed the walls to prepare estimates.

To help all these contractors find our place, we installed temporary house numbers on the church. Do churches ever have house numbers? Maybe the church sign was evidence enough of a worshiping congregation, but we needed something more definitive. I wanted to build the permanent number sign, but my idea required using a saw, and Tyler said he had more important things to do than cut circles of wood, so I found what I wanted on Etsy.

Clear signage came in handy when the stone for the fireplace was delivered—by a semi-truck with its own crane! That got the stone to our front door; St. Johnny carried it armful by armful into the sanctuary.

One day when Tyler wasn't feeling well, I was promoted to foreman. Make that *temporary* foreman.

Unlike Tyler, who could operate power tools, I tended to more pedestrian tasks. That day included two trips to Home Depot, one to pick up the sander for St. Johnny to use on the upstairs floor, and a second to drop it off. You-Can-Call-Me-Al tended to miscellaneous carpentry tasks (such as trimming out the upstairs belfry door and repairing holes in the hardwood near the back door).

Between errands, I laid out the tile rug to be set into the kitchen hardwood using two boxes of mixed tiles. You-Can-Cal-Me-Al didn't want to choose the design, so I laid it out dry and took a picture. While I was at it, I laid out the tile feature for above the stove. I then touched up the spiral stairway, which got a little scratched as it was screwed into the church.

My short stint as boss resulted in forward progress and no maiming, so I think it was a success.

My tile rug prompted You-Can-Call-Me-Al to poke around the subfloor where it would eventually be tiled between the stove and sink. He determined that the 126-year-old subfloor couldn't support the tiles, which could mean they would flex when someone walked on them and then crack. I had to make another trip to Home Depot, No. 4 just for that week.

I had become a regular at the local Home Depot, the nearest big-box home improvement store. Before this project, I would have told you big-box clerks were uninformed flunkies, but the clerks at this Home Depot were awesome. The cashiers always tracked down someone to help me load whatever I bought (which was invariably heavy). One of the flooring guys once offered to help after seeing only my behind sticking out of a pallet of tile on the floor. The paint mixer and I were on a first-name basis. But it was the lumber guys whom I really appreciated. They would help me find the wood and screws on

Tyler's list and usually load my purchases into a cart.

On this trip, Tyler told me to buy three-quarter-inch plywood with a cement board underlayment. The helpful clerks in the lumber department (I had two this day!) told me it didn't exist. I had long since given up on trying to translate, so I called Tyler and handed my phone to one of the clerks. Turns out, I needed *two* things: half-inch plywood *and* quarter-inch cement board.

St. Johnny had a different task every day. Frequently, it involved moving construction materials or sanding or using the Shop-Vac, but in early July, he earned his keep by digging ditches in the backyard. Tyler had devised a way to coax water away from the foundation, but he needed to lay puffy drainage piping in ditches. This was not easy work, but we feared the next fifty-year rainfall event. To finish the basement, it had to remain dry.

A few days later, Tyler asked St. Johnny to edge the sidewalks, a project that appeared to have not been done for years. This task was less urgent than the drainage project, but it was satisfying to see the before, during and after all in one day.

We'd found plenty of work for You-Can-Call-Me-Al, too, as he was equally skilled using a tile saw and any number of wood saws.

One day, I stood on the balcony pickling the last of the planks for the upstairs ceiling. I wore headphones, listening to National Public Radio, while quietly rolling diluted white paint on wood.

Tyler worked in the master bedroom with a table saw and a nail gun, assembling the beadboard on the closet wall.

You-Can-Call-Me-Al played the radio at a volume that didn't quite overwhelm the sound of his tile saw when he modified a fireplace stone. He was finally making progress on our twenty-foot fireplace after a couple of false starts with unacceptable mortar. The stone guy suggested a type he'd used for an outdoor firepit, but when we tried it, the stone would still come off twenty-four hours later. This might have been OK for a three-foot-high fire pit, but we eventually learned (from a Home Depot guy), that we needed mortar for a *vertical* application. When laying stone twenty feet off the ground, you do *not* want it to fall off, lest you kill someone. Still, You-Can-Call-Me-Al built only about three or four vertical feet of fireplace a day so it would dry level.

    I enjoyed this sort of meditative work. Roll, roll, roll of the paint. Pithy NPR observation about the history of Chinese food. Whirr, whirr of a saw. Pop, pop, pop of a nail gun. The swoosh of mortar on the back of a hunk of stone. Whoomph, whoomph, as You-Can-Call-Me-Al occasionally used a rubber mallet to coax a piece into place. Then more of the same. My grumbling stomach was the only gauge of time, calling me to lunch.

33
ONE WHO IS FAITHFUL IN VERY LITTLE IS ALSO FAITHFUL IN MUCH

WE SPENT SO MANY months thinking of the church as a worksite, a project, a financial puzzle and unending to-do list, we had forgotten it was our home.

Home. The very word makes a person breathe easier. This place—this sawdusty, tool-infested, unfinished blank slate—would soon to be our home, a place of refuge, a thing of beauty, a space to put up our feet and enjoy a roasted cup of coffee or an ice-cold beer.

There was a moment at the beginning of summer after we'd finally squished the spiral stairway into the church and erected it in the corner, when I was reminded—ah, yes, this place is special.

And then we went back to sanding floors.

But, as fortune had it, we went with the same spiral stairway company to fabricate our balcony railing. And when they installed the railing at few weeks later, those same feelings came rushing back. I think it was the instant gratification. Instead of building a hundred walls or applying twenty coats of paint or driving back and forth to

Home Depot, the railing got installed in less than two hours, and then it was finished. All that was left for us to do was dust it.

"This is really ours," Tyler said as we sat by ourselves in our rolling office chairs in the great room at the end of the day.

"It's going to be beautiful," I said.

"Yup."

We were in a good place, figuratively as well as literally. As we coasted down the side of the mountain that was finishing the floors, we had something finished to admire at the end of many days. One day, it was the antique newel post topper for the spiral stairway.

It's the scene at the end of *It's a Wonderful Life*. After seeing how the world falls to pieces without him, the angel restores George Bailey's life. Zuzu's petals are in his pocket; to his relief, his daughter exists. He runs through the snowy streets of Bedford Falls, greeting all the buildings by name. He bursts through the front door of his house to find the bank examiner and local sheriff, whom he greets with a smile and a "Isn't it wonderful—I'm going to jail!" He happily leaps up the stairs, accidentally yanking out, kissing and carefully replacing the railing post ball on the stair post—for the *third* time. And he chuckles before he's reunited with his beatific children and his wife, who has summoned the whole town to turn out to help address his financial woes.

He really had a wonderful life, that George Bailey.

And a nice railing post ball. Kissable!

Now we had a nice post ball, too.

When the stairway was installed, the hollow center poll just had a cover. If someone removed the cover, they could drop something down the post, never to retrieve it twelve feet down. To fill the hole, we acquired a distinctive ball made of overlapping iron leaves.

The proprietress of the spiral stair manufacturer found the one-of-a-kind feature for us online (she was as big a fan of eBay as Tyler). A deal at $45. Described as an "antique, architectural salvage newel fence post finial," it was 10 inches wide and dated to the early 1900s.

A view from the top.

We won the auction and handed it off to the spiral team to paint it, which was a bit of a trick given the spaces between the leaves. They managed to paint both the inside *and* the outside to match our spiral and railings.

Ta, da! The ball on top really set off the spiral. So pretty, I could have kissed it.

AS SUMMER PROGRESSED, AN abundance of perennials bloomed in our yard. Surely the beautiful flowers blooming in the warm summer sun had been planted and tended to by members of the church at one time. We had demolished what we heard were vegetable gardens in the backyard when we poured the garage foundation, but a small flower garden on the side of the church displayed new color every month. In April and May, yellow tulips and yellow-white daffodils flashed their finery. In June and July, orange lilies and purple phlox signaled summer's heat.

The lilies caught the eye of Tyler's uncle. He knew their species well, having grown them in his own garden at one time.

"They are called Turk's cap lilies," he said. "They look like little turbans. If you fertilize them and take care to replant their seeds, they will be an even deeper color and grow huge!"

The garden was neglected for at least two years, when the congregation vacated the building. Now it was surrounded by mounds of dirt and construction materials. But soon, if not this season, it would receive more than Tyler's fleeting attention.

Meanwhile, the annuals Tyler planted in the old church sign flourished even as I let the sign itself languish. His marigolds and purple salvia looked like well-dressed Hollywood ingenues in front of the marquee that I hadn't updated since the Fourth of July.

Priorities.

BACK IN JANUARY, TYLER spent the month demolishing the rest of the interior of the church and wringing his hands about how he was going to take apart the twenty-foot ceiling of the sanctuary. But then he found our drywalling team that came to the rescue by tearing down the ceiling *and* putting it back together again. They also lent us scaffolding that was used to install the faux beams, the ceiling fans and the restored sanctuary chandeliers.

Oh, and the stone on the fireplace to the ceiling.

Thank God (and the drywallers) for that scaffolding.

But finally, months later, it was time to get it out of our great room. It obstructed the view.

You-Can-Call-Me-Al deconstructed it (single-handedly, which was a trick) and piled the scaffolding into the back of the pickup. Tyler returned it to the owner, and now we could see the finished fireplace in all its glory. Ironically, or perhaps just as it should be, the fireplace occupied the same place the red velvet curtain did behind what was once the altar, the symbolic representation of the place where worshippers throughout history burned sacrifices (and probably enjoyed the resulting barbecued animal flesh). We would burn natural gas and enjoy the dancing flames just as much.

Tyler also wrapped up another project that, like the scaffolding, had been sitting around for months: the pickled, planked plywood for the second-floor ceiling. Tyler started the project when we had the tubular skylights installed in the roof months ago, and then work lapsed for more pressing priorities. I finally finished painting the planks, and Tyler wanted them out of the way, so he and a helper nailed wood to the ceiling all day.

The ceiling when we bought the church consisted of beat-up ceiling tile boards. The new shiplap-like planks, even untrimmed, were a vast improvement.

Meanwhile, You-Can-Call-Me-Al replaced the old windows upstairs and trimmed them out. With the refinished floor, the vision for the second floor was finally materializing.

In fact, during the preceding month, You-Can-Call-Me-Al had replaced all the windows on the west side of the house plus the only one on the north side. Tyler guessed the old ones might have been in place for seventy years or more. The seals and gaskets were shot, and the wind blew right through. The new ones looked nearly identical, except the new ones had two panes instead of four. Their insulation value was vastly improved.

WE KEPT YOU-CAN-CALL-ME-AL busy. Tyler wanted all the trim out of the way to finish sanding the sanctuary floor, so You-Can-Call-Me-Al started to use it up. He solved some of Tyler's sense of urgency by building a shelf in the sanctuary for all that sixteen-foot-long trim rather than hauling it to the basement.

He first trimmed out the baseboard and windows in the master suite and, among other details, he hung the linen closet doors and trimmed them out. Shaped like a cramped confessional without the screen between, those strange little cubby holes leftover in the master suite floor layout had become handy closets for sheets and towels. All we needed were shelves, doorknobs and coats of paint. We now could envision the closets instead of strange voids in the two-by-fours.

You-Can-Call-Me-Al also trimmed out our master bedroom tray ceiling with crown molding and tin salvaged from the basement ceiling. Originally, I had hoped to show off the original tongue-and-groove wood ceiling inside the tray, but Tyler determined he couldn't repair its holes. Instead, we covered it in tin, which added an historical appearance, and painted it since it looked dirty against the bright white of the ceiling. Tyler installed high-tech rope lighting that changed colors into the tray's crown molding and could be controlled from a phone app—because he's a romantic like that.

AFTER CONSIDERABLE DEBATE ABOUT how to install carpeting over the edge of the balcony, the actual installation on a warm day a couple of weeks before Labor Day went well. The off-white Snowflake with a silvery pattern looked luxurious and meant only white wine drinkers were allowed.

We covered our light-colored carpet with industrial carpet wrap for temporary protection from construction dust and contractors' boots. Imagine a giant, three-foot wide roll of super-sticky Saran Wrap. Great concept. Tricky execution.

Tyler tried rolling it down himself, and even with his strength and wingspan, it was impossible. This was a two-person job.

He held the giant roll while I yanked it out with both hands in four- or five-foot lengths, balancing the flimsy sheet with one hand and cutting it with a knife with the other. Then, on my knees, I stuck it down along all the edges. Frequently, the stuff would stick to itself. There was no going back. That piece was garbage.

After twenty minutes, I felt a splash when I yanked the plastic off the roll. Tyler, standing over the roll, was sweating on it, and when I yanked the sheet, droplets of his perspiration popped up at me.

Exercise and a shower, too. Double duty.

The sticky on this stuff was truly industrial strength. Even a month later, it stuck to the carpet, protecting it from dirt.

WITH THE FLOORS IN the master suite finished, it was time to install the lower cabinets of the bathroom vanity.

But first, Tyler had to assemble them.

Tyler ordered these cabinets months ago from an online retailer. They arrived in nearly a dozen boxes one Sunday night in April at eleven o'clock—near as we can figure.

The boxes certainly weren't there earlier when we locked up the church and headed back to the rental house. Long after Tyler fell asleep, the church's security alarm sounded, and Tyler groggily answered the phone when the security company called to determine if the alarm was an emergency.

We had, by this time in the project, experienced plenty of false alarms. We knew from the experience of driving by the church at night that our headlights in the windows would trip the motion sensor. We had become a little immune to the security system's push notifications on Tyler's phone. But rarely had an alarm progressed to a live phone call from the security company.

Nope, he didn't trip the alarm, he assured the caller. Must be a prowler. Tyler pulled on a T-shirt and shorts—no time to locate underwear so he went commando. He stepped into his slippers. He located his car keys. I wished him luck from the comfort of our bed. When he headed back to the church, he found no prowler but a dozen large boxes stacked in front of the main entrance.

How odd.

A little detective work revealed the boxes held our online cabinets.

While grousing under his breath about the retailer's peculiar delivery system, Tyler began stacking them in his pickup to haul to our rental unit when a cop arrived.

I'm no policeman, but I can only imagine the officer found it strange that a bedraggled man would be loading his pickup with boxes in the middle of the night outside a church that was widely known in the village to be a construction site.

Of course, Tyler—who had sleepily dressed in a hurry—didn't have his wallet or ID with him.

He proved his ownership of the church by punching in his security code and unlocking the door. He and the officer tiptoed through the church looking for the housebreaker who set off the alarm but found nothing. Whatever small talk Tyler made while on patrol must have assured the officer that, yes indeed, he was the owner not an interloper, and the cop made his getaway before Tyler could talk him into helping load the boxes into the pickup.

We assume the cabinet company had hired a fly-by-night delivery company. Literally. And the delivery company thought it would be OK to leave the boxes outside the church at eleven o'clock.

In any case, these boxes of cabinets sat unopened in the rental unit for a couple of months before Tyler hauled them back to the church basement to assemble them.

Compared to sanding floors, putting together cabinets was easy work, but Tyler required all day to put together the drawers and cabinet pieces for our 132-inch bathroom vanity. In the basement, they looked black, and I initially thought we had received the wrong ones, just like with the errant kitchen cabinet. But in daylight, our espresso-hued cabinets were the perfect color. (The other thought I had when I saw the assembled cabinets for the first time was, oh yeah, we need knobs for those cabinets. Another item for the to-do list.) After the countertop was installed, the upper cabinets in cream would flank the gently arched vanity mirrors on order from the glass guy.

When Tyler's uncle visited a few days later, Tyler looped him into helping assemble the cabinets for the mudroom and laundry room. (Mental note: More cabinet hardware needed.)

Ah, yes, the laundry room. Oh, how I missed a nice, clean laundry room I could call my own. When we lived in the RV, I used a laundry room at every campground, some fresher smelling than others. In the rental house, I used the dank, scary cellar laundry room with an exterior entrance. I was tired of other people's laundry rooms, tired of collecting quarters and tired of lugging bulging baskets of clothing from place to place.

My new laundry room was inside my walk-in closet. Talk about convenient—no hauling clean or dirty clothes anywhere but across the room. It would be so convenient even Tyler would be able to throw in a load of laundry occasionally!

Looking back through the mental file, we realized neither of us had ever purchased a new washer or dryer. We always inherited them in the houses we purchased, or we splurged on used models because as far as appliances go, washers and dryers were usually repairable. But with the laundry in the master closet, we wanted the appliances to look as good as they functioned, so we had determined we would splurge on a matching pair for the "chome."

Shortly after assembling the cabinets, Tyler and I went shopping while we waited for the sanctuary floor to dry. We weren't looking specifically for appliances, but we had laundry on our minds. A big, pink sign plastered on a floor model dryer caught our attention: "Display Blowout!" We couldn't refuse the price, plus, we would get an 11-percent rebate. So we bought the matching washer, too. On top of everything else, we saved an $80 delivery fee since we hauled them ourselves. We tasked the painter with doing the closet first, persuaded the electrician to drop by with a GFI outlet, and a few days later, I fetched the washer and dryer.

As usual, we experienced a tiny hiccup during installation that required two emergency trips to the hardware store, but in no time, we had an operational laundry room. It was the first, fully functional room in the house.

Never had it felt so satisfying to wash a load of clothes.

34
THE GOLDEN CALF

IN EIGHTH GRADE, MY stepson's English teacher assigned an exercise to create similes for every color of the rainbow. My stepson is smart as a whip (see what I did there?), but not exceptionally creative. His first attempt was something like "as green as grass" and "as yellow as the sun." I pushed him to try again—to think of unique similes. I recall being inordinately proud of his teenage simile for orange: "As orange as my fingers after eating a bag of Cheetos."

Pretty descriptive, right? You know that unnatural orange, made of neon seasonings and various dyes named with numbers and lethal to clean clothes and furniture. Very clever. As orange as *that*.

Well, that was the color of our sanctuary floor after we stained it.

Wait, back up—Driftwood stain turned the floor orange?

Not exactly.

We thought we had settled on Driftwood stain after testing a small area. After buying a gallon, Tyler tried it on a larger area and judged it as too green. He sent me back to Sherwin-Williams for more samples. His uncle and I spent nearly two hours getting three more quarts of custom-mixed stain, and still Tyler didn't like them. Too dark, he decided.

At this point, I refused to go back to get more stain just to have him reject it, so Tyler went. He was a man on a mission, determined to get this enormous floor stained so he could move to another task. When he was told he'd have to wait a couple of hours to get a custom mix, he chose what he perceived to be a lighter colored stain from off the shelf: Golden Oak. He had had enough with quarts to test; he bought two gallons of it.

It was our first mistake. It was the wrong color.

He applied Golden Oak to one thousand square feet of 126-year-old sanctuary floor. That was perhaps our second mistake, not considering the age and dryness of the floor. It drank up that stain like it was the Sonoran Desert. One hundred percent saturation.

After it had dried, and we looked at it the next morning, it was … well, golden oak. Not exactly what we were going for, but not too dark, either.

Then Tyler applied his sticky concoction of Douglas fir sawdust and polyurethane to fill the cracks. That was our third mistake. The polyurethane emphasized the red in the Douglas fir. If you remember your third-grade color wheel, you know yellow plus red equals orange. We had combined Golden Oak and red Douglas fir, and the result was as orange as my stepson's fingers after eating a bag of Cheetos.

We tried to like it. We told ourselves it would improve after Tyler light-sanded again. We were committed. We could make this work. I even applied Golden Oak with a watercolor brush to the edges of the fireplace and the base of the spiral stairway while lying on the floor.

After getting an ant's eye view of the entire expanse during that tedious task, I called Tyler who had stolen a few moments away from the work of the church to attend a local mud bog race.

"I'm sorry, honey, I just have to tell you this," I said as gently as I could over the roar of the off-road engines. "I hate the floor in the great room. It's orange. That's all there is to it. And orange isn't part of our color scheme. We have to do something about it."

"You know what this means, don't you?" he asked with as little rankle as he could pull together. "It means sanding the floors down to the wood again. Is that what you want to do?"

"There are no other options?" I pleaded. "Can't we try another coat in a different color?"

"No," he said. "I applied poly to the floor. We're past the point for another stain. We have to sand it all away."

"Well, then, yes, I guess so," I said. "We have to. I hate it. I can't live with an orange floor."

The mistake cost us hundreds of dollars in wasted Golden Oak, floor sander rental and sandpaper.

Frustrating, no doubt, but not the end of the world.

Tyler and his hired man St. Johnny spent another week—and the money to rent sanders and buy sanding paper—sanding away a thousand square feet of Golden Oak. (At least the seams were filled—we wouldn't have to perform that step again.)

Another stain color was required. The Douglas fir by itself was too red, so we couldn't go with the natural polyurethane-only look we chose for the maple in the bedroom and the pine upstairs.

This time, we went to Sherwin-Williams *together*. With a sample of Douglas fir flooring. The clerk—the one who had already mixed three different samples for me—was fresh out of gallons of clear base stain. He couldn't mix any colors for us. He sent us down the road to the next Sherwin-Williams. Along the way, Tyler suggested we try a stain-polyurethane mix that, in theory, would be more sheer than stain alone.

We took our wood sample to a Menards, which still carried the Minwax brand that Home Depot was feuding with Sherwin Williams about. We asked the paint clerk (who was surprisingly well-versed about staining wood floors) to test a couple of colors of 1-Step wood stain plus polyurethane on our sample of Douglas fir.

We walked out with five gallons of Acorn Brown 1-Step.

This new hue was significantly darker than Golden Oak, but definitely not orange. It did not dawn on me until much later that acorns grow into oaks (hopefully not golden oaks). The tallest oak in the forest was once just a little nut that held its ground.

Tyler and I spent ninety minutes on a Saturday afternoon applying Acorn Brown to the sanctuary floor. Unlike stain alone or polyurethane alone, this was a two-person job. Tyler smeared on the stain with a lamb's wool mop, and I followed behind him with a synthetic deck paint pad, making sure it was evenly applied. Sometimes I just held the dripping lamb's wool mop over the bucket while *he* used the paint pad—because he was *not* interested in doing this a third time. The stain-poly was tricky to work with because unlike clear polyurethane, sloppy work is evident. Missed spots and errant drips are easy to see.

But we turned on an eclectic mix of '80s pop and classic rock music, embraced the sweat and used only two gallons of Acorn Brown. It was dark. But brown, not golden and not red. And—thank goodness—not orange.

I thought we were done (finally!), and I planned to relax the next day—a Sunday. We had just finished using a product that described itself as 1-Step, after all.

As usual, Tyler woke up before me and inspected our work in the quiet morning as sunlight poured into the windows. I stayed in bed, thinking about how good my first cup of coffee would taste.

He returned to the bedroom and announced that we would have to apply another coat. Right. Now.

I tried to talk him out of it. The rest of the world was going to church or sleeping off a hangover or reading the Sunday paper, and I wanted to join the rest of the world in a typical Sunday morning activity. But after pouring the first cup of coffee, inspecting the floor myself and consulting the fine print, which clearly stated two coats might be required (1-Step, ha!), I agreed. Our showplace wood floor needed another careful coat.

Tyler turned up the music again (jazz this time), and we commenced getting sweaty. I never got breakfast—only coffee so I was extra grumpy when we finished. But we were really and truly finished. It looked good!

We needed to protect the beautiful flooring because the old church required a lot more work and a lot of contractors would be traipsing around. Tyler bought a couple hundred dollars' worth of Ram Board, heavy-duty cardboard that can be rolled out like a red carpet to provide temporary floor protection. On Monday, we rolled it over most of the sanctuary floor.

Monday evening at about 11, just after I retired for the night, Tyler's phone pinged, indicating motion detected inside the church. Sometimes headlights from passing vehicles set off the motion detector so this was not unusual. But I was lying wide awake, so I looked at his phone notification and was alarmed to see a pile of trim scattered all over our newly stained sanctuary floor.

I shook Tyler awake. "Something happened," I said as I dressed with the clothes on the floor.

"Huh? What? What happened?" he said.

"The trim fell down! Our floors!"

I ran over the church (Tyler chided me later for not letting him lead the way), and he followed a minute later. I flipped on the sanctuary lights, and we took in the scene. The sixteen-foot-long trim stored on a temporary shelf in the sanctuary was all over the floor. Our beautiful finished floor! The weight of the trim broke not the shelf but the window trim to which it was screwed. It had fallen with a mighty clatter.

We went back to bed, a little crestfallen, but when we cleaned everything up the next morning, we found only one big ding in the floor and only one broken piece of trim. As with so many events on our reconstruction, timing was everything. Fortunately, the shelf yielded in the middle of the night when no one was around, and the floors were thirty-six hours post-staining, so they were dry and

An expensive pile of fiddlesticks.

covered by Ram Board. Divine Providence was overseeing our project.

Back to work.

35
THE ROAD TO DAMASCUS

As we wrapped up the flooring part of *Phase Three: Drywall, Paint & Flooring*, the painter arrived. Truth be told, he showed up a little sooner than was convenient. You-Can-Call-Me-Al was still nailing trim in place, but this was not something to grouse about after some of the flaky contractors with whom we had dealt. He showed up, first of all, and he showed up sooner rather than later, so we were happy.

Early on, I imagined Tyler and I would paint the interior of the church ourselves. We had succeeded in painting the first floor of the first house we owned. Tyler hired out the work of painting the ceiling, and then he painted all the walls, leaving me to put paint and ladders in place, fetch more buckets and paint inconspicuous walls in the closets and the powder room.

But Tyler was tired—he had so many other things he could do, and he didn't trust me to precisely cut in the line between the walls and ceiling (I had proven to have an unsteady hand). We decided a professional could do it right and more quickly than we could accomplish. He collected quotes from two recommended men, and settled on the one with the thick, wavy gray hair of a Greek god. This one had dropped by more than once to inspect the church, and when we chatted about the features of the old trim around the sanctuary windows, his attention to detail impressed me. At the time, I noticed nothing unusual about the volume of his voice.

It wasn't long, however, before he earned a nickname: Low Talker.

Low Talker derived his name from a character on the '90s TV sitcom "Seinfeld." Her lips would move, but Seinfeld and Elaine couldn't hear what she said. To be polite, they would just smile and nod. As the plot evolved, Jerry smiled and nodded in agreement to something Low Talker uttered, only to find out later to his horror he had agreed to wear one of her designer puffy shirts on a TV appearance. Ha, ha, ha.

This character trait is not good for a contractor, and certainly not with a painter who frequently consulted the spouse he perceived to be making paint color decisions. If you smile and nod in agreement to something, you better be sure you heard correctly or soon you'll have a wall that's the wrong color.

So I said, "What?" A lot.

For the record, Tyler didn't have the same communication problems. Only I said "what?" after every sentence. Was the problem Low Talker's soft voice or my poor hearing? Those who know my family health history might pin the fault on me, but I maintain Low Talker was a man who spoke softly and carried a big paintbrush.

It became apparent right away paint needed to be plentiful. We started with eleven gallons of wall paint: five gallons for the trim and two for the wainscoting. Only a few days in, I returned from the paint store with another two gallons for the wainscoting and three more for the trim.

If you're counting, that's twenty-three gallons of paint.

That number made me glad I wasn't the one painting.

LOW TALKER BEGAN WORK in the master suite, specifically the laundry room, which I was eager to get finished and washing and drying. After he'd painted several walls, I realized that I'd chosen the right color of gray, a light gray inspired by Behr's Evening White but mixed by Sherwin-Williams. It made me happy just walking through the rooms any time of day. The trim, a white inspired by Behr's Bleached Linen, popped against the gray. And the wainscoting, a tan inspired by Behr's Arid Landscape, brought warmth to the scene. Low Talker also painted the tin inside the master bedroom tray ceiling with Arid Landscape.

The painter then tackled the second floor, where he sprayed two coats of polyurethane on the pickled plywood ceiling. This was a horrible, stinky job. At first, I thought he was just a sweaty guy—painting was hard work. But eventually, after I asked St. Johnny about how hot it must be on the second floor, we both realized Low Talker wasn't covered in perspiration. It was much easier for him to get clean at the end of the day of spraying paint around when he first coated exposed parts of his body—like his flowing locks—with baby oil. No wonder his hair looked as soft as his voice sounded.

For Low Talker to paint the rest of the second floor, You-Can-Call-Me-Al got busy installing trim. I chose a simpler trim style for the second floor than for the sanctuary; I wanted more of a farmhouse look there.

Among the items You-Can-Call-Me-Al trimmed out was the interior leaded-glass windows Tyler and I selected months before to add decoration to the balcony wall while adding natural light from the second story to the sanctuary. Tyler was quickly emptying one of our rental units, and the carefully packed leaded glass windows were transferred to the church to be installed. The windows had the simple farmhouse trim on the inside and more ornate trim on the balcony side. The glassy artwork transformed the holes in the drywall into light-dancing features over the tub in the second-floor bathroom and along the balcony wall. Their installation confirmed we had made progress, yes, beautiful progress.

THAT SUMMER, HOT AND humid days were many, and sawdust or paint fumes floated in the air. Tyler began most days by flinging open the double castle doors and leaving them open all day. An enormous industrial fan ran constantly, either spewing our dust into the street or cooling the men working inside.

The open doors had an ancillary benefit: they welcomed visitors. We had so many, in fact, our castle doors could have been revolving doors. I wouldn't have guessed sawdust could have such an upside.

Our ongoing work continued to lure interested former church members, neighbors and other curious observers, and we rarely let anyone get away without a grand tour. It was so much more fun showing people the work we had *actually performed* instead of pointing to where we *planned* custom vanities, a spiral staircase, leaded glass windows and a grand balcony.

Some visitors bore gifts. A neighbor heard what we were up to and offered us some of her yard's abundant perennials. Tyler was thrilled. She gave him directions to her nearby home, and he excitedly told me about her offer. As we were concentrating on sanding floors, we didn't make it to her house right away. A couple of weeks later, she dropped by with a trunk load of divided hostas and something called four o'clock flowers she had harvested. All we had to do was plant them, which St. Johnny dutifully did on our backyard garden that was producing cucumbers and tomatoes in abundance. I imagined my mother, active in her local garden club, might do something similar for a foreign sojourner, and I found the woman's gift to be such a generous gesture of welcome. And hers wasn't the only one. Other friends, old and new, offered intangible cheerleading about the house and tangible additions to it. Another acquaintance of my corporate days offered us decorative grass from her yard; one day when we were in her area, we stopped by and dug up great hunks of it. Far-flung friends talked about making trips just to see us (and the house, let's be honest). Their kindness was just the encouragement we needed after so many months of hard work.

As neighbors dropped by to peek inside, we thought about looking outside.

All the windows in the sanctuary had obscured glass. Not frosted, exactly, but some sort of cloudy glass that prevented parishioners from gazing out the windows and daydreaming during sermons. Conveniently, it also prevented thieves and other marauders from peering inside, too, so we left it in place during demolition and restoration.

But now it was time to replace the obscured glass with clear glass and let in the sunshine. Also, we wanted the sashes painted, and we might as well replace the glass first. We had every window in the sanctuary removed and hauled to the glass guy's workshop for replacement. Meanwhile, You-Can-Call-Me-Al added quarter round to the frame edges, and Low Talker caulked the cracks. They vacuumed up decades of dust and pine needles stuck in the top of the frames, easily twelve feet off the floor. Surely, no church member had ever bothered to dust up there since the 1940s when the orientation of the sanctuary changed from east-west to north-south.

The windows came back to us with sparkling clear glass, and Low Talker lined them up along with wall-like sentries to paint them.

ABOUT THIS TIME, I witnessed the strange details one must pay attention to when one is renovating a hundred-year-old church. In this case, rehabbing the doors.

We had replaced the exterior doors to the entryway, but a second set of double doors divided the entryway from the sanctuary. At one time, when there was no entryway and only exterior steps, these doors now between rooms might have been the exterior doors, so they were one-and-three-quarters inch thick. We wanted to replace the top wood panels with glass, so we could see our entryway from the sanctuary. But like so many wishes that weren't horses, this was not easily done. The door was a single solid piece of wood, and even You-Can-Call-Me-Al, with all his carpentry experience and tools, was skeptical he could cut out these holes. Even if he succeeded, he wasn't sure about trimming out the glass again.

Much debate ensued. We shopped for alternative doors and discovered quickly we would have to buy (and wait for) custom ones

Our doors with windows, ready for paint.

because our ancient doors were extra thick and two inches taller than modern doors. You-Can-Call-Me-Al, who didn't want to ruin our doors with a mistaken cut, reminded us how much more insulating modern doors would be.

But we didn't want to wait (or waste perfectly good doors) so we urged You-Can-Call-Me-Al to cut holes in the doors so Low Talker could paint them with the rest of the doors.

You-Can-Call-Me-Al gamely tried.

And succeeded. ("It wasn't easy!" he told me later.)

Our original doors could be painted with everything else and glassed. Another reuse project on track.

36
THAT WHICH IS LEFT SHALL ESCAPE

WE HADN'T GOTTEN RID of anything significant, except for layers of wood flooring while we sanded, since the demolition phase of renovation months ago. But we did find an interested party for our old fire escape.

A former church member astutely observed that the fire escape was not an attractive addition to the street side of the church. We agreed.

Tyler tried peddling the fire escape to various potential buyers—anyone who had a second story was a potential buyer—but he met with little interest. Then he mentioned it to Reroofer, the agile young man with the distinctive red beard who repaired the roof of our belfry and helped us insulate. Yeah, Reroofer said, he needed a deer stand.

OK, a great way to recycle.

The deal required Reroofer to dismantle and haul away the two-story solid steel fire escape himself. Instead of viewing this as a burden, Reroofer found this prospect fun.

One Monday morning in August (so he would have plenty of time for modifications before deer season), Reroofer showed up with a buddy in separate trucks.

While Reroofer and his compadre determined their plan of attack, I removed the paint from one of the doors we found in the church so it could be painted by Low Talker, our painter. This was an effective distraction from the ruckus occurring around the corner of the house.

Reroofer and his friend cut the stairway into three pieces. At one point, they used a truck and a rope to pull things apart, but I couldn't tell you what tools they used.

The fire escape during removal.

I didn't really want to know how they were accomplishing this task, so I didn't ask questions and I didn't hover. I prayed. I prayed no one would get hurt, and my house would remain standing.

I quickly realized my project was a no-go. The rotting door couldn't be salvaged. A few hours later, my prayers about the fire escape were answered.

You win some, you lose some.

Hauling away the fire escape in pieces required a few trips, even with two trucks. But by beer:30, Reroofer had a new deer stand, and Tyler and I had a clear view of the side of our house for the first time.

37
SO SHALL YOUR STORAGE PLACES BE FILLED WITH PLENTY

WE WERE STUCK ON Phase Three of our project—Drywall, Paint & Flooring—for so long, I'd forgotten Phases Five, Six, Seven and Eight existed, but I remembered clearly what we had been working toward during those long days sanding wood floors: cabinets! Finally, we'd arrived at *Phase Four: Cabinets & Appliances.*

Oh, we had been picking around the edges for some time. We had bought the display kitchen and received a quote for having it delivered. When we heard the number, Tyler and I agreed it would be much cheaper to rent a U-Haul and perform the heavy lifting ourselves. That day back in March was filled with numerous references to Devo and *Lost in Space.*

"Crack that whip!"

"Danger, danger, Will Robinson!"

We whipped it good, and we didn't bust anything; we earned our soup that day.

In the time between buying the display kitchen and picking it up,

I worried I wouldn't have enough kitchen gadget storage space, but handling every single cupboard and drawer disavowed me of that notion. Since the church wasn't ready for cabinet installation when the remodeling firm was ready to get rid of their display kitchen, we handled every single cupboard and drawer *again* when we moved them from the rental unit to the church, but it was an exciting day that signaled we were done sanding floors. (Did I say "done"? We weren't done, exactly, but instead of churning the ice cream, the next time we sanded we would be putting a cherry atop the sundae).

Installing the laundry cabinets and the master bath vanity were the other bites we'd taken on in the cabinet phase, but really, nothing compared to that kitchen. We diddled with the upper cabinets and additions we'd purchased during the rainy week of the longest days of summer. By the end of August, however, we were *still* waiting for the replacement cabinets in the right color (that retailer was *not* going to like our review—the firm epitomized recalcitrant).

In total, our kitchen cabinets were a Rubik's Cube. Without instructions, we moved around parts of the display kitchen, added a few pieces drawn from various sources, and now we had to figure out how to put them back together and get them level. Tyler, You-Can-Call-Me-Al and I conferred several times that day, poring over the pictures we'd taken of the display kitchen when it looked like it was supposed to, instead of how it looked in pieces on the floor of our sanctuary.

That was the problem with doing it our way. We had a lot of jerry-rigging to do.

When a regular homeowner purchases a custom kitchen, someone comes to measure, draws up plans with illustrations and sends instructions to the installer. We measured, more than once, but our installation prep ended there. This left these loose ends:

 —We switched cabinets on either side of the sink so the wine rack would face the beverage bar.

 —We eliminated the shelves and drawers and moved the glass-doored cabinets to either side of the stove. The cream-colored shelves were moved to the blue beverage bar; they required painting.

—We shortened the tongue of the island and added cupboard doors so we could use the storage space. When cabinet doors in the wrong color arrived, our painter Low Talker spray painted them, and I glazed them. Ditto for the cupboard above the refrigerator.

—I painted yards of kickplate and quarter round to match both the cream-colored and blue cabinets.

—We ended up with a leftover drawer. You-Can-Call-Me-Al noted it would fit perfectly on the floor beneath the wine rack for corks.

—We planned for a wider stove than in the display kitchen, making the stove vent obsolete. Fortunately, we acquired a different one. But it was brown. We couldn't decide if we wanted to leave it or paint it.

Oh, the stove vent.

We had purchased the stove hood as part of the castle door deal. The door seller had a strange variety of stuff in his garage, including the enormous wood stove hood. Tyler got him to throw it into the deal. This was long before we found the display kitchen and long before we purchased the 36-inch wide stove on Craigslist, so we tiptoed around it in the basement for months.

It seemed like an incredible deal, until I saw the tab for the vent. The hood was just decoration. To make it operational, we needed a vent in the correct size. Tyler found a new one he liked. Cha-ching.

No matter how good your vent, you need a duct to transfer the smoke (or whatever is coming off your cooktop) to the outdoors. During the mechanicals phase, Tyler thought ahead enough to get ducting from the hood to the outdoors. Cha-ching.

The vent needed to be inside the hood, and that required You-Can-Call-Me-Al's expertise. Cha-ching.

And to make a vent operate, we needed electricity.

We put the electrician to work. Cha-ching.

Naturally, it wasn't a simple connection. It didn't work on the first try, so we would need to remove the vent, solve the problem, and try again. Cha-ching.

The incredible deal was turned into a money pit. Or money vent, I guess. Poof, money floating from the chome through the stove vent ducting.

And then there was the refrigerator.

There had been no refrigerator in the display kitchen. I guess display people don't need cold food. But we were real people, and ice cream was a requirement, not a negotiable.

When we designed our kitchen, there was a perfect 37-inch-wide nook on the left side of the kitchen's back wall; the congregation had a custom cabinet in the space that we guessed stored bread and wine. This slot was maintained when Tyler installed the header to support the balcony. The drywallers did their work, and we were set to shop. Except with five-eighths-inch drywall, our slot ended up 35-and-three-quarters-inch wide. A 36-inch refrigerator would not fit.

That's OK, refrigerators come in a variety of widths. And while we were shopping for the washer and dryer, we found one. It was 35-and-five-eighths-inches wide. We liked it because it had more capacity than some 36-inch-wide ones (*so much* more than a skinny 32-inch-wide or 34-inch-wide refrigerator). It would be snug fit perhaps, but hey, we had an eighth of an inch to spare. We signed on the dotted line to set up a delivery date.

I suppose you know where this story is headed.

Back at the church we measured two times what we *should* have measured the first time.

We did indeed have 35-and-three-quarters inches at the *top* of the opening. But we had only 35-and-a-half inches at the bottom.

At one point, Tyler, known to use brute force on obstinate inanimate objects, said he'd shove it in one way or another. I'm sure he *could* have.

But he reconsidered and called the drywallers. They came by in a few days to replace the five-eighths-inch drywall with quarter-inch drywall, thereby buying us a whole inch of play, top *and* bottom.

Our painter Low Talker painted the slot just in time for the delivery.

No brute force required.

Experience taught us that one refrigerator wouldn't be enough. In our previous home, we liberally used a used refrigerator in the garage, especially when we entertained. This time around, we designed room for not one but two additional refrigerators—one for beer and pop and one for wine. Once we added our Drinkpod water cooler and a coffee maker, surely we would have enough space for beverages for everyone. Including a beverage bar in the kitchen design was one of my favorite design ideas.

As was his wont, Tyler ordered both refrigerators online, and they arrived packed in multiple layers of plastic and cardboard. The beer cooler was dented (slightly), and the wine cooler's door was askew.

A bit of complaining yielded discounts on both. Tyler fixed the wine cooler door with 57 cents in new screws. We were happy with this result. It meant every appliance in our new kitchen was purchased used, at a discount or on sale. Given the extras required for the Craigslist stove hood, this was good for the Tequila Budget (with plenty of space to ice tequila in the future!).

Both refrigerators were installed with only a little bit of finagling.

We were finally ready for countertops. Tyler called the countertop company to take measurements.

MEANWHILE, I HAD BEEN working on the dressers that would become the vanity for the upstairs bathroom. After I painted them, most of the drawers wouldn't close anymore, so I sanded edges. I also dragged my eBay crystal knobs to the hardware store to find appropriately sized screws.

You-Can-Call-Me-Al installed the dressers in the bathroom, created fillers and built a ledge for the makeup table in the center. More work was needed; You-Can-Call-Me-Al would have to modify the drawers for the sink, I would have to paint all the added bits and pieces, and we needed mirrors. But like the kitchen, this vanity was ready to be measured for countertops.

THROUGHOUT CONSTRUCTION—ESPECIALLY after drywall—people asking about the window in our closet amused me.

No, we did not design a window into the closet.

But the hole at the end of the closet *looked* like a window for a while.

Instead, it was a slot for a bank of cabinets in the mudroom. They were designed at a height that would allow us to place a pew beneath them. Yes, a church pew! Tyler had owned this pew for decades; at one time, he shortened and refinished it. It sat just inside the front door of our previous home so people could sit to remove or put on their shoes. It would serve the same purpose in the new mudroom, which led from the garage.

One of our design rules required storage built into every room, and the mudroom was no exception. A quick look at design magazines and blogs will tell you every homeowner's headache is the "drop zone" in the entryway forever filled with clutter. A single little pew wasn't going to cut it. But a bank of cabinets to store keys and purses, shopping lists and shopping bags, flashlights and lightbulbs might do the trick.

Tyler assembled the cabinets, and You-Can-Call-Me-Al installed them and trimmed them out. Suddenly, the empty maw into the master closet smiled like an old man with new teeth. No one would ask about our closet window anymore.

LIKE WITH OUR BALCONY railing, the installation of our countertops was quick and satisfying. A week after the experts came to measure, they returned with finished stone and manhandled it into place. Because of the complexity of our kitchen island, they dry-fitted the granite during that second visit and returned a few days later to glue the finished pieces into place.

There was only one hiccup: part of the beverage bar did not fit the first time. It had to be removed and refinished. Moving massive pieces of quartz and granite is not for the faint-hearted. At least four men were involved with every piece. I was reminded yet again about how heavy construction materials are, and grateful for the named and nameless men who helped us move items into the church.

It was a banner day when You-Can-Call-Me-Al put up the kitchen backsplash. I adored how it turned out, tying together so many different colors in the kitchen all in the rustic style of Paramount Flooring's Havana.

The feature area above the stove was laid out with the placement of the Deco Mix in mind. I wanted You-Can-Call-Me-Al to use the four-by-eight Sugar Cane and Havana Sky tiles randomly, but he wanted a bit more direction, so he laid them on the countertop first and let me reorganize them "randomly." I used mostly white with the cream-colored cabinets and mostly blue with the blue ones.

At first, You-Can-Call-Me-Al warned me he might not have enough tiles. I popped into the church every hour to check on his progress—I think You-Can-Call-Me-Al suspected I was checking on him, but I was admiring the tile (and his work). In the end, I had ordered the exact number of boxes required. I chose white grout, which coordinated beautifully with the trim color elsewhere in the room. When he was finished, I swooned. I was in love.

The backsplash for the stove—without the stove.

When the countertop guys and You-Can-Call-Me-Al completed their work, I would tour the church in the evenings, when everyone else was gone, and quiet had descended on the place. I would pass my fingers along the cool, smooth stone of the countertops and, depending upon the room, I'd imagine brushing my teeth, chopping vegetables or sipping coffee. We soon would have an operational bathroom, bedroom and kitchen, which meant we could move in. All we needed now was a few tweaks by the electrician and by our plumber Glimfeather, who was on toilet duty, too. We were on to *Phase Five: Finishing.*

38
THEY PREPARE THE TABLE, THEY SPREAD THE RUGS

TYLER WAS A LATE August baby some fifty years ago, and he woke up early on his birthday the year we renovated the church.

It was half past 3 o'clock.

Which was an eye-opener even for him.

He was tired, but couldn't sleep, and his joints ached. Six weeks of all-out effort since our last break had taken a toll on his body.

I understood only a fraction of his complaints because I was still half asleep, but I clearly remember I couldn't even squeeze in a "happy birthday, honey" before he said he was a "stressed-out wreck."

Wrangling various contractors, with whom he didn't always see eye to eye and who argued loudly, made a thousand decisions a day exhausting. On top of that, he felt the pressure of a self-imposed deadline to apply the last coats of polyurethane to the floors before we left to camp over the long Labor Day weekend. Weeks ago, I made dental appointments this day for the both of us at 8 o'clock.

Birthday boy wasn't beginning his day happily.

Maybe buying and renovating a church wasn't such a good idea, I thought in my sleepy haze punctuated by Tyler's tossing and turning.

He finally got out of bed an hour later, and even though I really wanted to fall back to sleep in our warm and now motionless bed, I didn't get the chance.

Tyler bellowed from the kitchen, "Where is the filter cap?!"

We used an AeroPress manual coffeemaker (it really makes the best coffee), but sometimes we lost the filter or the filter cap in the garbage when we dumped the used coffee grounds. Apparently, whoever used the coffeemaker last the previous day—or possibly me when I cleaned up the kitchen (though, surely, I couldn't have been so sloppy)—dropped the filter cap in the garbage. I had efficiently taken out the garbage the night before, which meant I had to get out of bed to help look for the lost cap. This led to us digging around yesterday's cold coffee grounds and other detritus in a garbage bag outside.

I might have raised my voice in complaint.

At 4:45 a.m.

On Tyler's birthday.

After waking up more and resolving the coffeemaker debacle, Tyler suggested we bring our insulated cups of java inside. He dragged the rolling office chair and a folding chair into the center of the sanctuary, where sunshine now streamed through the now-clear-glassed windows. We were alone before any contractors had arrived.

Low Talker, our painter, had finished the trim and walls of the sanctuary the day before. The room looked bright and clean. Even though various tools lie scattered, like they had nonstop for nine months, we could envision how the completed room would look.

"We've come a long way," I said, attempting to coax out the optimistic morning Tyler I knew and loved.

He reluctantly cheered up. It was hard to resist, sitting in the huge, sunshine-filled room we would soon be living in.

"It's going to look kick ass," he said, with an emphasis on "kick."

"Happy birthday," I said.

"It's about time," he said.

"I couldn't get in a word edgewise while you were complaining," I said.

"I'm just tired," he said.

"We just need to power through a few more days," I said. "Then you'll get a break."

"I know," he said. "It'll be worth it."

Tyler's birthday wasn't the only occasion that week overshadowed by work at the church. A few days after Tyler marked another year, we celebrated a milestone wedding anniversary: ten years.

Since we bought home goods for the church like Home Depot shopping addicts, we agreed we didn't need to exchange anniversary gifts, but I requested earlier in the month that we mark the occasion by dining out. Tyler obliged by making dinner reservations.

When our anniversary arrived, I realized I would be spending the entire day on my hands and knees. Handwashing every square foot of the wood floors so Tyler could apply the last two coats of polyurethane before we left for the Labor Day weekend.

If I didn't do this, all the dust and tiny paint splatters on the floors would be forever encased in a layer of shellac, reminding me of my sloth and sloppiness.

I donned a pair of kneepads and began on the second floor. At about 10 o'clock, I was sure we would not achieve our goal, because the floor of the sanctuary was still covered in ram board, miscellaneous cabinets and tools. But while I washed the pine upstairs, Tyler and St. Johnny cleared and vacuumed the sanctuary so by 1:30 (when I finished the upstairs and the main floor master suite),

I moved to the enormous empty open-floor-plan great room.

I earned a repetitive stress strain in my shoulder by performing the same sweeping wiping motion with a wet rag a thousand times that day. Hand mopping sawdusty floors meant refilling my wash bucket several times for each room. At the point, the only running water in the church was in the basement, so I made many trips up and down two flights of stairs. I also scraped off paint splatters where I found them with sharp implements stored in my pockets (which, not infrequently, poked me, too). Fortunately, our painter prepped well, so there were few drops of paint to remove.

I finished washing at 4 o'clock, just in time for a much-needed shower before dinner, while Tyler wrapped up the first coat of polyurethane. To be specific, it was the third coat, but it was the first of the final two coats if you're counting down, which believe me, we were.

We dined on hard-earned steak and pasta and toasted to our anniversary bonds which, against all odds, had strengthened during our renovation odyssey.

Though unfinished, the kitchen never looked better.

The next morning, we surveyed the results before Tyler applied the final coat of polyurethane. We decamped elsewhere and left it all to dry. They way everything looked was the best anniversary gift ever. In the morning sun with the lights on, the kitchen literally glowed. The sawdust and tools were gone, and the floors gleamed.

I tiptoed around in my bare feet, taking pictures like a pro with both our phones so we could share the results with every person we might encounter over the long weekend. We were so proud of ourselves. The pain and effort were worth it.

SOME PROJECTS THAT WOULD be considered minor in any normal renovation hogged time in this one (refinishing the floors was Exhibit A). But window coverings, too. We didn't want to see the neighbors all the time, and they didn't want to see us all the time either ("home is where the pants aren't" is not an internet meme for nothing). One or two or four blinds was a small project. Hanging fourteen blinds, some from twelve feet high, required all day.

Once they were hung, the windows took on a new feel. Instead of being wide-open public windows, they looked like windows that belonged in a home. I liked it.

We hung basic white wood-like blinds in all the windows except the master bedroom, where Tyler hung light-blocking Roman shades. Well, he hung them in *one* of the bedroom windows. The other window presented a dilemma. One of the corners was eclipsed by the bottom of the stairway; hanging this shade straight would require some jerry-rigging, which would come later. Until then, we hung a paint-splattered drop cloth in the window.

THE ELECTRICIAN RETURNED TO install light fixtures and electrify outlets. He had wired the place months before and hooked up some of our lights and fans, but when we walked through the church in the evenings, we used flashlights to see where we were going in most rooms.

First stop: the kitchen. Most of the can lights were already operational, but he finished work and hung our island pendant lights.

Next up was the bedroom. I could hardly wait to hang crystals on the nightstand chandeliers that once hung in the sanctuary. I washed what felt like a hundred of them only to discover I had enough for only one chandelier. It looked lovely. I spent over an hour looking for the other crystals we had salvaged during demolition. But I came up empty. I had stashed them too well. That night I dreamed they were in the cargo trailer. When I poked around in there, they rose to the surface like a beautiful bubble. I washed the contents of the box and had exactly enough crystals for the second chandelier.

I also discovered I had failed to order lights needed for the back stairway, the laundry room and the water closet. I went back to the Lighting Savant to peruse his piles of catalogs; more light fixtures went on order.

GLIMFEATHER THE PLUMBER returned. He still was a fan of strange hours (Sundays, Friday evenings) but he didn't linger until 2 o'clock in the morning anymore.

It was so odd for me to see a man washing his hands in one of my sinks. For months, I had no sinks. Then for weeks, I had no faucets. And for days, I feared running the water. (Was the drain connected yet? Did I dare find out?). When I witnessed the plumber washing his hands, I knew the system was operational. Glory be.

The plumbing in the kitchen was nothing particularly special (unless you consider a pot filler special) though I was inordinately excited about our new garbage disposal and dishwasher. It was the master bath plumbing that had me singing like Carly Simon: "An-tici-pay-yay-tion … is making me wait."

Coincidentally (if coordinating multiple tradesmen is ever coincidental), the vanity in the master bath came together in about forty-eight hours a few days after the countertop was installed. You-Can-Call-Me-Al installed the tin ceiling and flanking cabinets, Low Talker painted the tin, Glimfeather installed the faucets and the glass guy installed my elegantly arched mirrors. We weren't quite done—primarily, we needed lights, outlet covers, towel rings and knobs like an apothecary cabinet maker—but we got mighty close. That double sink vanity made me want to brush my teeth. I would never have to share a mirror again!

While he was there, the glass guy spent several hours installing our coveted glass shower door. The one we drooled over so many months ago when as we tried to make the numbers work. And the rainfall showerhead–oh, oh, oh! Years prior, my brother-in-law had installed a rainfall showerhead in the home where he and his sister lived. It was divine (and theirs wasn't even in a church), and I knew what I was missing. How I longed to stand under those water drops for an entire afternoon.

Instead, I tracked down boxes of towels to wash them and stack them in my linen closets, which Tyler had filled with shelves and Low Talker had painted. Very soon, we would be using these towels to dry off after washing our hands and taking showers.

BESIDES SHELVING IN ALL the various cabinets, we needed to install closet rods before we could move in.

We reused the closet rods that came with the hall closet, and Tyler hung a standard closet rod in the upstairs closet in minutes. The master walk-in closet, with nearly twenty-five feet of horizontal hanging space, required a bit more effort.

Tyler was inspired to use half-inch steel plumbing pipe for rods.

It was strong, cheap and eminently customizable. I liked the industrial vibe so much that I'd chosen cabinet pulls and closet light fixtures to match. I researched standard closet measurements to achieve the most efficient use of space. One morning, Tyler took his measuring tape inside the closet and dictated measurements to me. He ordered pipe fittings online, and he called up the nearby big-box store to have pipes cut and threaded to size.

When everything arrived, we laid it all out on the bedroom floor, a bit confused about where to begin. Which pipes were forty-two inches long and where were the forty-four-inch ones? Is this one a vertical pipe or a horizontal pipe? Which pieces do we screw together first?

After the first attempt, we realized we needed more five-way pipe fittings. And the ceiling and floor weren't perfectly parallel, so the plumber shortened some of the pipes onsite with his pipe cutter-and-threader. As with all construction projects, this one also required grunting and sweating, but the stud finder and electric drill came in handy. As far as items on the honey-do list went, this one was easy. Presto, change-o, the plumbing pipe turned into closet rod.

I had lived for two years in a camper or a tiny rental house, neither of which had more than a few feet of clothes hanging space. I had been proud of myself to downsize like that. In truth, I had gotten rid of a lot of out-of-fashion and ill-fitting items, but several boxes of very nice clothes had been packed away, waiting patiently to be worn again. I was in heaven, admiring something as simple as closet rods.

A few weekends later, Tyler and I installed shelving inside our master closet. The closet rods were great, but only half the story. Shelving would make the space above our heads useful. Much measuring, sawing and drilling ensued, but we accomplished this necessary project, too, with only one mishap. While sawing a hunk of shelving on a table saw, Tyler lost his grip and the hunk hurled itself into his stomach. "Ooph!" he exclaimed in a manner eerily similar to Skipper on *Gilligan's Island*. For a week, he had a perfectly rectangular bruise across his torso (fortunately for me, I earned no blame in this). Just another badge of honor earned by renovating a 126-year-old church.

With shelving and coordinating baskets installed, my master closet could now neatly contain all my purses, scarves, workout gear and swimwear.

ON TO THE FLOOR coverings. You'd think we had the most difficult part done once Tyler applied the last coat of polyurethane to the refinished floors, but no. Wood floors are, oh, so chic, but they are not cozy. Rugs are *de rigeur,* and choosing rugs is not for the timid. Google "how to choose a rug," and you'll get 113 million pieces of advice. Tips on finding the right size sift to the top, so anyone with access to the internet and a few minutes can figure that out. Choosing a material, a design and a color paralyzed me. These were not towels or curtains that could be easily changed if they were wrong—a properly sized rug covers a lot of real estate. And if I didn't like what I purchased, cha-ching. Good rugs weren't cheap.

The bedrooms were the first to get rugs (which saved us the trouble of moving beds). Tyler's favorite approach—shopping Amazon—led him to Houzz, where he found rugs for the second-floor guest room and our master suite. He sorted through hundreds of options, narrowing them to three, and made me choose.

On the second floor, where the trim was white and the walls were gray as in the rest of the church, my accent color was seafoam green. I knew I wanted to use a handmade quilt I'd won in a raffle on the bed (it was quite a prize for $5 in raffle tickets), and its main color was crimson, so a shade of green would complement it. I also planned to put my antique steamer trunk at the foot of the bed, and Tyler had once had it painted for me by a Rockford, Illinois, artist as a gift. The color scheme was cream and blue and seafoam green. For the rug, I chose a muted traditional design in gray and greenish, big enough to cover the floor beneath the bed and the walkway to the bathroom.

I agonized for weeks about the color scheme for our master bedroom, mostly because I was too cheap to buy new sheets. We had good quality sheets for the king-sized bed in khaki and in a white-and-blue print. Either would work just fine in our master, but I didn't have a decent quilt to match. (I am the sort of woman who likes to match her bra and underwear, too, even though no one except Tyler ever sees them.) I ended up with an all-white bed-in-a-bag with a comforter, knowing I wanted a lighter weight quilt to fold at the foot of the bed (eventually, I found a great deal on a navy blue one). Later, my sister gave me a set of matching decorative pillows as an accent. For a rug, I settled on a mottled gray, black and turquoise rug.

For more than a month, our new dining room table sat on a bed of furniture blankets as we weighed our rug options. One evening, as Tyler forced me to adjudicate while he paged through literally hundreds of rugs on online retailers' websites, we struck upon a jute rug with formal navy striping. I liked the texture of the twine-like substance (ease of cleaning remained to be seen) and the simplicity of the design that was on the edges, not the center of the rug (what's the point of a center design when the table covers it?). When the rug arrived, we wasted no time replacing the ugly furniture blankets. Classy replaced crass in about ten minutes.

My internet-shopping husband wanted me to choose a rug for the "living corner" of the great room, too. He narrowed the search parameters to a particular size and color and still we could have paged through two million options. Nothing spoke to me. Then I began questioning the color. Then I wondered if I really wanted that size. Every choice looked right. Then they all looked wrong.

We'd already made one rug choice for the corner of the great room that contained the fireplace and sectional. Or rather, Tyler did. During one of his early morning shopping trips (some people shop the internet at night while consuming liquor—Tyler did his damage armed with coffee before anyone else got up), Tyler ordered a special rug.

A huge package of unknown origin (at least to me) arrived one day before we had even moved in. As Tyler unpacked it, he exclaimed, "Oh, it's the bear rug! Check this out," as he unfurled a huge, furry, strangely shaped mat.

Indeed, it looked a lot like a bear rug—only the fur was polyester, and it didn't have any teeth.

After we made an offer on the church but before we closed the deal, we toured a house on a Parade of Homes. I spotted a bear rug (a real one) in one of those million-dollar homes, and I told Tyler we *had* to have one in the church. This was a unique textural piece that would be right at home in a former church in southern Wisconsin, I thought. What's cozier than curling up on a bear rug in front of the fireplace? Tyler remembered.

"How much did you spend on *that?*" I asked, loving that he remembered, agreed we should have one and shopped for and bought it, knowing I would approve.

"Only two hundred bucks!"

When we moved in, we rolled it out in front of the fireplace almost right away. It did look right at home. Only the robot vacuum cleaner, which got tied up in it every time it vacuumed, protested.

We had a rug for the fireplace, just not one for the sectional. And I felt like I had to coordinate whatever we chose to go under the sectional with the rug in the dining corner, and the tile rug in the kitchen and the bear rug in front of the fireplace, and—oh, yeah—we had carpeting on the balcony, too, and technically, the balcony is part of the great room, right?

This is when paralysis set in. I couldn't decide. I just couldn't. Tyler and I visited a furniture warehouse store, a discount store, a mass market store and at least three antique shops. We looked for the right chairs to set in front of the fireplace, and oh, if we could find a living room rug and a sofa table and a couple of end tables, well, all the better. And we could use about a half-dozen lamps, too. Nothing was right, and we hadn't spent a dime all day. The day's shadows grew long. When my stomach started growling and Tyler's happy hour flag began fluttering in his mind, we wandered around the sprawling showroom of a regional furniture dealer.

The salesman showed us a pair of chairs that we could special order in just about any color or fabric. I was ready to choose anything, just to tick something off the to-do list. Tyler was so tired, he just sat in one of the chairs admiring the swivel mechanism. I talked Tyler into a latte-colored leather for the chairs, and I impulsively chose a geometric-patterned rug that ticked all the color boxes. Exhaustion had inspired action. Delivery was scheduled for twelve weeks hence.

AMONG THE FINISHING DETAILS I enjoyed watching come to fruition was the door to our granddaughter's playhouse, the space under the eaves we'd named for her.

More than once, I was amused to see a grown man working in that little five-foot-high space. The drywallers installed drywall, and the painter painted it. I sanded the floors with the edging machine (it was less amusing when *I* was the one working on my knees).

Tyler recycled the old closet door that had led to the opposite eaves and sported a hand-lettered sign on the closet door warned: "Do not open." He removed several layers of paint until he revealed the last layer—a distressed sea foam green that I loved. He cut it to size, and I applied a couple of coats of clear polyurethane. He attached it to our granddaughter's playhouse with some vintage-like black hinges; all we required now was a cool doorknob, which Tyler soon found on eBay. Our soon-to-be-walking granddaughter would find this little room to be just her size.

The space was like falling through a rabbit's hole into Wonderland. Much later, we would install a window in the little room, looking out over the balcony. Tyler found a mirror, a looking glass if you will, enclosed inside a pair of gothic wooden doors. He removed the mirror, and we used the doors to cover the playhouse window. We were getting to the end, and I was reminded of the King's advice to Alice: "Begin at the beginning and go on till you come to the end; then stop."

39
THE TRIALS OF JOB

As we encountered challenges small and big, we talked about them. Constantly. We were a one-note two-man band.

Early on, our wry son-in-law joked about starting a competing blog called "Everything Wrong with the Church" to reveal all our mistakes we didn't want to share with the world. Then I think he realized how little I left out when I was broadcasting our every move. This chapter is for him.

We had been cruising along, making a lot of decisions by hook or by crook, and we had arrived at the point where our lack of design plans exacted a price in time or money. Or both. The finishing phase was where the rubber hit the road.

The size of the refrigerator nook, for example: We measured incompletely and ended up re-drywalling the nook so the fridge would fit.

This would never happen to a house builder who built the same five house plans over and over. Key word: plans. The same goes for a custom home builder; an architect would have determined all measurements before a single nail was driven. We weren't home builders, and we were arrogant enough to believe we could do an architect's work (we had a floor plan—what more is there?). As the saying goes, we didn't know what we didn't know. If we had a written plan, we still might have ended up with a crooked wall here and there, and we might still be making decisions by the seat of our pants, but we wouldn't be redoing work. Now, in the finishing phase, a quarter inch—or foot—made the difference between something fitting or not. Missing steps meant going back to retrace them.

On top of our lack of plans, we pushed toward occupancy, so Tyler sometimes had a half-dozen men working in the church at once. He and I wrote checks like we'd never write checks again. The Tequila Budget was long ago busted. And if the street in front of our house didn't look like a construction zone before, it did now. Timing issues—this task was required before that task could be finished— were bound to arise.

Someone—we're not pointing fingers here—screwed a hole in the electrical wiring behind the beverage bar. When the electricity didn't work, we pulled out both beverage fridges to troubleshoot. Two hours, gone. While we had everything torn apart, Tyler added insulation to the plumbing running up an exterior wall. Maybe in this way, a mistake prevented a problem. This was how we had to think to keep frustration from outrunning hope.

The upstairs bathroom was particularly vexing.

When I unpacked the fixtures for the vanity, a knot formed in my stomach. What I had unpacked was beautiful, but I knew instantly the wiring—around which had been drywalled and painted—was in the wrong place. The electrician did the best he could with the direction he got—from me—but I was wrong. The wall would need to be ripped into, re-drywalled and repainted.

Both a standard shower stall for that bathroom and a standard glass door had been delivered in March, so the stall could be installed before we built walls around it. When You-Can-Call-Me-Al began installing the door, he realized it was too tall. After rummaging in an inches-deep pile of receipts, we remembered we'd purchased it at Lowe's. Thank goodness, we learned the big-box store had a lenient return policy. I boxed the door back up, drove a half hour to Lowe's, stood in line twenty minutes to return it, purchased a new door with Tyler's specs and drove back to the church. You-Can-Call-Me-Al set to installing the new door before determining it was now the correct height but the wrong width. Back to Lowe's. Apparently, "standard" came in a variety of sizes.

On the last day of our plumber Glimfeather's work, he brought two helpers and powered through plumbing details. In the final hour, he announced he was nearly done; he only needed to install our distinctive Kohler bathtub faucet. Where did I want it to be installed again? We surveyed the tub, and I fixed the point. I went about some other task, leaving him to his work, only to be called to the tub a few minutes later. The faucet—a beautiful one we'd coveted, ordered and paid for in April—was designed for a vanity sink, not a tub. "It'll take forty minutes to fill your tub with that faucet," Glimfeather said. "The water will be cold before you're done." Alas, the plumber's work was not done after all. We'd have to track down the correct faucet, and he'd have to come back (twice).

In one of his last acts, Glimfeather determined the faucet in the powder room—the one we'd acquired for an amazing deal in a display vanity—didn't have all its parts. During the test, water sprayed everywhere. A fail. Another vendor complaint would have to be issued. Another reason to see Glimfeather again.

Then I had buyer's remorse about the trendy glass cut-out handle I'd specified so precisely for the master shower door. After it was installed, and I admired it repeatedly, I noticed it was impossible to use without leaving fingerprints. This was a mistake that couldn't be fixed with a new coat of stain or a store return. There was no going back. Windex and I would be getting familiar.

We fired up our zone cooling system that would cool only the master suite instead of the whole church. It worked great, but then we noticed cool air shooting from the mudroom vent. It dawned on me that the HVAC guy, way back when he installed ductwork, saw only two-by-four walls; the back door didn't yet exist. The mudroom—with its maple wood floors—probably looked like part of the master suite back then when it was really an entryway to the sanctuary.

When it rained, it poured, as the old figure of speech goes. It applied literally, too. Another monsoon befell us, this time while we were trying to enjoy some free time over Labor Day weekend. It washed out our boating plans *and* our basement.

The basement was still flooding on the regular. It appeared that Tyler's inventive drainage techniques, executed via a lot of back-breaking digging by his hired man St. Johnny, had resolved the leaks on the south and north sides of the church. But he hadn't finished work on the east side, where huge piles of dirt we'd salvaged from the school's parking lot still stood as monuments to Tyler's distractions inside the church. Rain barrels and rock were purchased, and St. Johnny dug man-sized holes to accommodate them.

We crossed our fingers until the next rainfall, and then it happened. Rain poured out of the sky. Tyler peeked out the window, and the gutter on the east side of the house looked like an active firehose, shooting water eight feet out into the yard. He braved the heavy rain to secure the elbow at the bottom of the gutter. Ugh, he'd forgotten to secure that section with a screw. He reconnected the pieces of gutter so all the water from roof now shot into his drainage system, not the yard. But some of the early deluge, alas, made it into the basement.

The finishing detail that made me thunk my forehead with my palm came not with an element of the church, but with a piece of furniture. This a project spread itself over a couple of weeks and required attention from both me and Tyler.

The beat-up headboard and footboard we found on the side of

the road? We would need a guest bed sooner rather than later, so I painted it one weekend. The project put me in the way of contractors who required space or basement access, but it needed to be done. I ran out of paint before I finished, so I used some leftover paint in a close match to finish the back (no one would ever know—unless they read the blog about "Everything Wrong with the Church"). When it dried, St. Johnny and I hauled it upstairs, taking care not to ding the drywall.

Through a friend, we sourced a barely used queen mattress set that came with a bed frame. We counted ourselves lucky because our benefactor of the headboard and footboard did not bestow us with the frame. Tyler and I hauled it to the church, and as we were about to shove the box spring up the back stairs, we realized it wasn't going to fit (this was a throughway designed for Sunday schoolers, not queen-sized box springs). OK, so we enlisted a few contractors to help shove it over the balcony railing the next morning.

As we assembled the bed frame, we realized it was designed for a headboard only. There was no way to attach the footboard. OK, so Tyler jerry-rigged a solution, spray painted it and hauled it upstairs. Because it was jerry-rigged, it required an inordinate amount of grunting and number of screws to assemble. OK, Tyler grunted and succeeded. He and St. Johnny lugged the box spring into place ...

And Tyler called me upstairs.

"Your bed doesn't fit," he said in summons.

"Okayyy," I said slowly. "Whaddya mean 'my bed doesn't fit'?" I had measured the headboard and knew it would be a tight fit for nightstands, but I also figured I could find a creative solution (what's Pinterest for anyway?). I joined him at his side, looking at the bed.

"It's not a queen headboard," Tyler said. "It's a king."

We had plucked it from the street and unloaded it into our rental unit. I had moved it to the church to paint, and I touched every square inch of it. St. Johnny and I had moved it upstairs. I had *measured* it to determine what kind of nightstands would fit. Tyler built a frame on it to fit a *queen* mattress. And not until the mattress was in place did we realize the headboard was *king sized*.

Um, yeah. That headboard is too big for that mattress.

Do you suppose we were a little distracted?

The queen mattress with the king headboard looked ridiculous.

"Well, I guess we'll be moving this down to the basement when we finish a bedroom down there," I shrugged. There was no modifying it. "One of our guest beds in the basement will be a king, I guess."

All these finishing mistakes, they were small things. The oven fit perfectly. The kitchen sink worked like a dream. The chandeliers hung beautifully in the bedroom. The shower drained like it should and felt like a luxury to use. So many things fell into place, even without a documented plan.

So the headboard was the wrong size. It made for a good story. Who's to say it wasn't meant to be?

40
REBUILDING THE TEMPLE

As autumn slipped through our fingers, Tyler eyed the calendar and began work on the belfry and shortly thereafter, the "Garage Mahal."

Our move-in was unlike any you would ever see on HGTV. The big reveal on those home improvement programs features flowers on the countertop and pictures on the wall. The project is *done* done. *Our* move-in would include no chocolates-on-the-pillow touches. We had no switch plates. We had no floor registers. We had no cabinet knobs. If we had doorknobs, it was only because they were still attached to an original door (of which there were few). Many cabinets and closets had no shelves, and if you've ever really bothered to consider your cabinets and closets, they're nearly useless without shelves. Every vase, every piece of wall art, every basket and organizer I owned was packed in a box or a bin, which were tucked into every available corner, waiting to be unpacked.

But Tyler couldn't concentrate on these details, at least not yet. October loomed large. The days shortened and grew cooler. One day,

You-Can-Call-Me-Al, who'd worn denim shorts to work on the church all summer, showed up in jeans, and he looked like a different person. The belfry required attention and the garage needed to be built, and Tyler had limited time to get these projects accomplished before outdoor work was uncomfortable if not impossible. Reroofer arrived, too. Reroofer, the bearded young man who secured the roof beneath the bell, was no longer bearded but still willing to work on our belfry. He climbed up inside the tower and began tearing off siding from the top down to reveal the real problems—and the real beauty—of our belfry.

A peek beneath the aluminum siding revealed the beautiful original diagonal wood siding and decoratively detailed cedar-like shakes—and the window we could see from the inside but had been covered by aluminum on the exterior. Reroofer revealed the truth of the structural problems so we could see clearly what we had and how to address it. The belfry never looked so naked, and the pilings holding up the bell looked as spindly as a wet dog after a bath. From afar, the 126-year-old four-by-fours looked like toothpicks, and they didn't look so great up close either.

On Day 2 of reconstruction, You-Can-Call-Me-Al spent the entire day vacuuming up decades of animal carcasses, nesting material and animal feces in the space between the interior ceiling on the second floor (where the trap door was, above the window) and the roof beneath the bell that Reroofer repaired the last autumn. You-Can-Call-Me-Al filled bag after bag of gross detritus. In every single corner, animals and insects had lived and died. This is where Stan the Squirrel—the mummified resident Tyler found when he first inspected the belfry—had existed. Stan had chewed away many boards.

This cleaning allowed the men to see what they had to work with and what needed repair. They also used the floor in this anteroom as a staging area for tools, nails and lumber.

Day Three of the belfry reconstruction project dawned with

Something had chewed nearly through
the angled boards supporting the pilings.

warmish weather and a lumber delivery. A truck with a crane dropped a literal ton of lumber in our backyard, most of it for building the garage, but some of it for the belfry.

The goal of the day was to sheath the eight pilings of the belfry with new lumber, thereby reinforcing them and revitalizing the strength sapped by decades of weather and animals.

This was a four-man job. You-Can-Call-Me-Al was Nail Man. Standing on the narrow ledge outside the bell tower with a nail gun, he called measurements down to Tyler. Tyler was Cut Man. He cut lengths of wood with a table saw on the ground. He then attached these pieces of lumber to a rope on a bricklayer's wheel acquired and installed by You-Can-Call-Me-Al. You-Can-Call-Me-Al pulled up the planks and attached them at the top of the pilings. Meanwhile, Reroofer was the Middle Man. He stood on the ladder all day attaching the planks *inside* the belfry. St. Johnny helped Tyler on the ground and frequently ran smaller items and tools that couldn't be hoisted up to the second floor, where Reroofer retrieved them.

In the afternoon, Tyler had me buy more bolts, enormous pieces of metal bigger and longer than my fingers. I paid more for *each bolt* than I would have for most fancy drinks at Starbucks. These were substantial fasteners that meant business.

None of the men sat for more than a few minutes all day. You-Can-Call-Me-Al balanced on the narrow ledge, Reroofer stood on a ladder, Tyler maneuvered mighty planks on the ground and St. Johnny scurried around, picking up after them.

Four o'clock, the customary quitting time, came and went. Five o'clock came and went. These guys had a system going, and they were determined to finish the job. Six o'clock, and my stomach rumbled. Even I, who had been sitting at a desk most of the day handling arcane paperwork, was hungry.

The men wrapped things up about half past six. All eight pilings now sported new sheathing all the way around. The belfry had a new-car smell about it.

I attended an evening class nearby and returned an hour later. I found evidence that Tyler had fixed himself his favorite comfort food—macaroni and cheese—and I peeked in the bedroom: Tyler was snoring softly.

The following day, You-Can-Call-Me-Al and Reroofer climbed back up into the belfry to wrap the now heftier pilings in waterproof net. While he was up there, You-Can-Call-Me-Al tested the heft by ringing the bell.

Reroofer rang the bell when he was repairing the roof beneath it the previous fall, but he did it carefully and by hitting the stationary bell. Now, You-Can-Call-Me-Al stood on the ledge of the bell tower, grabbed the circular crank and pulled. (This is the mechanism to which a rope is usually tied—we removed the worn-out old rope intending to replace it with a new one of impressive diameter). The bell swung, and the clapper made contact.

Tyler and I stood on the ground, watching to see if the tower swayed. Standing on the tower and confident of his work, You-Can-Call-Me-Al assured us it was solid.

He rang the bell wildly.

The tower stood immoveable.

Our bell sounded full and melodious. It hadn't been rung so enthusiastically for years, and it was lovely. I watched, smiling widely.

A passerby asked me if we planned to ring the bell at three o'clock in the morning. Maybe she was worried.

"No," I said. "But maybe at midnight on New Year's Eve."

"That would be OK," she said.

OK? That would be awesome!

You-Can-Call-Me-Al tested our bell a few more times. No police showed up, so the neighbors must have been either happy to hear it or willing to bear it.

Reroofer now went to work in his specialty—finishing the flat roof beneath the bell. He performed this work once already, back in autumn, but all that had been pulled apart to repair the pilings. He spent a solid week traipsing up the ladder with various construction materials—plywood, aluminum, waterproof sheeting and more—to do whatever a good and proper roofer does. He dodged a recalcitrant squirrel who'd taken possession of the nook *above* the bell and insisted Reroofer was trespassing. For the most part, Reroofer simply ignored the squirrel's chattering, but he noted to himself and to us that the filling the roof above the bell would deter squatters.

Reroofer attached the rope to the wheel of the bell so standing on the roof to ring it wasn't required. The same day, a pair of my friends visited so I celebrated by inviting them to ring it with me. They demurred. "You really ought to be the one to ring it the first time," one said.

I yanked on the rope once, and I could feel that it wasn't hard enough to get the clapper to make contact. I was too timid.

"Do it again!" they said.

I pulled again, this time with gusto, and the bell rang out. My eyes grew as wide as my grin, to the delight of my friends.

Later, Tyler climbed the steps to ring the bell himself. He was not so timid as I had been. He pulled the rope and rang the bell three or four times, satisfied with all the work that got him to this reward.

Church bells, of course, are not usually rung just for fun. In the strictest sense, the primary purpose of ringing a church bell is to call parishioners to services. "In a broader sense the bells produce a pure musical sound that stirs the hearts of all who hear them," according to an online FAQ I found about ringing bells. "The uplifting sound transcends any artificial boundaries of sect or religion. Most of us love to hear them whatever our beliefs—because they stir something deep, perhaps something deeply spiritual, in all of us. And we are grateful and want to continue the tradition."

Since it was the sort of signal that could be heard across town, I thought I should develop some sort of guidelines for bell ringing. Traditionally, bell ringing was used to announce or signal special events such as weekly services, according to the FAQ. They also rang as flood or fire warnings, messages to douse fires for the evening, warn that the town water supply had been polluted (perhaps by a drowned animal), or to signal the harvest or new year. Bells also were used to announce times of great joy, such as weddings, or to express sorrow, such as at funerals. I thought perhaps we could get away with ringing the bell to welcome visitors (so we could show it off, of course), for family birthdays (though I wasn't sure I trusted ringing it once for every year of life—I had a 103-year-old grandmother after all) and for the new year (because that could be expected).

And every time we would ring our bell, George Bailey's Zuzu would be celebrating with the angels: "Every time a bell rings, an angel gets his wings!"

Behold the regal bell pull.

WE HAD A LOT of leftover rope on the bell pull, which I asked Tyler about. I wondered if this was his typical "go big or go home" approach to buying in abundance or something else. He said he was pondering threading the rope through the closet to the main level. At some point, he intended to attach to the end of the rope an ornate bell pull he'd found on Ebay. The designer, a sailor with a knack for knots, lived in the United Kingdom and had fashioned a crown at the top of the elaborate bell pull. "This particular crown most resembles the King George crown having six legs and an ermine fur cuff," he wrote in his description. All of it was made of nylon rope, some of it painted. It would be a dignified ornament for our bell rope.

With the repairs complete and the bell operational, we would revisit the exterior of the belfry the following summer when Tyler rented an articulating boom lift, cheaper and more mobile than a crane. You-Can-Call-Me-Al rode in the basket to the top to install a new spire, and he used it to re-side the belfry and to repair and paint the cedar-siding shakes.

For now, Tyler wanted to concentrate on a new project: the garage.

41
Sixty cubits long, twenty wide and thirty high

How to build a garage in ten easy steps:

1. Pour concrete.
2. Nail together and erect two-by-six walls.
3. Sheet walls with plywood and wrap with air- and water-repellant building wrap.
4. Order roof trusses.
5. Hire crane to set roof trusses.
6. Sheet roof with plywood, roof felt and an ice-and-water barrier.
7. Install soffit and fascia.
8. Shingle.
9. Install doors and windows.
10. Install siding.

If it were as easy to do as it was to write about it, everyone would build their own garage. Not everyone does. But Tyler was not everyone.

As he turned his attention to his garage, Tyler discussed the project with You-Can-Call-Me-Al, the man whose experience and skills made him Tyler's right-hand man. You-Can-Call-Me-Al, who had been willing through months of construction to work without written plans, was nonetheless more comfortable using them.

"Don't you have blueprints for the garage?" he asked.

"No," Tyler said. "I've never had plans for any *other* garage I've built."

Tyler and I joked later than I should draw his ideas on notebook paper with blue ink, hand them to You-Can-Call-Me-Al and say, "Here's our blueprints."

Thus, Tyler and crew embarked on forming a garage from the ether of ideas.

Naturally, this was no basic two-car garage. Fiddlesticks! What would my go-big-or-go-home husband do with such a tiny structure? He couldn't even contain all his screwdrivers to a single drawer in his tool chest! He certainly couldn't contain all his man-cave dreams—and tools for a lifetime—to a standard garage.

To be fair, Tyler created plans for the footprint of the extra-deep four-car garage to acquire a building permit. This allowed us to pour the cement foundation in the spring, and it would cure all summer. As we enjoyed happy hour drinks around a picnic table on the what became our temporary summer patio, we marveled at how well the water drained off the driveway. We knew we had a good foundation.

While Reroofer worked on the roof of the belfry, You-Can-Call-Me-Al and Tyler built ten-foot-tall garage walls with two-by-sixes. In what I imagined an old-fashioned barn raising to be like, the two men would fold in helpers when necessary to set up a wall. One morning Tyler roped in a couple of railing fabricators who stopped by to measure for an interior railing, and often Reroofer, You-Can-Call-Me-Al's son and St. Johnny would lend a hand.

Over a week, skeleton walls were built just in time for the delivery of the roof trusses. These, too, had plans of a sort. Tyler specified the size, and the factory constructed the triangle-shaped roof supports. Because the garage was large, these trusses were too. The pile of forty-four feet long trusses filled nearly the entire driveway. The weatherman also delivered. The day dawned sunny and clear, if a little breezier than one might like.

The morning we set the trusses, Tyler—who dreamed of this huge garage for most of his life and had grown sick and tired of constructing anything and wanted to see progress—said, "If we get through today without anyone getting hurt, I'll be happy."

I knew then that this work was tricky, trickier than most of what we had performed in our project. If Tyler was measuring success by lack of injury rather than by dumpsters filled or two-by-fours used or square footage sanded, then this must be serious business.

The crane moved the first truss into place as gently as a crane can.

The enormous roof trusses required a crane to lift them from the ground, one by one, and set them on the walls. A full crew of men—five plus Tyler and the crane operator—had been summoned. You-Can-Call-Me-Al and Reroofer straddled ladders and makeshift footings to help place and secure the trusses, while the other men dashed around below. Because cranes and skilled crane operators are, shall we say, not inexpensive to rent, everyone was moving fast and efficiently to not waste time, which was money.

For the most part, I couldn't watch. I sat at my computer inside. I heard the regular sounds of engines and hammering and men yelling, praying I wouldn't hear anything more urgent or worrisome than that.

I didn't. The crane left to do crane-type work elsewhere in less than four hours. No one was injured. The trusses sat properly in place.

Tyler was happy.

WHILE TYLER AND HIS crew worked on a big and noisy project, I worked on projects small and quiet.

Switch plates and outlet covers, for example. Rather than paying the electrician to install dozens of switch plates, which required no particular talent, Tyler put me on the job. On the main floor, we chose a sleek metal-look alternative Tyler sourced from eBay rather than standard white. I spent ninety minutes screwing on plates before I ran out of the right shapes and energy. I was only half done.

I also unpacked box after box of cookware and serving ware. Cast iron, stainless steel, nonstick, porcelain. Crystal, ceramic, glass, bamboo. Oval, round, rectangular, decorative. All the large, fancy and heavy pieces we didn't bring with us in the RV but couldn't bear to part with were now unpacked and homes found. I fantasized about using a butter knife. Such an inconsequential but lovely flourish I could offer guests once again. For the butter. Which would be served in a ceramic butter dish instead of Tupperware. This small thing made me happy.

And oh, the simple joy of a real wine glass. When we traveled in the RV, I drank wine from plastic glasses unless I dined out (and, believe me, I appreciated using glass when I had the opportunity).

Glass glasses were so much more civilized, sophisticated and aesthetically pleasing than plasticware. I unpacked all but one of our glass wine glasses intact and stowed them in the cabinets of our new beverage bar. A few days into the garage construction project, my clever father installed a plethora of cabinet organizers, including the stemware holding rack that turned my wine glasses from functional pieces into art.

TYLER WAS DETERMINED TO finish his garage. But Mother Nature had other plans.

The day after the garage trusses were set, it rained. And the day after that. And the day after that. Tyler and his posse wrangled with passing showers over the following days, but they made steady progress nailing plywood to the roof, then roof felt and the ice-and-water barrier and finally black shingles to match those on the church.

At one point, we needed to finally demolish the structure that protected the back stairway (I sometimes called it a lean-to, but it wasn't strictly leaning against anything—it was the cover for the back stair). I was inside the church when it was razed, and at first, I thought something terrible had happened. There was a mighty clatter. Then another. The men pried great hunks of roofing material and siding from the church, leaving behind the welded back-door walkway over the back stair. After clean-up and sweeping, all evidence of the lean-to disappeared. The main floor back door and the basement door led to the garage as if that had always been the case. Only a railing around the steps going downstairs was missing.

The men installed some of the windows and the garage's exterior doors. The largest garage doors hadn't yet been purchased, and the window openings of the planned three-season porch in the fourth stall of the garage were boarded up. Those windows would be installed later, probably in the spring. Tyler had grand plans for this mancave porch, but he would wait for warmer weather.

On a sunny autumn day, Tyler rented an earth mover so he could finally redistribute all that glorious black dirt he acquired months before. He also smoothed the side yard of the garage for a patio to be built the following summer. He planned a cozy firepit, too. This patio would one day provide access to the beautiful outdoor space. We could peer out the windows to see the garden planted by parishioners. But as a church, there was no porch, no patio, no deck—even the front door spilled out onto the public sidewalk. This three-season porch and outdoor patio was designed to remedy this missing amenity.

What's a mancave without a refrigerator, right? During a trip to Menards, Tyler ran across the deal of the century. Menards was peddling a used refrigerator. For months, he would send me to the Dollar Store to get another bag of ice to chill the beer for the contractors' happy hour when the heavy lifting was finished. "Another bag of ice?" I complained, not infrequently. When Tyler called me and asked if he should buy the refrigerator on sale for *nineteen bucks,* I never uttered a faster "yes!" We paid for the fridge by saving on three weeks of ice.

Our electrician stopped by—not for a beer, but to deliver a gift: a pair of lawn chairs he'd snagged for as good a deal as the refrigerator Tyler picked up. The electrician thought they would look right at home on our patio. We accepted his thoughtful gift. As he observed our mammoth garage structure, he remarked, "Your garage is bigger than my house."

He wasn't the only one to notice the Garage Mahal. A neighbor stopped by, echoing the electrician's comments: "Your garage is bigger than most of the houses here."

Point taken. The garage was about 50 percent bigger than the rental house we had lived in over the winter. Two blocks from the church, that rental house was in a neighborhood dotted with other rental units. To be fair, the neighborhood was also home to two impressive Victorian homes and a house that once served the town's hotel.

Friends who saw pictures used words like "ginormous" and "massive." It was big, no doubt, but I didn't feel it was outsized. At least our chome garage was *behind* the house instead of jutting out in front of it. I remembered how Tyler had filled the sanctuary with tools. used during demolition and reconstruction. They needed to be stored somewhere. Also, we had large vehicles (even so, we had to store the RV elsewhere because it was too tall and long for any standard garage). It might have been conspicuous now, but once the garage was sided to match the rest of the church, it would blend right in.

I would rather spend money on a big garage than a red convertible. If that made Tyler happy, it made me happy.

THE FINAL DOORS TO be installed were the garage doors. The garage door guy showed up and motored through the installation, one section at a time from the ground up to the windowed top section. Tyler chose brown doors. He consulted me but we'd talked about so many options, I was a little surprised when I drove up upon returning from grocery shopping.

The garage door guy also installed garage door openers (that could be operated by our smartphones!), but we weren't able to use them to drive our vehicles inside because the garage wasn't yet up to code. The workers till needed to drywall the exterior of the church that was inside the garage. Drywall acts as a fire barrier, which is required between the attached garage and the residence. (If our building inspector was a stickler about anything, he was picky about fire barriers). So despite having an enclosed garage with a shingled roof and operational garage doors, we parked our vehicles outside until the drywallers could perform their magic.

While they were here, the drywallers fixed the vanity wall in the second-floor bathroom that had been torn apart to install proper wiring for the light fixtures. That's what *I* was excited about: we were turning our attention back to the interior of the old Methodist church.

42
BECAUSE YOU HAVE KEPT MY WORD ABOUT PATIENT ENDURANCE

TYLER CALLED THE BUILDING inspector to ask him to drop by to inspect the church.

"We're hoping to move in this week," Tyler said.

Move. In.

We had a flushing toilet and a shower. The bedroom needed only a bed. The kitchen had a sink, a fridge and a hole for the stove. We were within a hair's breadth of having the operational bathroom, kitchen and bedroom the building inspector told us nearly a year before that we would need before he would allow us to occupy the church.

The next morning before the sun had completely risen above the horizon of our village, Tyler and I stood in our master bedroom gazing at the ceiling where he showed me the wonders of the high-tech rope lighting that had been tucked into the crown molding of the tray. Tyler fiddled with the app on his phone, changing the colors like he was operating a disco ball. I spied movement out of the corner of my eye. The building inspector stood in the doorway to the Hall of History.

"Come on in," I said. "Check out our ceiling lighting."

He gamely observed our superfluous bedroom lighting. The last thing the building inspector cared about was our disco vibe.

I skedaddled, leaving the foreman to show off our work and acquire a permit.

A few minutes later, Tyler handed me a piece of paper that specified we were the proud recipients of a temporary habitational permit. All that was outstanding was listed as "life safety," that being smoke detectors (which were installed later that afternoon) and handrails on the stairways.

We could move in! We could move in! I carefully folded and filed our permit, smiling ear to ear.

This was the relay handoff for which we had been sprinting.

That was a Tuesday. The permit allowed to sleep in the church/home, but we didn't yet have our big, beautiful king-sized Sleep Number bed. With all the distractions of construction, finishing and cleaning, it would take until Saturday to assemble all the pieces of the bed.

We accomplished the job in relative privacy on Saturday. Planning ahead, we rolled out a new rug and dressed the bed in new sheets and blankets.

With our gleaming chandeliers, the rustic feature wall and our funky nightstands made from safes, our master bedroom looked like one straight out of Pinterest.

We rewarded ourselves by showering in our new shower. At the same time. Our first shower in the church! We were giddy. I told my mother this later, and she said, "I don't want to know that." And I said, "All we did was get clean!"

We just got clean, I swear. Assembling Sleep Number beds was hard work. And we still needed to be at Lowe's to return upstairs shower door No. 2 (three times, the charm).

Our inviting nighttime haven.

We celebrated with sushi at a Japanese/Chinese fusion restaurant (sort of like we were now living in a church/residence fusion home). The establishment had apparently invested in the "happy fortunes" box of cookies because Tyler's fortune said, "Your present plans are going to succeed," and mine said, "The current year will bring you much happiness."

When we got home, Tyler fired up the television in the bedroom, and we snuggled under the covers. I wasn't interested in whatever was on TV. I stared up at the tray ceiling, romantically lit in a soft blue (the rope lighting touted "sixteen million colors!"). I took in the careful workmanship, the straight corners, the well-painted tin. I marveled at the quiet of the church; outdoor noise was muted and, when we weren't tiptoeing around creaking the floors, so was the interior. Our chome was so peaceful when no one was wielding hammers and drills.

It felt like home.

I fell asleep easily and dreamed sweet dreams.

We woke up the next morning, feeling refreshed after sleeping on our favorite bed. A Sunday. I found this somehow significant, even though we weren't conducting any services. First day of the week. First day living in the church.

Ahh, the beverage bar, ready for patrons.

First task: making coffee at the beverage bar. The extra-deep counter had room for all our coffee-making paraphernalia, and a little sink to rinse off the Aeropress. But on this day, Tyler brewed a whole pot. We sat at the island—because we'd hauled in the barstools when we brought in our bed—and we enjoyed our comfortable seating. I saw everything with new eyes because I was no longer planning it or walking by it in mid-construction. I flipped the light switches, I stood over the countertop, I ran the faucet to rinse a cup. It felt weird.

When the time came, I walked over to the Congregational church only a block away to worship. I said a little prayer of thankfulness.

I spent the rest of the day hanging clothes. Clothes that had been in the rental house. Clothes that had been in the RV. Clothes that had been in storage for two years. It was a good thing we'd created so much hanging space. While I hung clothes, I also washed them. How novel! My new washer and dryer hummed quietly as I unpacked long-forgotten dresses, suits and sweaters.

MONDAY DAWNED. IF EVER a man could be labeled as a rolling stone, it was Tyler. He gathered no moss on this day, two days after we first slept in the church. The movers were scheduled to arrive at 8 a.m. The guys from the electronics big-box store had also confirmed they would arrive with Tyler's new television between 8 and 10 o'clock. And, just to make things interesting, Reroofer worked on the belfry that morning.

I supervised the movers who would empty one of our rental units and our cargo trailer. First object of interest: the used six-burner stove we'd scored on Craigslist and stored since early spring. It was time to haul it into the church.

She was heavy, that stove (everything seemed heavy at this point), and the movers earned their pay hiking it into our pickup at the rental unit, back out of the pickup at the church, up the entryway steps and into the kitchen. A few gymnastics were required to hook up the gas behind the stove and exit this space again, but Tyler and one of the movers persevered. Tyler reattached the oven door and fired up the gas. Remember, we'd purchased it used and had never hooked it up to natural gas because we had no place to do so. Had we acquired a good deal? Or a bum one?

Burner One ignited. Burner Two ignited. Burner Three ignited. Four, Five, Six and the oven, too. We were cooking with gas, baby!

The operational stove proved to be a turning point. I could now move all our food into the church. I unpacked boxes of cookware—soup pans, woks, cookie sheets! Instead of cooking in a tiny RV kitchen or a poorly equipped rental house, I soon could whip up creations as I used to. I dreamed of stews and chilis, muffins and cookies. It was autumn, and I would have been drawn into the kitchen anyway. Now I could use this enormous new stove in my properly equipped kitchen, and I was inspired to chop and dice like never before.

The movers and I transported dozens of boxes of books, office supplies (we had an abundance of boxes labeled vaguely as "office"), home décor and odd boxes of speakers, speaker wire and "cords." When we'd moved from our previous house nearly two years before, I distinctly remembered dumping a literal ton of paperwork and boxes of weird wires. But still, we had a lot. Soon, Tyler would sort through all these extension cords, phone chargers and computer connecting wires. Among the ephemera, he found one of my old cell phones which he plugged in to recharge.

Meanwhile, the big-box store guys arrived. Tyler had installed the television bracket above the fireplace with a typical overabundance of caution. Whatever hung on that bracket would never come down. Ladders were erected, a bunch of plastic and cardboard packaging was removed from the state-of-the-art TV, and with great care, two guys secured it in place. Within a few minutes, rich pink flamingos in high definition strutted across Tyler's enormous television. The hairs of every feather were visible. Just like in a commercial, he was glued to the screen while chaos ensured around him. Joanna Gaines would never approve of such a monstrosity, but Tyler was pleased.

We had gotten rid of most of our furniture when we moved out of our house, so when we moved into the rental house over the winter, we needed somewhere to recline in the evenings. We bought an enormous sectional that we barely squeezed into the tiny rental house. Now, in our great room, it looked normal sized. We would buy other chairs and pieces, but for now, all Tyler required was this sofa, situated to take best advantage of the fireplace and TV.

Once the movers completed their work, boxes everywhere surrounded me. I chose to start unpacking in the dining corner of our great room because we expected visitors: my stepdaughter, our son-in-law and our granddaughter were coming for dinner, and I wanted to entertain on our new dining room table.

The table and a china hutch had been delivered a week before. Both were enormous, and I was glad I wasn't one of the guys hauling it. We found them at a nearby importer situated on a farm in the middle of nowhere. Most of their goods were imported from Asia, so the farm had a wide selection of stone Buddhas and Hindi gods, but it also offered unique jewelry, colorful dishware, one-of-a-kind furniture, handwoven rugs and cotton bedding.

When we moved out of our old house, we'd vowed never to buy new un-upholstered furniture again after selling off so many pieces for chump change, but the legs on the teak table at the importer were just the unique touch we wanted in a rustic table. We'd never find something so cool on Craigslist.

This also went for the china cabinet that was the perfect size for the corner of the great room. I'd never owned a piece of furniture like it, and I longed to display the china I inherited from my grandmother when she moved from her home. As I unpacked her china, a box of my own china and another of pink Depression glassware my mother gifted me, I realized this was a *big* china hutch. I had more than enough display space.

We found six dining room chairs at a nearby mass-market retailer. Tyler picked them out, and I was amazed at how well these chairs matched our teak table, which I dressed in table runners my mother sewed for this purpose and a tray of candles I found among packed dishes.

Tyler made a huge vat of spaghetti for dinner, our first opportunity to entertain—truly entertain, during which drinks were offered and we sat in chairs around a table—in the church, now our home. As usual, he made enough for an army even though it was just my stepdaughter and her husband (my granddaughter was eating solid food, but certainly not spaghetti). We recycled the leftover sauce over spinach lasagna rollups when his mother and her significant other joined us for dinner two days later. It made me so happy to sit around the table, mostly relaxed, enjoying the company of family. A few days later, a friend gave a housewarming gift of a hand towel emblazoned with the words, "Meals & Memories are made here." It was such an appropriate sentiment for my new kitchen situated inside a former church where spiritual meals of bread and wine had been served for more than a century, potlucks by the hundreds, congregation gatherings over funeral potatoes, barbecue, pie and other baked delicacies. We were carrying on the tradition.

IMAGINING HOW AWESOME YOU'LL be at making sure your guests are comfy and cozy and actually executing your ideas, as it turns out, are two different things.

Sure, we had a nice bed. But when we entertained our first overnight guests, we didn't even have a door for the guest room. And that wasn't the worst of it.

Our first overnight guests were Tyler's mom and her mate. They were excited to see our work, and we were excited to show it off, so they visited a few days after we moved in. They were forgiving of our unfinished spaces and the boxes everywhere. We pulled together real dishes for dinner and we had the guest bed assembled for sleeping.

The next morning, we asked and listened carefully to learn how we could make the guest experience better.

"Oh, well, I'm such a light sleeper anyway," Tyler's mother began. Uh-oh.

She said a car alarm woke her up in the middle of the night, keeping her awake for an hour.

Tyler and I exchanged puzzled looks. We hadn't heard any car alarms. In fact, our room was so well insulated, we hardly heard any street traffic. Hmm.

She went on to say the car's owner must have tried using a Dremel tool to get inside his car. "Hum, hum, hum," she re-enacted the sound.

Her mate nodded in agreement. He heard it, too.

How odd, Tyler and I said to each later. We were skeptical. We heard nothing. "Maybe the belfry lets in more noise than we know," I suggested. "Maybe we need to sleep up there and see how noisy it really is."

The next night, Tyler hogged the covers and I couldn't get comfortable, so I crept upstairs to try the guest bed.

At two o'clock, I awoke to an alarm. As I got my bearings, I realized the sound was a cellphone. I first thought Tyler was playing a trick on me to get me back to bed, so I got up to investigate. The sound was coming from the kitchen, which was right below the second-floor guest room. I tiptoed down the spiral stairway to find my old cell phone ringing and vibrating on the granite countertop.

I switched it off and realized my mother-in-law hadn't heard a car alarm the previous night, she heard my phone alarm. And the Dremel tool? It was the reverberation of the vibrate buzz on the granite countertop. Tyler had pulled my old phone out of a box of cords he unpacked a few days before to find all his stereo parts, and we plugged it in to see if it still worked. In all the time it sat idle, it somehow confused a.m. with p.m., and it had been going off—for an hour—every night at 2 o'clock because long ago I had an alarm set to give my dog (who had been gone seven months) her afternoon epilepsy pill.

We never heard the phone, but without a door on the balcony to the guest room, the sound carried clearly. As Sergeant Sacker made famous in 1979's *When a Stranger Calls:* "We've traced the call … it's coming from inside the house!"

Turning off the phone fixed this problem, but our early guests endured other hardships and inconveniences.

The bathroom doors lacked locks. The pocket doors on the powder room and guest bath didn't yet have handles. And while the toilet, shower and sink worked in the guest bath, the tub remained dry. We still didn't have the proper faucet to turn the big basin into an oasis. And vanity mirrors? Oh, those were waiting for vanity lighting, which was waiting for proper wiring and then cosmetic surgery to the drywall. My mother, who gamely got ready the first morning she visited without any mirrors, was inordinately grateful when I lent her the makeup mirror from the master bath (an act I should have performed sooner).

Also awkward for guests: Our beautiful French doors leading to our bedroom lacked window coverings, revealing our bed (and whoever was in it) to the hall. A guest using the back stairs walked right by these doors on their way to or from their own sleeping quarters.

The sleek new railing replaced a functional but ugly picket fence.

Thankfully, our early guests tolerated these not-quite-finished touches. We did manage to install one finishing touch, railings which, if it didn't make things cozier, certainly made the guest bedroom safer.

When we purchased the church, the back stair was protected with not a railing, but a picket fence. Perhaps this was a clever reuse of suburban nostalgia, but it was *not* pretty. We couldn't get rid of it fast enough, and during construction, we navigated the back stair without any railing at all.

The same fabricator who did our balcony railing replaced the fence. The guest room railing was similar but without the basket spindles. They also made a coordinating black handrail for the stairway.

DESPITE THE MINOR INCONVENIENCES, visitors still came. When a far-flung friend from my corporate days visited, she likened the church to a mecca. (Mecca, for those interested in the origin of words, is the city where Muhammad was born; many Muslims believe it's important to make a pilgrimage to Mecca at least once). My stories about the renovation stoked her curiosity, and she felt she had to see the church in person.

After the tour and my many comments about how much work this required and how we figured out that problem, she marveled, "How did you avoid killing each other?"

This was a concern early on. Home construction projects have been known to end marital commitments.

"I guess I'm more flexible than some wives, and Tyler has better taste than some husbands," I said.

As our contractors will attest, we raised our voices with each other more than once as we remodeled. Usually, one (or both) of us was just tired and cranky. But rarely did we disagree vehemently about our goals. Tyler was an excellent salesman who could get me to see things his way, and I had figured out how to appeal to Tyler's better instincts when the situation required. If he won the argument, well, then the results were probably better anyway.

MOM AND DAD CAME for another visit and helped us plow through the seemingly endless boxes. "When we drove by Home Depot," Dad said, "They had a sign that said, 'Tyler and Monica, We Miss You!'"

Oh, ha, ha. Yes, our visits to the store were fewer, but had in no way come to an end. (Shortly after Mom and Dad left, I made two trips to Home Depot in a single morning).

When I offered Mom a drink and recited the options, she said, "Oh, your aunt will be pleased. She thought your beverage bar only offered coffee, beer and wine, and she doesn't drink any of those, but I didn't know you had water, too." Indeed, the Drinkpod in all its filtered glory had been installed and dispensed crystal-clear water in three temperatures: cold, room temperature and hot. Mother learned its ease of operation and helped fulfill drink requests for the remainder of her visit.

My parents also came bearing delicious gifts of harvest: fresh buttercup squash from their Minnesota garden, two kinds of apples from Dad's orchard, honey from their property they rented out on the plains of North Dakota, jars of homemade applesauce, homemade chokecherry jelly and real maple syrup collected and cooked by the pastor who had once confirmed me.

A more-enduring gift than the abundant harvest was my dad's expertise with a cabinet hardware jig, a device for installing cabinet knobs. He spent his "free" time installing more than fifty cabinet knobs. When we moved into the church and I asked Tyler about when he would put on all our knobs, he said, "Rome wasn't built in a day." Rome wasn't finished when Dad left, but at least I could properly open all my cabinets.

Mom proved her prowess, too. She helped me unpack a dozen boxes of office supplies (yes, you might say they are our obsession), and she made an apple Bundt cake for a pair of friends, one of whom spent her birthday visiting me and the church. I was grateful for the Bundt pan I had unpacked, for my evenly heating gas stove and for the decorative cake plate on which to serve it—things I didn't have in the camper for nearly two years.

The evening before they returned home, Mom and Dad helped us remove the super-sticky plastic wrap from our balcony carpeting. Removal was as farcical as the application, but we persevered. Mom helped me assemble the legs for the balcony chairs, which I had gallantly retrieved from the store weeks before but hadn't had a chance to put together.

Mom and I recovered our breath while trying out the new chairs and taking in the balcony view.

"Now I have to find a lamp for up here," I said.

"Where are you going to plug it in?" Mom asked.

"We have an outlet in the floor," I said, looking down to locate it. "At least, I think we do."

We looked between the chairs. We looked under the chairs. No outlet.

"Oh, my goodness, they carpeted over it," I said, feeling the floor to locate the outlet through the carpeting.

We didn't find it that way either.

I later mentioned the omission to Tyler. "Oh, the electrician forgot that outlet," he said. "The carpeting installers wouldn't have known to leave a hole for it. We'll have to do it later."

Ah, later. Another "later" project. There were many of these "later" projects. Later, we would finish the entryway. Later, we would build a pantry and cabinetry for the back wall of the great room. Later, we would paint the interior of the belfry and make it a library. Later, we would hang pictures on all the walls and Hall of History.

Later.

THE AUTUMN RAINS PREVENTED Tyler from working on his garage. Rather than being frustrated, it pleased him. For a change, he was happy to take a break from sawing wood—so he could saw some wood on the sectional in front of his enormous TV. Zzzz. He also spent time setting up the great room sound system and threading speaker wires through the basement.

He tested his sound system when a couple of his musically inclined friends from way back and their wives visited. While we lingered around the dining room table (we might have been basking in the glow fueled by excellent tequila), Tyler blasted The Rolling Stones.

"If you start me up, I'll never stop."

The sound was impressive. This was a former church sanctuary, after all, designed for big sound.

"You make a grown man cry."

Tyler laughed. Our friends laughed. I laughed, too. A get-together like this was exactly why we'd purchased the church.

"Kick on the starter, give it all you got."

We couldn't hear our laughter over the music. This was impressive inside, but how did it sound *outside?* What would the neighbors think?

I left the table, making a path to the powder room. But instead, I ducked out the back door instead and walked to the front to hear how the music sounded outside.

Sounded just fine. I could hear Mick Jagger. He could never stop by now. But even passersby on the sidewalk wouldn't be likely to complain—unless they complained they weren't invited.

COZINESS CAN BE DERIVED from candles and comfort food, says Meik Wiking in her book about the Danish concept of *hygge*.

I had vowed to work comfort and coziness into the design of the old Methodist church conversion, and I knew I could get there with soft throws pillows and by serving hot coffee, cold drinks and good food to guests.

But what about the church itself? Especially that wide open sanctuary?

Pull up a chair. Can I get you something to drink?

When friends visited the church in those early days of living there, they frequently said something along the lines of, "It's cozier than I thought it would be." (More than one visitor stood in the great room, turning around to look at everything and refused to be hurried to the next stop on the "tour." Two visitors said taking it all in gave them goosebumps. One woman who was married in the church wept tears of joy as she stood in the transformed sanctuary. I loved giving tours to people who had last seen the church when it was falling apart.)

I credited Tyler's brilliant balcony, which had the kitchen beneath. By pulling the kitchen into the great room, we took a bite out of the openness and had created a cozier gathering place. The space no longer felt imposing and formal, as it might have been as a worship. Instead, it looked and felt like a home.

Guests would often gather around the tongue of the island (it seated five) to nosh on treats or appetizers while I puttered around the kitchen. The hanging seeded-glass pendants splashed light over us as we enjoyed good food and each other's company.

Family, food and fellowship—exactly the life I imagined in our new home.

On the other hand, our only living room seating was the sectional. Six people could sit comfortably on the L-shaped couch, but it was a little awkward when that was the *only* place to sit, which I suppose is why some people gravitated to the island. We would remedy the seating arrangement in due time, but we worked on making the church cozier and livable with many other small projects in those early days.

I established cozy in my office. Guests wouldn't use this space, but *I* would—every day.

In our previous house, my office occupied the smallest bedroom. It was usually filled to the top with paper of all sorts—books, magazines, files, notebook paper, printing paper, loose papers, mail, greeting cards I treasured, greeting cards to send and stationery … I was a papyrophiliac. This drove Tyler just a bit crazy. He successfully encouraged me to upgrade from newsprint to digital editions of my favorite newspapers (yes, I subscribed to two), but I still adored paper anything and hesitated to let it go.

When we moved out of that house, I trashed and shredded a literal ton of paper. The experience was freeing. I felt so much lighter physically and spiritually one, too, but getting rid of *a lot* of paper didn't mean I wanted to forego *all* paper.

I stored some of that treasured paper (books, primarily) and lugged around the rest in the RV we lived in for nearly a year. My corner desk was a triangle that had enough space for my computer and a pen caddy. It was difficult working that way, and when we finally moved into the church, unpacking and putting together other rooms before doing my office made me grumpy. I longed to have my own paper-centric space back.

We chose the back corner of the second floor for my office because most of the time, I was the only one who would see it (paper piles everywhere—how fun!). My nook's window overlooked the elementary school playground across the street. Children's voices made me happy and reminded me of the window in my old office that overlooked the basketball court in our former neighbor's driveway where children frequently spent time shooting baskets.

When I finally had time to assemble my desk, the hardest part was finding all the parts. My desk was actually two desks made of sheets of glass and a whole lot of metal tubing. I first feared legs were missing, but a little digging revealed the missing parts in the closet—maybe the movers stashed them there, or maybe I did and I forgot. So many moving parts.

I spent the day with an Allen wrench and successfully reassembled both desks, Their L-shape fit perfectly in the corner. When my mom visited, we unpacked a dozen boxes labeled "office supplies" into the eaves behind my desk, and *ta da!*, I had a real office again with a real desk and plenty of room to pile up paper. I was in heaven, or at least enjoying the rarified air of the second story of an old church, and that was just fine.

MY SISTER, WHO FOLLOWED my every move on Facebook with enthusiasm (like a good sister should), had been privy throughout the construction to a string of secret pictures and previews. Frequently, she implored: "More pictures." It was easy to oblige, thanks to Verizon and smartphones. When we talked, the church and our work was all I could prattle about.

But until October, she and her family hadn't seen the church in person. She and my brother-in-law were busy parents to three busy boys, and they lived seven or eight hours north of us. Finally, a long weekend break—and the prospect of an operational bathroom and guest bed—offered the perfect opportunity for four of them—my oldest nephew was off to college—to pay us a visit.

Sister came bearing more of Dad's homegrown apples and an obscene amount of Halloween candy. And gushing. Lots of gushing. Music to my ears. Even the fifteen-year-old, who probably couldn't care less about Auntie's crazy church house, was complimentary. And my ten-year-old—a doll! He carved a Halloween jack-o-lantern to decorate my church sign.

But despite the string of pictures I'd shared with her, few were "before" shots. Nothing to brag about there. After seeing our work in all its semi-finished glory, she wanted to be reminded of how far we'd come, so I took her down memory lane with a slideshow on my computer. Printed photos? So last century. Check out these pixels of dust, paneling and old carpeting. *This* is what this place *used* to look like.

AFTER MY SISTER AND her family left, Tyler relaxed for the first time in months. We both had long honey-do lists: thresholds, paint jobs, trim work, furniture painting, decorating, missing screws, missing doorknobs, furniture buying and more. My wish list for Tyler was three pages long. On one hand, we lived in a semi-finished space. On the other hand, we had earned the break we when Tyler got the fireplace going one rainy autumn day.

Tyler supervised a fireplace installer, meaning he sat on the couch while the installer connected the gas and built the fake logs. Most of the project—like punching holes through the bricks and snaking the venting through to the roof—had been completed during construction; only the last 10 percent was left. Within ninety minutes, fire roared. ("I could have done it," Tyler said, "but it would have taken me a lot longer"). With a click of a remote, flames danced, warming the old church as the days grew shorter and the evening chillier.

Snuggle up, honey.

Sitting in front of the fire wearing wool socks and drinking hot tea—now *that's* hygge. The timing of our move couldn't have been better for taking advantage of the coziness. Almost exactly a year before, we were living in our RV in Tyler's cousin's yard, watching snowflakes fall and buying propane a hundred dollars at a time.

"What are you thinking?" Tyler asked as I gazed at the dancing flames.

"I'm thinking about how much we got done in the past year. I'm thinking about how perfect everything is." I took a breath as I sipped my tea.

After moving in, you fill a house with memories. But, of course, we had a head start. The church itself had accumulated decades of memories as generations of faithful worshipped, baptized, wedded and were sent off to another plain. And we had made a year's worth of memories as we transformed the sacred space into a cozy home, one swing of the hammer, one pass of the sander, one sweep of paint at a time.

"I'm thinking about how it was worth the wait."

Epilogue

THE INTERNET IS FOREVER.

The former church we now call home once hosted meetings for Alcoholics Anonymous, and about twice a month, someone rings our doorbell about half past 7 o'clock on Tuesday asking about the weekly AA meeting.

"Nope, it's not here anymore," we say, conscious of the lack of anonymity represented by one of us standing in our open doorway. "AA meets at the church around the corner now." And we offer directions to the nearby Congregational church.

We admit our powerlessness over old web listings that show our address for Tuesday evening AA meetings. If it's got "meeting," "recovery" or "AA" in the web address, it might list our house as the meeting locale in the search results.

That's a weird thing about living in a former church. What with the belfry and the church sign, our home looks like we might still be a religious space, so no one can be blamed for knocking. No one has shown up for a Sunday morning sermon, but FedEx still gets confused about delivering packages to an address assigned to "First

Methodist Church" and we've had a couple of people drop by looking for the Loaves & Fishes food bank, which parishioners hosted in our basement.

I don't mind.

Those infrequent confused visitors are beautiful reminders that our home was once a community hub, a place where people met and extended their hands to support each other. Coretta Scott King once said, "The greatness of a community is most accurately measured by the compassionate actions of its members."

The compassion shown by our community has truly blessed us. Our friends, old and new, continue to visit and make nice comments about our work. Former church members still request tours, to which we readily agree, and they bring us gifts that we probably don't deserve but are, more appropriate *in* the church than out of it—doors once part of the building, light fixtures, altar plaques, quilts, Christmas tree skirts, cookbooks. A year after we moved in, we hosted an open house for neighbors, former church members and contractors, and more than a hundred people showed up. We didn't have gloved waiters or kegs of beer as we might have envisioned, but we requested donations to the local food pantry. Our supporters contributed more than 600 pounds of nonperishable food items.

We love living in our little village, and I look for opportunities to host get-togethers of the Library Friends or meetings for the Congregational church around the corner. If you want to find friends in a small Midwestern town, buy a historical site and lovingly renovate it.

As with any home, we never run out tasks. The summer after we moved in, we finished the garage, built an outdoor patio, finished the exterior of the belfry and restored some of the original siding. The basement still stands empty (though finally dry!), awaiting its finishing into a mother-in-law's apartment.

I don't mind this list of things to do. When you quit living, you're dying. The best thing about renovating a 126-year-old church was not a new home, but a sense of accomplishment. Tyler and I with creaky knees and the Tequila Budget believed we could turn a decaying church into a picture-worthy house, and we did, when just about everyone who loved us and everyone who met us were skeptical. We rock.

We didn't finish the church for $248,600, like we estimated when we created that first tequila-fueled budget before putting an offer on the church. I quit adding at $286,000, and the garage still wasn't finished. But we certainly spent less than we did on our first house, the cardboard box, and we now are the proud owners of a higher quality building. After handling all the pink insulation, I'm proud to tell you the chome costs less to heat and cool than that old cardboard box, too.

People often ask us if we knew what we were getting into when we bought such an old building. I didn't really know; the fairy dust of HGTV and Pinterest obscured my vision. But Tyler did. And I had faith in Tyler, which turned out to be well placed. His hands touched nearly every element of the demolition and reconstruction, and what his hands didn't touch, his eyes watched as he supervised the hands of others. He's my Big Sexy, and because of him, I'm living the big time, as Peter Gabriel sang, "I will pray to a big god, as I kneel in a big church."

We joke that we go to church every day now. It's true in the literal sense, but it's true metaphorically, too. If one goes to church to feel closer to God and experience the company—spiritually at least—of other believers, I feel that way every day I spend in my Church Sweet Home.

Acknowledgements

THERE'S AN OLD JOKE that illustrates that God helps those who help themselves. A young man with more debts than friends goes to church and prays, "Dear God, please help me win the lottery. I really need the money, so please help me win." When he doesn't win, he goes back to church and implores "Why? Why aren't you listening to me?" And God responds: "Buy a lottery ticket!"

I bought a lot of lottery tickets and have won many times over as Tyler and I turned the 126-year-old Methodist church into our home. The parade of talented contractors we enlisted is long, and I'm grateful to all them. Thanks also go to the former members of the church, especially the Rev. Lucinda and the Hill sisters, who welcomed us, told us stories and gave us pictures and beautiful objects that had once been in the church or deserved to be there. And thanks to Kathy V., who walked by our construction site with a thumbs up so many mornings and helped us pull off our open house.

Similarly, I thank the friends, acquaintances and new friends who read my blog day by day as we were working. Their encouraging words helped us so many days when we were dirty, tired and disgusted. They helped remind us we were on the right track and to keep going.

I thank the stars for my editor, Robert Fraass. He did with words what Tyler did with wood; Robert demolished the worthless bits and polished the good parts, transforming my manuscript of weak phrasing and lazy clichés into a readable thing of beauty.

Because of my mother's encouragement, you are holding this book. Dad is a big supporter who helped us put finishing touches on our home, but Mom is my biggest fan, and she knows exactly how to encourage me to finish the book without pissing me off. Thanks, Mom.

About the Author

MONICA LEE IS THE author of *The Percussionist's Wife: A Memoir of Sex, Crime & Betrayal*, a fitness memoir *How to Look Hot & Feel Amazing in your 40s: The 21-Day Age-defying Diet, Exercise & Everything Makeover Plan* and a piece of historical fiction about how she learned to French kiss when she was 15: *Truth, Dare, Double Dare, Promise or Repeat: On Finding the Meaning of "Like" in 1982.* She is a personal historian, blogger and writer who helps her husband make money by filling out boring insurance paperwork, but her real love is writing. Follow news about *Church Sweet Home* (the book) and her other works at http://mindfulmonica.wordpress.com or catch up with her everyday life on her blog at http://minnesotatransplant.wordpress.com. For updates about the chome and lots more before-and-after pictures (in color!), check out http://churchsweethome.com

Reading Guide

What's the biggest project you've ever completed? How was it similar or different to renovating an old church? What aspects of Monica's story can you most relate to?

Would you react with envy or horror if a friend told they were buying a church to turn into a home?

Do you believe in ghosts? Do you think ghosts haunt old churches?

Church Sweet Home included a belfry that required a lot of attention and money to repair. Is it a good use of resources to spend them on superfluous decoration?

Tyler and Monica lived in a camper and a tiny rental house while they worked on the church, and they moved into a semi-finished space. Would you have the patience to do the same?

Which characters in the book did you like best? Which character would you most like to meet?

MONICA USED PHRASES FROM the Bible for chapter titles. Do you think this was an inspired choice or a sacrilegious one?

MONICA'S MISSION STATEMENT FOR her home was "We strive to create a comfortable sanctuary in the modern world, built solidly and maintained orderly." What is the mission for your home?

MONICA SUMMARIZED HER DESIGN style as "rustic transitional punctuated with elements of warehouse, farmhouse, barn house and house of worship." How would you summarize your interior design style?

TYLER'S STEREO SYSTEM WAS an important finishing touch to the chome. What songs does this book make you think of?

DID YOU LEARN ANYTHING about renovation or decorating from this book that you might apply in your home?

Made in the USA
Monee, IL
08 May 2020